ADVANCE PRAISE F

I0880425

EVERYTHING IS EVERYTHING

"In *Everything Is Everything*, Steve Jones has given the great Zelig-provocateur-enabler of sixties rock the tribute he deserves: eclectic, surprising, and opinionated, in prose of immediacy and brightness, and with the laughter kept in the final mix."

—**JONATHAN LETHEM**

"In 1966, music was up for grabs. Through close, astute examination of groundbreaking albums recorded that year, Jones reveals the shadow cast by producer Tom Wilson, the unlikely visionary connecting dots, erasing genres, and opening doors at this pivotal moment."

—**ALAN LIGHT**, author of *Don't Stop: Why We (Still) Love Fleetwood Mac's "Rumours"*

"Pop music got on a whole new trip in 1966, and Tom Wilson was the conductor. Jones's fascinating book illuminates this oft-overlooked figure and his crucial involvement with some of the era's most important artists and albums."

—**DAN EPSTEIN**, author of *Stars and Strikes: Baseball and America in the Bicentennial Summer of '76*

"Two books rolled into one: an exploration of Tom Wilson, understudied maverick and industry mainstay, and of 1966 in pop music via the array of groups he produced. This works because of the intricacy, thoughtfulness, intelligence, and prodigious research that animate these pages."

—**ERIC LOTT**, author of *Black Mirror: The Cultural Contradictions of American Racism*

"A kaleidoscopic portrait of a chaotic and creative year in popular music history organized around one of the most neglected and influential producers of the era, *Everything Is Everything* is everything and more."

—**LOREN GLASS**, author of *Carole King's "Tapestry"*

"In *Everything Is Everything*, Jones does something rare in cultural criticism, correcting several prevailing myths about the explosion of creativity in the sixties and shedding welcome and long-overdue light on producer Tom Wilson."

—**JIM DEROGATIS**, author of *Let It Blurt: The Life and Times of Lester Bangs, America's Greatest Rock Critic*

"Wow!"

—**MARSHALL CRENSHAW**

"The currents of popular music swirled into each other in 1966—shaped by the soft-spoken and untrammeled producer Tom Wilson. Jones's *Everything Is Everything* offers an eye-opening and ear-opening tour of these forces at a pivotal experimental moment."

—**SEAN WILENTZ**, author of *360 Sound: The Columbia Records Story*

EVERYTHING IS EVERYTHING

STEVEN E. JONES

EVERYTHING IS EVERYTHING

TOM WILSON AND POP MUSIC IN 1966

STANFORD UNIVERSITY PRESS • STANFORD, CALIFORNIA

Stanford University Press
Stanford, California

Library of Congress Cataloging-in-Publication Data
Names: Jones, Steven E. (Steven Edward) author
Title: Everything is everything : Tom Wilson and pop music in 1966 / Steven E. Jones.
Description: Stanford, California : Stanford University Press, 2026. | Includes bibliographical references and index.
Identifiers: LCCN 2026006886 (print) | LCCN 2026006887 (ebook) | ISBN 9781503647626 cloth | ISBN 9781503647909 paperback | ISBN 9781503647916 ebook
Subjects: LCSH: Wilson, Tom, 1931–1978 | Sound recording executives and producers—United States | Popular music—United States—1961–1970—History and criticism | Sound recording industry—United States—History—20th century
Classification: LCC ML429.W567 J66 2026 (print) | LCC ML429.W567 (ebook) | DDC 781.6409/046—dc23/eng/20260225
LC record available at https://lccn.loc.gov/2026006886
LC ebook record available at https://lccn.loc.gov/2026006887

Cover design: Michele Wetherbee
Cover photograph: Tom Wilson by Charles Steiner © 1967

The authorized representative in the EU for product safety and compliance is:
Mare Nostrum Group B.V. | Doelen 72 | 4831 GR Breda | The Netherlands | Email address: gpsr@mare-nostrum.co.uk | KVK chamber of commerce number: 96249943

To the memory of Wayman E. Jones (1936–2026)

CONTENTS

ACKNOWLEDGMENTS

Many thanks to Erica Wetter for her savvy and creative editorial guidance. Thanks to everyone at Stanford University Press who worked to produce this book, in particular Caroline McKusick. For some time, friends and family have listened to me pitch this project. Many were interested and offered encouragement, among them, Molly, Peter, Rebecca, Ken, and Sylvia. Trusted colleagues Paul Jay and Paul Youngquist responded just when I needed them most. Author and music journalist Dan Epstein took seriously my idea for the book, which really meant a lot. Celebrated rock musician and singer-songwriter (and soon-to-be documentary producer) Marshall Crenshaw provided feedback on my plan for the book, then shared bits from his own ongoing research as I was writing it. Other musicians taught me things I needed to know, two trumpeters in particular: James Suggs, who keeps Hugh Masekela's music alive in his own repertoire, and Jimmy Owens, who shared his story about making the *Batman and Robin* album with Sun Ra. Producer, musicologist, and Tom Wilson expert Irwin Chusid responded to queries and read part of an early draft. I'm grateful for his honest criticism—indeed, everyone interested in Tom Wilson owes Chusid an enormous debt. The New York Public Library Archives and Manuscripts helped with some not yet fully transcribed materials among the Lou Reed papers. I found Sun Ra's scrapbook at the University of Chicago's Hanna Holborn Gray Special Collections Research Center. This book began with the first album I ever bought, *Batman and Robin*. My Batman fandom predates my involvement with most of the music discussed here, and my brother Jeffrey aided and abetted that fandom and shared other interests over the years. Finally, Heidi never stopped supporting my research, writing, guitar playing, and record collecting (and me).

INTRODUCTION

EVERYTHING IS EVERYTHING, 1966

Bob Dylan, "Like a Rolling Stone" (1965); Simon & Garfunkel, "The Sound of Silence" (1965)

THIS IS A BOOK IS ABOUT AMERICAN POP MUSIC IN 1966. NOT 1967, THE year of the Summer of Love, and not 1964, the start of the British Invasion, but what I think is an even more interesting year, 1966: when go-go dancing met the electric blues, bubblegum pop met underground rock, free jazz met psychedelia, and they all morphed into one another like fluid blobs in a liquid light show.

The chapters that follow explore that fluidity. I look at how genres mutated and fused or replaced one another in the spotlight. The focus is on albums, and 1966 was a landmark year for albums: the Beach Boys' *Pet Sounds* came out in in May; Bob Dylan's *Blonde on Blonde* appeared in June; the Beatles' *Rubber Soul* topped the charts and, in August, the group's *Revolver* came out, a genre-diverse milestone that included psychedelic and Indian sounds, backward tape-loop guitar and sitar parts. Those albums were massively influential, and a lot has been written about them. I don't spend much time on them, beyond referring to them occasionally for context. Most of the albums I consider registered only modestly on the sales charts, though some have since become recognized as important and influential. But each had its listeners, and each made a difference. Their very existence, adjacent to the more famous records, changed music history.

History, including music history, often unfolds through such juxtapositions, as musician/DJ/director Amir "Questlove" Thompson argues. It's important to look at the juxtaposition of different tracks, he says, because "often, the most interesting things" are found "tucked between the things that everyone knows, serving as counterweights and commentary."[1] I think the same holds true at different scales for different albums, artists, genres, and scenes: how they are juxtaposed, and what's between them, matters for how they are understood. A lot of interesting music is produced out of juxtapositions, and often out of constructive oppositions. In 1966, some of the most interesting music-making took place "off the charts": both literally, through emerging styles and genres not yet recognized for their commercial potential, and figuratively, by veering off the mental maps most people have when conceptualizing the musical landscape. We need to look beyond or to one side of blockbuster albums of the year by the Beach Boys, the Beatles, Bob Dylan, the Rolling Stones, or the Supremes to appreciate what was adjacent to those albums and to understand how that adjacency itself allowed for meaningful differences to emerge.

Consider the timing: Frank Zappa's *Freak Out!* was released the same week in June 1966 as Bob Dylan's *Blonde on Blonde*. On TV in prime time, *The Monkees* premiered in the fall, about a month after *Revolver* came out. In the spring, the Velvet Underground were playing in Andy Warhol's experimental multimedia show, the Exploding Plastic Inevitable, in downtown New York City just as the Batman craze was blowing up, thanks to the hit TV show that had premiered in January. When it came to blockbuster albums, we have to remember that Herb Alpert's Tijuana Brass's *Whipped Cream & Other Delights* topped the charts around the same time as the Beatles' *Rubber Soul*. It was all happening simultaneously. Even if listeners and viewers were not fully aware of them, influences were flowing up from underground and avant-garde circles into pop music and mass entertainment and back again. Artists and albums later relegated to the edge of the frame mattered a lot at the time to fans, critics, and other musicians. And the ripples they sent out sometimes changed music history, even if they were nearly erased from that history.

The heart of this book is the story of an influential but now relatively unknown record producer, Tom Wilson. A Black man from Waco, Texas, he attended Fisk University, then transferred to Harvard, from which he graduated cum laude in economics. Still in his twenties, he formed his own record label; after a short run, he moved into positions at Columbia Records and MGM/Verve. Put simply, he affected the whole course of American pop in the 1960s and early 1970s. 1966 was Tom Wilson's annus mirabilis, when he helped to create folk-rock, brought underground and avant-garde music into conversation with pop music, and fostered a number of hybrid experiments in jazz, pop, blues, and psychedelia. He produced some of the most influential and significant albums of that year, including first albums or key albums by a diverse range of artists, such as Bob Dylan, Simon & Garfunkel, the Blues Project, the Velvet Underground, Frank Zappa and the Mothers of Invention, Hugh Masekela, and Eric Burdon & the Animals. As a producer and A&R (artists and repertoires) executive, Wilson practiced as well as preached a radical eclecticism. I made his favorite catchphrase—"everything is everything"—the title of this book because I think it characterizes the most important trend in pop music in 1966: an exploding genre eclecticism, accompanied by a sometimes desperate search for authenticity. (More about Wilson below and in the chapters to follow.)

That focus on "everything," that sweeping eclecticism, was a commercial as well an aesthetic matter. Radio formats were becoming increasingly specialized at the time, FM and AM stations began to diverge in their content, opening the way for album-oriented "freeform" programming on FM.[2] Radio stations and record companies imagined an ever more segmented audience, then made changes to record production and marketing that helped to produce and reinforce that segmentation. This was no happy flowering of diversity. It was more like a jostling, competitive arena in which musical genres were often defined against one another, through opposition.[3] Around 1966–1967, for example, we start to see "rock" music differentiate itself from "pop." When rock 'n' roll first emerged in the 1950s, it was as a *kind* of pop music.[4] In my title and throughout this book, I use "pop music" in the broad sense, as an umbrella term covering various popular genres, including rock, and an expanding eclectic range of subgenres and genre hybrids. Sometimes the eclecticism of 1966 was the result of a band's or a producer's rejecting a genre label and staking out an alternative territory, as when the Velvet Underground deliberately avoided folk and blues, for example, and anything that might sound like commercial pop. By the mid-1960s, musicians, producers, and marketers also increasingly distinguished genres and audiences in terms of the "vertical" cultural divide between the popular and the underground, the commercially successful and the hip.[5] Some musicians tried to have it both ways, to make music that could be heard differently by different audiences. For obvious commercial reasons, some producers and record companies encouraged such double-voicing to appeal to multiple audiences.

Reflecting these trends, the overall trajectory of American pop during 1966 was from folk to blues to rock hybrids, including folk-rock and blues-rock, to psychedelia. R&B and newly identified soul music in many cases followed the same trajectory—as when the Chambers Brothers produced a form of psychedelic soul, for example; or Sly Stone and other musicians recorded gospel-flavored R&B. In some cases, as with Parliament and James Brown, mutations within the soul and R&B traditions led to the rise of funk. Even in these cases, the trend toward psychedelia included a wide swath of pop music.

This book's chapters follow that route, that overarching trajectory. Given that arc, genre eclecticism was one obvious tactical response, a way to make something new by grafting or combining genres. As the end of the year approached, this often took the form of mixing various pop genres in the musical blender of psychedelia. Behind it all was the widespread search for some form of authenticity in the go-go era.

THE PROBLEM OF AUTHENTICITY

The idea of authenticity in American music, the ideal of keeping it real, is deeply entangled with histories of race, minstrelsy, folklore studies, and the differentiation of genres, as Karl Hagstrom Miller argues.[6] In the late nineteenth and early twentieth centuries, the music of the American South was segregated by genre—the blues, for example, came to be thought of as essentially Black and was subsumed into the marketing category of "race" records. So-called old-time music, on the other hand, was seen as essentially white. By the 1920s, catalogs, record bins, and marketing reflected the segregation. An increasingly stark "musical color line" was drawn and enforced by the burgeoning music industry, tied to the sale of recorded music.[7] In the early twentieth century, the work of collecting field recordings and the concurrent rise of folklore studies was built on and reinforced a similar genre and race-based segregation. "Authentic" or "country" blues, for example, played on acoustic guitar and sung solo by Black musicians, was sought out and valued over mere pop standards, mainstream music that had been widely known and played.

This folkloric urge to sort followed from the popularity of blackface minstrel shows in the nineteenth century. Although it might seem the epitome of the inauthentic, minstrelsy had often claimed to represent Black culture in a kind of ethnographic way.[8] Indirectly (and ironically), the minstrel tradition "taught that authenticity was performative."[9] Robert Johnson, to cite one well-known example, had played a variety of musical genres, basically anything he heard on the radio, including the pop tunes of his day. But his music was increasingly shoehorned into the pseudo-ethnographic genre, the (Black) blues.[10]

Despite this history, the *ideology* of authenticity, the illusion that one might find a self-identical, authentic mode of musical expression that transcended commercial categories, continued to drive pop musicians, listeners, producers, and decision-makers in the music industry through the twentieth century. Indeed, as Michael Serazio has argued, "[a]uthenticity has always been an obsession of pop music."

> From blues and folk to rock and rap, artists, critics, and fans alike have endlessly hungered for the "real" and rejected that which sounds, looks, and above all, *feels* "contrived, pretentious, artificial, or overly commercial."[11]

As Serazio puts it, "authenticity is not actually real"; that is, it's an ideology, a set of beliefs that obscures the material and social relations the music industry is built on. Musical authenticity is something made and something sold.[12] But the obsession with it is very real, and it only increased as the music industry coopted authentic music as part of what it marketed to consumer-listeners.[13] So, it makes sense that the search for something real and authentic in pop reached a fevered pitch in 1966, a year dominated by Batman, Andy Warhol, and the Monkees.

In the chapters that follow, I look at various ways musicians and bands sought authenticity, especially through experiments with genre. For the Blues Project, a couple of founding members came out of the folk music and jug-band scene in Greenwich Village. The band was fully formed when another member was added, Al Kooper. He had come from the world of pop songwriting and session work. He had worked at 1650 Broadway in New York, near the famed Brill Building and part of the hitmaking system associated with it. The Blues Project's earliest impulse was to shift from folk to folk-rock, and from traditional blues to electric blues and blues-rock. But as the band's name implied, theirs was a pseudo-folkloric "project" to "revive"—or sustain and promote—the blues, which they took to be deeply rooted in Black culture. Serious devotees, they joked self-deprecatingly about being on a "blues crusade." But they were often uncomfortable, even embarrassed, by the cultural appropriation their project involved. This was one reason they began to write and play a variety of hybrid genres, searching for a form more their own: folk-rock, blues-rock, and, finally, a vaguely defined psychedelia.

Every musician in the chapters that follow underwent similar changes in 1966. For Sun Ra, the question of identity was turned inside out. Born Herman Poole Blount in Birmingham, Alabama, he was reborn as the artist Sun Ra from Jupiter, arrived on Earth via the interstellar spaceways. Authenticity was a matter of being true to his own highly constructed and imagined artistic vision. For the Velvet Underground, being real meant not being phony, saying no to folk music, to the blues, to mainstream pop, to develop like a photographic negative an avant-garde, underground credibility. Frank Zappa was a satirist who mocked the whole idea of authenticity, the pretense of sincerity, while flaunting his indifference to commercial success and thereby claiming his own kind of artistic integrity above the fray. Trumpeter Hugh Masekela rejected stereotypes of Black and African creativity, aiming instead to capture the genre diversity of the modern African diaspora. Eric Burdon, out of Newcastle, was an earnest devotee of Black American blues and R&B. In late 1966, he moved to America and sought a new identity as an artist. With the help of psychedelics (and inspiration from both Frank Zappa and Tom Wilson), Burdon turned inward, writing and singing what he called the "blues of [his] mind." Like many others at the time, he psychedelicized, and thereby internalized, the quest for authenticity.

CONTEXTS, SOCIAL AND POLITICAL

The internalization of the quest for musical authenticity was one response to the widespread cultural disillusionment with communitarian politics. The tide of utopian speculation and social experimentation had crested and was receding by the time all the publicity started around the Summer of Love in 1967. At that crest, the mid-1960s were a tumultuous time in American politics and culture—a cliché that's true. The period saw a generation of upheaval in just a few short years: the escalation of the Vietnam War; the draft and antiwar resistance; major political assassinations; the pursuit of peaceful or violent revolution; communal lifestyles and changing sexual mores; changing gender roles (to a limited degree); experiments with psychedelics; the exploration of Eastern religious practices and non-Western music; the ongoing civil rights movement, including *after* the Civil Rights Act of 1964 and the racist reaction to it; and the rise of Black Power in the second half of the decade and the often violent reaction to that rise. The Black Panther Party was founded in 1966; BPP leader Fred Hampton was killed by the police in 1969. Much of the music of the time was topical and explicitly referred to these events; some aimed to intervene. There were antiwar songs and antiracist civil rights songs and songs celebrating sexual freedom or drugs as countercultural expressions. For the most part, I don't spend time juxtaposing music with social and political headlines. For something like that approach, you can see Jon Savage's book, *1966*, a thorough chronological survey of the singles charts that year, alongside historical events, month by month.[14]

My aim is different. I don't think we can trace any simple or unmediated connection between a headline about a social or political event and a given record or song, beyond noting topical references in lyrics. Don't get me wrong: historical and cultural contexts are vitally important. Art is always "in context," one way or another, whether consciously or not. Music is a product of the culture and, in turn, helps to produce the culture. It is inevitably, if sometimes obscurely, marked by the politics of its day. But in this book, I treat pop music not as an unmediated "reflection" of the times, or as journalism with a beat, but as art, as a series of creative acts (recording an album, for example). This involves paying attention to form and sound, trying to understand pop music *and* some of its contexts through close listening. If we want to understand the connection between music and drugs in 1966, for example, we need to really listen to psychedelic rock records—and not only read the lyrics. The music—including its forms but also the timbres of specific instruments it is played on—is worth exploring in detail, with contexts interwoven with the exploration.

For practical purposes, I focus almost exclusively on American pop, though of course American pop was already part of a global music business. But as we're reminded by the term "British Invasion"—the takeover of American sales charts of records by British bands in 1964–1965, records often inspired in the first place by American blues and R&B—national cultural boundaries were still imagined as being significant at the time. It was not always easy for British musicians to get their hands on sought-after American blues and R&B records, for example, and listening to them helped to construct an idea of American culture, however superficial.

Also, I focus on albums, not singles. As Jon Savage notes, "1966 began in pop and ended in rock"—a corollary being that, at the beginning of the year, "the single was still king," just in terms of record sales. But that wasn't true for long.[15] The cultural dominance of the 7-inch 45 rpm record didn't survive the year, as Savage goes on to show (though of course singles did). By the middle of 1966, the 33⅓ rpm LP, the album emerged as the dominant form of recorded music when it came to artistic achievement and cultural influence, to what was cool and what counted. The albums I focus on, almost all of them produced by Tom Wilson, form a pathway through the year, like brightly colored 12-inch cardboard steppingstones.

This is a selected list of key albums from 1966, not every album released that year. The book follows a playlist, one I've designed to tell a story, which I think happens to be the central story of pop in 1966. It's about the transformation of genres, the creation of hybrid genres, and the marketing and consumption of these to make something authentic at a moment when pop music seemed increasingly manufactured and fake. Behind it all was a question: was authentic music even possible in the go-go era? The real question is: why did it seem so important to so many at the time?

Maybe authenticity mattered so much in 1966 precisely because it seemed increasingly impossible. Pop art; plastic go-go boots; diversifying radio formats, including the emergence of "progressive" or "underground" FM radio; the multiplication of musical genres; the increased use of electric instruments, especially the guitar but also various synthesizers, distortion pedals (the wah-wah pedal was invented that year), and tape effects (which went along with the increasing use of the recording studio as the uber-instrument, thanks to the Beatles); mind-altering drugs; and immersive light shows and high-volume live performances—things all came to a head that year. In response, so did the pursuit of the elusive ideal of authentic artistic expression: indeed, this mattered more than ever in a year dominated by Andy Warhol and the Monkees, pop art and commercial pop.

ONLY IN IT FOR THE MONEY?

As a way to contextualize some of the issues at stake, consider two iconic album covers from just after 1966: the Beatles' *Sgt. Pepper's Lonely Hearts Club Band* (1967) and Frank Zappa and the Mothers of Invention's *We're Only in It for the Money* (1968). Most everyone knows the Beatles' image, a collage made of cutouts of famous figures from history alongside contemporary influencers, standing behind the band members as if for the portrait of some bizarre club. It's a satire of the whole idea of group photos, whether of clubs, bands, classes, platoons, or teams.

Fewer people remember the Mothers' parody, created in 1967, an image that became the inner gatefold for their third album. We may be tempted to cast the Beatles as the straight men, the naive targets of Zappa's satire. The Fab Four, whom Zappa had accused of merely updating rock 'n' roll for trendy commercial purposes (he said they played "Chuck Berry a go-go"), appear in full psychedelic garb in their *Sgt. Pepper's* group photo, wearing the kind of thrift-store Edwardian era uniforms popular in hip boutiques at the time, with droopy mustaches and holding brass instruments, as if they were the titular band. The Mothers' assemblage/collage includes similar-looking public figures from history and from the 1967 present, but also more obscure persons and some vaguely menacing examples, like film stars from the black and white era, *The Twilight Zone*'s Rod Serling, and Frank Zappa's high school coach, along with an eclectic group of musicians—Edgard Varèse, Elvis Presley, Jimi Hendrix, Captain Beefheart, Big Mama Thornton. In the collage, they all appear to be standing with the Mothers, who are dressed in half-hearted drag, with pigtails, minidresses, gowns, and boots, staring defiantly at the camera.

Zappa's gatefold image was a satire on the Beatles' satire. It was meant to one-up the Liverpool band's own cheeky attitude toward history and what the British call "heritage." But in its own way, Zappa's parody is also a performance of sincerity, a way for the self-described composer to flaunt his own musical roots, as weirdly eclectic as they were, and to satirize the sham of the music business that seemed to exclude such creative eclecticism—while still taking part in that music business (if not *only* for the money). The two images actually represent a contest over artistic credibility, over *relative* authenticity. Zappa reportedly telephoned Paul McCartney for permission, or at least a blessing, for the parody image. McCartney said that he was fine with the parody but that Zappa would have to deal directly with the lawyers at EMI. Zappa later told the story to emphasize his belief in artistic freedom and to imply that McCartney had deferred too readily.[16] Interestingly, McCartney has always pointed to the Mothers' previous album, 1966's *Freak Out!*, as a key inspiration for *Sgt. Pepper's*, alongside the Beach Boys' *Pet Sounds* from that same year. Even during recording sessions for *Sgt. Pepper's*, which began in 1966, McCartney reportedly declared, "This is *our Freak Out!*"[17]

In the end, MGM's lawyers on Zappa's side decided that the image would have to go inside the album, as the gatefold instead of on the outer cover of *We're Only in It for the Money*. Despite that compromise, by producing it at all, Zappa was claiming the greater artistic integrity. The whole incident reflects fundamental tensions that had bubbled up in the previous year, between art and commerce, commitment and selling out, making meaningful records and just selling consumable "plastic ware" (as the Byrds put it, in their 1967 hit, "So You Want to Be a Rock 'n' Roll Star").

ENTER TOM WILSON

Take another look at that surreal group portrait for Zappa's *We're Only in It for the Money.* One figure stands off to our left, over at the furthest edge of the frame: a tall Black man with a goatee, his right hand thrust Napoleon-like into the breast of a buttoned-up high school letter sweater, gazing calmly at the camera.[18] That's Tom Wilson, the first producer for Zappa and the Mothers of Invention. He discovered the band at the Whisky a Go Go in Los Angeles in 1966 and immediately signed them to MGM/Verve. He then arranged for the label to support the production of that experimental double album that meant so much to Paul McCartney, *Freak Out!*

This book began for me with a very different album produced by Wilson, a *Batman and Robin* record. It was the first album I bought with my own money. It had a bright comic-book cover and was obviously made quickly to cash in on the Batman craze of 1966—that's when I first purchased it from the dollar bin in a supermarket. As an adult, I learned that it was made by a group of anonymous studio musicians that included the great jazz innovator, Sun Ra, and members of one of my favorite bands of the 1960s, the Blues Project. I also learned that the record was produced by someone named Tom Wilson. I'd never heard of him at that point, but I would soon discover that he had produced Bob Dylan, Zappa, and many more important musicians of the time. My education about the *Batman and Robin* album started with the radio station WFMU's blog. I first learned about Wilson from a website created by a DJ at the station, Irwin Chusid.[19] I decided to write this book after following breadcrumbs left by Wilson, moving from one album to another, listening online at first, then through streaming services, and eventually hunting down vinyl copies of the albums and poring over their cover art, liner notes, and photos associated with them. Wilson was the connecting link. I came to see how his story sheds light on important issues facing pop music in that pivotal year.

Hugely influential in the 1960s, Wilson died in 1978 at the age of 47 from a heart attack, a complication of Marfan syndrome. Today he's barely known to the general public—although that may soon change. Chusid's pioneering website has inspired a number of online articles and blog posts, some of which include lists of albums Wilson produced, like the list that structures this book. As I write, there are two different films in the works about Wilson: a biopic endorsed by his estate, and a music documentary produced by the rock musician and singer-songwriter Marshall Crenshaw. Online, there's a podcast out of Waco, Texas, Wilson's birthplace, that explores his story.[20] And finally, a recent book of essays, *Everybody's Head Is Open to Sound*, edited by Anaïs Ngbanzo (2025), addresses Wilson's significance in a handful of original chapters by jazz and pop critics, with the addition of reprinted interviews.[21]

It might seem tempting to think of Wilson as a Zelig figure.[22] After all, he was everywhere in 1960s pop, hiding in plain sight out at the edge of music history's frame. It's true: Wilson pops up in historical photos, films, and audio clips. For example, we see him standing, 6'4", in the background on a London rooftop, wearing an overcoat, dark shades, and a fez as Dylan flips word cards for "Subterranean Homesick Blues"; or sitting off to the side of Dylan's upright piano, wearing glasses, leaning back as he listens to the folk singer play gospel-inflected licks that seem to be an early version of the song "I'll Keep It with Mine." (Both of those instances are from D. A. Pennebaker's 1967 documentary *Dont Look Back*.) He later makes a momentary appearance in Zappa's experimental film *Uncle Meat*. In one still photo, Wilson bends over to talk to a seated Dylan, who is wearing dark Wayfarer sunglasses in the recording studio. In a publicity photo for his radio show, *The Music Factory*, Wilson stands, arms spread between two flagpoles in front of an ABC sign in New York, in a white suit, with shades and a goatee. On audio, we have hours of talk and record spinning from that radio show, but there are also overheard bits like the opening of "Bob Dylan's 115th Dream," where Wilson laughs after a false start by Dylan, then calls a new take. In another photo, he's at work behind the glass, beside the mixing board, surrounded by a smoking Frank Zappa and other personnel. Wilson is talking on the phone, as he reportedly was during many recording sessions. In yet a different photo, he leans back in a chair, playing an acoustic guitar with the neck pointing up, lifted close to his ear.

A number of musicians have complained that he was too hands-off in the studio, more interested in his phone calls and his female guests in the sound booth than in the work of producing records. But just as often he's remembered as an astute, sympathetic, and skilled producer who allowed recording artists to be themselves. In fact, he was an instigator—the *producer* in more than one sense of a series of historic recording sessions involving a range of different musical genres. He was almost always engaged with the creative side of the recording process (of course there were some records he took on solely, or mostly, for business reasons).

Lately, it seems as if Wilson pops up everywhere, at least among music bloggers and music historians. But he was no Zelig. That reference to the Woody Allen character gets it exactly wrong. Yes, Wilson often shows up, just out of frame, at various historical turning points in the 1960s. But unlike the nebbishy Leonard Zelig, Wilson, according to most accounts, was usually the coolest person in the room. Neither insignificant nor obscure back then, he didn't just happen to be in the right place at the right time. On the contrary, he was an astute observer of trends and a catalyst of cultural events, a cool hunter and a scene-maker. From what he says in interviews and on his radio show, it's clear that he saw all of this as just part of his job. Wilson's title at MGM/Verve was Director of Pop A&R East Coast. He was a record producer in the technical sense; but he was also what was called at the time an A&R (artists and repertoires) executive, that is, a producer in something like the theatrical sense: an instigator, fundraiser, coordinator, and promoter of performers, gigs, and recordings, someone in charge of developing "talent" and repertoire.

The word "Pop" In Wilson's job title at Verve is doing a lot of work, in keeping with the typical usage of the time. Earlier in his career, he had begun with jazz. At Harvard in the 1950s, where he was studying economics but also working at the student radio station, WHRB, he founded the New Jazz Society. A notice appeared in the *Harvard Crimson* April 9, 1953, under the headline "Jazz Club Forms; To Meet Tonight":

> Establishment of a new jazz society, whose purpose is "to create an atmosphere here at Harvard that will foster an appreciation of the idiom," was announced last night by its provisional president, Thomas B. Wilson, Jr. '54. [. . .]
>
> Named the Harvard New Jazz Society, the group will "focus attention on all that's good in jazz, not only bop or progressive. Only our [sic: he must have said "Our only"] prejudice," Wilson stated, "is a catholicity of jazz taste."
>
> The group will hold an organizational meeting at 7:30 p.m. in the Lamont Forum Room. Wilson extends an invitation to "all interested in jazz and its recognition as an indigenous art form."

In retrospect, we can already see in this college newspaper announcement the producer's career-long core values. He seeks to "create" (an "atmosphere") and to "foster" (an "appreciation") of jazz (which he views in anthropological and genre terms, as an "indigenous art form" and an "idiom"). The appreciation will not be restricted to the Ivy League campus. He intends to make a whole scene, a musical community. The academic club will also operate out in the city, including local jazz clubs like Storyville and the High Hat, as well as the usual lecture and performance series on the Cambridge campus. The notice concludes that Wilson had already "experimented with" this scene-making "idea" for the Jazz Society a couple of months earlier. It's clear that he begins from a fundamental premise ("Our only prejudice") in favor of "a catholicity of . . . taste." That's "catholicity" with a lowercase "c"—meaning inclusive in a comprehensive way, embracing a wide range of things.[23] This anticipates his hipper personal motto for years thereafter: "everything is everything."

It was as a result of that experience with the New Jazz Society and in the clubs of Boston that he founded his own jazz label, Transition Records, in 1955. There he produced debut albums by free-jazz and avant-garde musicians Cecil Taylor and Sun Ra, among others. The recent graduate made use of the WHRB radio studio facilities and engineers to produce records for Transition.[24] He always acted as an A&R man as well as a studio producer, finding and developing musicians and promoting them before and after producing them, a role he would continue at Columbia Records, MGM/Verve, and then in the 1970s with his own Tom Wilson Organization. He stayed alert for new groups and new scenes, and the records he made sometimes helped to create the scenes from which they emerged. For example, he sponsored and produced a series of concerts at the Cafe Au Go Go in Greenwich Village, The Blues Bag, a phenomenon all its own that attracted a large audience and was reviewed in the *New York Times*, but was also the source of tapes that Wilson turned into the first album by the Blues Project, *Live at the Cafe Au Go Go*. Wilson found and fostered talent and found and fostered contexts out of which new talent—but also new forms and genres of music—could arise and thrive. He was a catalyst at every level, from booking personnel for recording sessions, to taking meetings with the marketing department, to conceptualizing rosters of artists and acts, albums and their contents, and—he especially seemed to enjoy this one—visiting happening clubs at all hours to hear new music or support his already-signed performers.

PRODUCING FOLK-ROCK

Two examples serve to illustrate Wilson's importance. These are relatively well-known stories involving famous musicians and iconic songs: Bob Dylan's "Like a Rolling Stone" and Simon & Garfunkel's "The Sound of Silence." Wilson was responsible for both—not just for the records but for the unique new sounds they demonstrated. The Dylan story is about his epochal shift from folk to folk-rock, usually referred to as his "going electric." It's one of the founding myths of rock history, a way of summing up a shift in the zeitgeist. You've likely heard it before: Dylan went onstage with a sunburst Fender Stratocaster and an electric band featuring Mike Bloomfield on guitar and Al Kooper on organ at the Newport Folk Festival in July 1965. He was booed by at least some in the audience. Folk-music godfather Pete Seeger may or may not have threatened to axe the power cord, whether over the genre of the music or how loudly it was played. On Dylan's tour that year, there were similarly hostile reactions to his new folk-rock sound, summed up in the ludicrously earnest cry of one British fan in the spring of 1966: "*Judas!*"[25]

It was partly Wilson's fault. He had just produced Dylan's album *Bringing It All Back Home* and, more recently, using essentially the same musicians, the single "Like a Rolling Stone." At the time of the festival, he was in the midst of producing the groundbreaking album *Highway 61 Revisited*, which would be released in August. About producing Dylan, Wilson said quietly, matter-of-factly:

> I didn't even particularly like folk music. I'd been recording Sun Ra and Coltrane, and I thought folk music was for the dumb guys. This guy, Dylan, played like the dumb guys, but then these words came out. I was flabbergasted. I said to Albert Grossman [Dylan's manager], "If you put some background to this, you might have a white Ray Charles with a message."[26]

Adding "some background" is an understatement for what happened in his sessions with Dylan. Pause for a minute and note that, for Wilson, the introduction of electric guitar, organ, bass, and drums, played by skilled session musicians, was a way to put Dylan (and his lyrical brilliance) into conversation with the R&B and soul tradition. Wilson wasn't out to imitate the Byrds or the Animals so much as to experiment with a sound that crossed boundaries of genre and race, driven by that "catholicity of . . . taste." When Dylan was asked later about Wilson's claim that he was responsible for the singer's going electric, giving him the "rock & roll sound," he laughed. "Did he say that? Well, if he said it . . .

[*laughs*] more power to him. [*Laughs.*] He did to a certain extent. That is true. He did. He had a *sound* in mind" (my emphasis).[27]

During the sessions in June 1965 for "Like a Rolling Stone," which would be released as a single and also appear on *Highway 61 Revisited*, Wilson selected players, made suggestions, then calmly orchestrated the results. Partly as a result of this high-level style of working, I think, he's treated unfairly by Greil Marcus in that critic's otherwise brilliant book on the iconic song.[28] Marcus implies that Wilson's production of "Like a Rolling Stone" was not as effective as the final mix made by Bob Johnston (after Wilson was dismissed) because, Marcus says, Wilson's "characteristic sound is not at bottom a rock 'n' roll sound; it's too clean, too discrete."[29] Marcus's description of Wilson's sound here is not wrong. But the implied negative aesthetic judgment seems arbitrary—we might even call it rockist—in its assumptions about the supposed superiority of a dirty (rather than "clean"), organically "whole" (rather than "discrete") sound. The judgment is perhaps anti-pop (and probably, in a different way, anti-jazz). It's revealing in its preference for a certain *kind* of rock 'n' roll sound. Marcus accuses Wilson's production of having "a harsh edge—the acrid tone that was everywhere in 1965, the sound of the time, if not the times."[30] I know what he means, but, again, I don't agree with the pejorative judgment. Most listeners would rightly call the Byrds' music from the same time jangly, if not exactly "acrid"—but that's not necessarily a bad thing. It was a pop sound that appealed to a lot of listeners at that "time," at that historical moment. In fact, it was a folk-rock sound.

Around 1965, a good deal of pop in various genres did sound, if not necessarily "harsh" or "acrid," a little *metallic*, sometimes even *tinny*. And it often involved a clean separation of instruments, as Marcus says, but these were also frequently mixed with echo and/or tremolo to produce a warbly, layered soundscape indebted to surf music, Phil Spector's wall of sound, and numerous studio string sections as heard on records at the end of the monaural era. Interestingly, even the Velvet Underground would later say that they were attempting to create a Phil Spector–style wall of sound with just their four-piece rock band. Echoey, layered, immersive mixes *were* the sound "of the time."

Marcus's criticism of Wilson's sound can also be read against the grain, as a backhanded, if unintended, compliment. The sound *was* of its time, of its own pop moment, and indeed suggested where pop was in that moment—and perhaps something about its context, the times. That reedy organ on "Like a Rolling Stone" *is* in some ways "harsh" in tone, and it certainly stands out separately from the mix at times. But, as Marcus himself says, "as the song goes on, the organ becomes the conductor of its own drama. For the song, it is the shaping hand."[31] The actual human hand that played that organ belonged to Al Kooper, who came to the recording session at Wilson's invitation, ostensibly just to observe, listen, maybe sit in on guitar. That last idea he gave up once he heard Mike Bloomfield play his newly purchased Fender. What happened next has become legend (and myth). During a break, he slipped in unnoticed behind the Hammond organ. On the tapes you can hear Wilson's surprise when he comes back from break and sees Kooper. He asks, "Hey, what are you doing there?" They both laugh, Wilson calls out the number of the take, and Kooper plays on the organ what would become the signature part of this soon-to-be famous song. As they listened to playback, Dylan insisted that the organ part be turned up. Wilson said, "Hey, man, that cat's not an organ player," and Dylan replied, "Hey, now don't tell me who's an organ player and who's not. Just turn the organ up."[32] There are two things to note about this event: first, hijacking that organ for "Like a Rolling Stone" was the beginning of Kooper's own long and storied career as a rock keyboardist and bandleader. Second, Kooper's organ was an *electric* instrument, the sound of which had become associated with R&B and rock 'n' roll, just as much a part of Dylan's new sound as Mike Bloomfield's electric guitar.

Like everything having to do with Bob Dylan, that story has been retold many times. I'll leave it there. In the next two chapters, however, I look at what was soon to be Kooper's new band, the Blues Project, whom Wilson was also producing at around the same time as the later Dylan sessions. Wilson produced "Like a Rolling Stone" at the crossroads of what had been until then relatively separate sounds, genres, and scenes. The result was a hit single, despite the song's length. Marcus focuses on the fact that Wilson was dismissed as Dylan's producer shortly thereafter, but Dylan himself always spoke positively about Wilson.

The Dylan story also reminds us of how important session musicians still were at the time, a fact that comes up repeatedly in this book. Even as the focus had started to shift at around the same time in favor of bands' writing and performing their own original material, a trend that would continue into the 1970s, session players were integral to the songwriting and publishing business and would remain so for another decade or so. At that point in 1965, Kooper himself still had one foot in the Tin Pan Alley system of music production. He had emerged out of early rock 'n' roll and doo-wop, and, tellingly, he operated for several years into the 1960s with two musical personas, one for the "weekend folk singer, under the pseudonym 'Al Casey,'" and the other, for the Tin Pan Alley songwriter working at 1650 Broadway under his legal name, "Al Kooper" (born Alan Kuperschmidt). He came to view this divided identity as inauthentic, however, and he credited hearing "Subterranean Homesick Blues"—another Wilson production—for awakening him to the possibility of playing folk-rock or blues-rock more or less as himself.[33] Kooper's musical double life wasn't unusual in the mid-1960s, as the earlier system associated with the Brill Building (with nearby buildings in midtown Manhattan) was giving way to a new model of creativity and hit-making. As late as September 1966, Kooper's bandmates in the Blues Project were still ribbing him onstage for cowriting a pop hit recorded by Gary Lewis and the Playboys, a version Kooper detested, "This Diamond Ring"—way back, they teased, "in his former life as a Tin Pan Alley songwriter, living in Queens."[34]

THE SOUND OF "THE SOUND OF SILENCE"

Another brief story about Wilson's mid-1960s sound. Like Al Kooper, Paul Simon was a young Jewish songwriter from Queens who emerged from the Brill Building scene, who also worked under multiple names, and was also produced by Tom Wilson. Coincidentally, Kooper and Simon used to play music together when they were teenagers.[35] Just after the recording sessions for "Like a Rolling Stone" in 1965, Wilson went into the studio and tried another hybrid folk-rock mix, in this case without the musicians' knowledge. Simon was in London pursuing a solo career and Art Garfunkel was studying uptown at Columbia University. Both were trying to move on from their recent efforts to make records when Wilson added electric instruments to their obscure single, "The Sound of Silence," turning it into a folk-rock song and a massive hit.

Wilson had first recorded the acoustic folk duo for Columbia Records on what he called his "experimental budget." The resulting album, *Wednesday Morning, 3 A.M.*, did not sell. But some college radio stations had started to play "The Sound of Silence," and Wilson realized that he could do something else with the track. The Byrds' folk-rock was one model for the sound. Dylan's recent work was another. Wilson hired some of the same skilled session musicians who had played on Dylan's record—electric guitars, bass, and drums—to record a rock layer for the Simon & Garfunkel folk song. The new sound kicks in with a drum fill following the first verse (just after the phrase "In restless dreams I walked alone"), but it's foreshadowed in the Byrds-style electric arpeggios dubbed over the opening verse. Guitarist Al Gorgoni did not use an electric twelve-string like Roger McGuinn's. He and Vinnie Bell just recorded multiple guitar parts—including the song's bluesy licks—onto a single track.[36] Gorgoni had played on Dylan's *Bringing It All Back Home*, and later in 1966 would play on the Monkees' "I'm a Believer." Much later, he would say that he didn't much like the *sound* of "The Sound of Silence." Actually, some accounts have said that Simon wasn't crazy about it either when he first heard the remix. But in a recent documentary, Simon says that he was indeed sent the song and tacitly approved its release.[37] Wilson was "so cool," Simon says, that he just assumed the producer knew what he was doing. The newly remixed single reached number one on the charts. The record company rushed to bring out an album in 1966, *Sounds of Silence* (*Sounds* plural), to try to cash in on the single's success.

Relistening now, I can't help but think that the remixed single may have been so successful in part *because* of its sometimes awkward sound, the way it wears its genre contradictions on its sleeve. You can plainly hear the distance between the born-acoustic song and the superadded electric tracks. I suspect others heard the song as I did back then, as a deliberate, rather than accidental, hybrid, an uncanny monster: folk-*plus*-rock. That was what made it cool, that friction. It may have been a sound Wilson happened upon, but it worked, representing the feeling of distance and wistful alienation in the lyrics. As Richie Unterberger puts it, the mix of electric instruments, drums, and echo "immeasurably enhances the haunting song's somber power, even if the musicians seemed otherwise to have little idea of what they'd achieved."[38] The tinny guitar parts are central to the song's effect. The added echo and multitracking resulted in something interesting for that time, a sense of layered depths, like a sonic archaeological site where you can hear traces of various musical presences haunting the final mix. Something like the same layered effect is also at the heart of Spector's famous wall of sound. But in Wilson's recording it's less monolithic, more as if the wall of sound(s) had been partly demolished, leaving irregular layers of wallpaper, brick, and stucco showing through here and there. Contrast is key, like the percussive smack and tinny twang of electric instruments alongside mellow fingerpicked acoustic guitars and vocal harmonies. It's as if the song's different potential genre-associated sounds are struggling against one another, and the final (re)mix captures echoes of the struggle.

GENRE ECLECTICISM AND THE ALBUM AS A FORM

This book is not a biography of Tom Wilson. (As I write, I'm looking forward to the biopic as well as the documentary.) But Wilson is at the heart of the book because his eclecticism and pursuit of hybrid sounds both reflected and helped to create a key trend of 1966: the eclectic multiplication and rapid succession of genres, a phenomenon closely bound up with the pursuit of musical authenticity in the face of an increasingly overwhelming music industry.

Wilson knew the music industry from top to bottom. He changed pop music by making albums that pursued an eclectic vision. This book's chapters are organized around albums that Wilson produced in 1966, which, taken together, help us to understand what was going on in pop at the time. Chapter to chapter, I follow Tom Wilson like a trusted guide, someone who knows all the scenes, knows what's happening. He pops up in every chapter, as I move from Batman, to the Blues Project, to Sun Ra and his Arkestra, to the Velvet Underground, to Frank Zappa, to Hugh Masekela, to Eric Burdon & the Animals, and end with the Monkees—the only musical act featured in the book Wilson did not produce.

As I said, the title of the book, "Everything Is Everything," was a favorite catchphrase of Wilson's, one he liked to repeat on his radio show, *The Music Factory* (1967–1968). It may sound like the common response of resignation to what is unchangeable, "it is what it is" (or the future-tense version, "que sera, sera"). Or like a cliché out of the psychedelic era about the cosmic oneness of the universe: his use of the phrase did coincide with the love generation and its over-the-top rhetoric. But the phrase also shows up in various sectors of Black culture in particular, in the discourse of the Nation of Islam, for example. And in music, it's found in soul, R&B, and hip-hop as the title of songs by Diana Ross (1970), Donny Hathaway (1970), and later by Lauryn Hill (1998, "What is meant to be will be"), and as the title of an album by Brand Nubian (1994). It can be heard, spoken, in the multilayered mix of the opening bars of Marvin Gaye's "What's Going On" (1971), and again in Kendrick Lamar's "The Heart, Part 5" (2022). For Wilson, "everything is everything" may have been a Black thing. But it also clearly had a universal musicological meaning. It was a manifesto of a cool but open eclecticism—that "catholicity of . . . taste" mentioned in the student newspaper article about his founding of the New Jazz Society. It's a way to say that being open to everything means everything.

It was also a manifesto of genre desegregation in an era of increasing differentiation of genres and radio formats. Where music companies saw commercial potential in audience segmentation, Wilson imagined a listener with eclectic taste, an ear for a diverse range of genres and sounds. In the terminology of the day, he would also have said that he was interested in a "mixed bag" of genres and styles, and of sometimes bringing some of them together in new ways. As a professional listener, Wilson followed Western and Asian music, high and low styles, underground and mainstream. His own career—in jazz, folk, pop, rock, and what later came to be known as world music, even, near the end working on an avant-garde R&B and reggae opera—makes it clear that a hybrid-promoting eclecticism was the soul of his own taste. In one radio interview, he spelled out the connection between the rise of long-playing albums and this eclectic ideal, which for him seemed to reach toward something like a new cosmopolitan world music:

> More and more, we're coming toward an operatic form and LPs, and I call it the Everything Is Everything type of music. And I think it's going to destroy a lot of barriers internationally between people because there will come a time, I think now when any national group can hear within the field of rock elements of international music, besides what we Americans have always been contributing to pop music.[39]

For Wilson, "everything is everything" is connected to the album as a form and has enormous implications for pop music, globally considered. The idea of an "operatic form" itself implies genre diversity and universality: the opera is the form containing a multiplicity of other forms.

As *Billboard* magazine briefly noted, May 21, 1966, Wilson was brought to MGM "to build up an LP operation and establish artists with consistent LP value," even "to try to change singles artists into album artists."[40] The possibilities of the album were crucial to Wilson's vision. Those possibilities included capaciousness—the way you could fit two long sides of music, a whole collection or "album" of songs or movements, on a single disc. In fact, the term "album" had been used in earlier decades for booklets with paper sleeves like pages meant to hold multiple recorded discs between leather or vinyl covers, like a photo album but for records. The rise of the 10-inch and then the 12-inch vinyl microgroove-format LP in the 1960s made possible whole albums on one (or two) discs. In its first decade or so, rock 'n' roll was a genre found on 45 rpm singles. By the end of the 1960s, thanks in part to the eventual rise of album-oriented FM radio, rock music was closely associated with the LP. Experiment and eclecticism in pop music were encouraged by the rise of the album as a (long) form. On his radio show, *The Music Factory* (program 7), Wilson defines the ideal as a kind of fluid genre transfer and exchange, "the transfusion of ideas back and forth between classical music, jazz, rock 'n' roll, rhythm & blues."

There's another kind of border-crossing implied in Wilson's eclecticism: it involves a "vertical" mobility between pop music and the avant-garde. "By 1965," as Jon Savage says, "pop culture was broad enough to include and exalt the avant-garde."[41] But it was not quite a settled relationship. We might say that avant-garde music—which included underground experiments and some contemporary classical compositions—and commercial pop were openly engaged in a kind of public dance, influencing and goading one another on. In another repeated line from the radio show, Wilson declared that he intended to play a range of music, "sometimes popular and sometimes *recherché*" (obscure or exotic). He meant that he would play both or either at any given time, and that sometimes he'd juxtapose them, setting off the popular *against* the *recherché*, staging small, productive confrontations, challenging assumptions about the limits of popular taste. Literary critic Irving Howe wrote in 1967 about how the middle class learned to consume artists' avant-garde "attacks" as "pleasing entertainments" and thus co-opted and assimilated the avant-garde, even if in a "vulgarize[d]" form.[42] But that was the whole point of at least one form of the avant-garde in the 1960s, pop art, especially in Andy Warhol's version: to erase (with a deadpan shrug) the kind of distinction of taste on which Howe's criticism depends. Pop art drew from and participated in that more pervasive underground attitude, associated especially with gay culture, camp. In the mid 1960s, mainstream America embraced pop art and, along with it, a mainstream version of camp, straighter and suitable for prime time. When *Batman* appeared on TV, January 12, 1966, at least a segment of the mass audience knew how to play along with the show's over-the-top camp and pop art signifiers. When *The Monkees* debuted at the end of that year, it could count on a similar audience response.

WORKING IN THE MUSIC FACTORY

Andy Warhol famously called his studio/salon The Factory. Tom Wilson called his syndicated radio show *The Music Factory*. Warhol's art provided an example of reframing and recontextualizing as a technique. Just as Warhol did with celebrity images or consumer-product packaging, Wilson helped various musicians reframe their roots-based folk music as jangly folk-rock, for example, or reframe their modern jazz as experimental Afrofuturism (in the case of Sun Ra), or express their jazz as a world music of the African diaspora (in the case of Hugh Masekela). He did this in part by borrowing and recontextualizing adjacent musical sounds, motifs, and conventions, from low to high (popular to *recherché*) and back again. His radio show was a promotional vehicle for the relatively diverse MGM/Verve catalog. But he often made something interesting out of the interviews and playlists anyway, giving the shows an underground radio feel with his free talk and self-reflexive humor about the whole absurd enterprise.

The show first aired on WABC-FM in New York, June 1967.[43] It was distributed to stations around the country on 12-inch vinyl discs, played directly to air from DJs' turntables. During many of the programs, Wilson riffed on the factory metaphor and made jokes about imaginary "slaves" who were laboring behind the scenes, taking lunch breaks, etc. In one recurring gag, he pretended to raise hogs and keep a barbecue fired up out back—as if he were just a slow-talking DJ at some border station—and laughingly offered to share soul-food delicacies with his guests. Wilson chose for the show's intro and outro a track that he had produced for *Freak Out!*, Frank Zappa's weird drone-and-chant piece, intended as part of a larger avant-garde composition, "Help, I'm a Rock." The repetitive music and chanted lyrics sound like a vision out of a nightmare or a fairy tale or a bad trip. It's also like a philosophy thought experiment: what is it like to *be* a rock? The tagline is repeated over a thumping bass and layered ambient noise. In context, it's hard not to think that it may have been a parodic response to Simon & Garfunkel's "I Am a Rock" from *Sounds of Silence*, or maybe it's just a parody of "rock" music in general, written by a semi-reluctant participant. Every time we hear it as the intro or outro to a program of *The Music Factory*, it's hard to avoid thinking of the song as Wilson's own sardonic cry for help from his position as a promotional DJ working for a record label that wanted everything set in stone. Ultimately, the choice of this song makes a statement about the kind of *recherché* underground rock that Wilson intended to bring into the mix on the show, despite the conditions of production he knew so well.

In the first *Music Factory* program, Wilson says that some people may view the band, the Mothers of Invention, as "camp" or "pop art," but he disagrees. This may seem like an odd thing to even bring up, from our own art-historical vantage. But Wilson took it for granted there might be a perceived connection between Zappa's kind of outrageous experiments and Warhol's work with the Velvet Underground and the Exploding Plastic Inevitable. The remark reminds us that one of the meanings of "pop art" as a modifier at the time was as a synonym for "sardonic"—as in a cynical prank, a hoax, or a put-on. Also, the Mothers were more a part of the art scene and Warhol was more a part of the rock scene than we may remember, and the comparison would have come naturally to the producer of the Velvet Underground. As I've already suggested, the name *The Music Factory* was likely inspired by Warhol's Factory in New York. The record he helped the Velvet Underground make came to define authentic underground music, defined in opposition to mainstream pop and rock clichés. But it did so in the form of a hybrid: avant-garde art-rock. Hybrid genres and forms were at the heart of pop in 1966. A folk-rock song, when it works, sounds like *both* kinds of music at the same time, as when the finger-plucked arpeggios of "The Sound of Silence" seem to strain against the overdubbed bass and drums, and the vocals and guitars seem to force the tempo of the rock ensemble to stretch and retract like taffy.

ONCE UPON A TIME IN THE 1960s

This book looks back at pop music in 1966. But for a moment I want to turn to a film, one that also looks back at 1960s music: Quentin Tarantino's *Once Upon a Time in Hollywood* (2019). Conflict between the cool and the uncool, the authentic and the phony, is one of the subjects of the film, a revisionist retelling of the Manson Family murders of August 1969. As in every Tarantino film, the soundtrack is obsessively curated. There are a few deliberate anachronisms, but most of the songs are from within a couple of years of 1969. The point seems to be to dramatize the conflict between pop from the middle of the decade and the increasingly dark psychedelic rock that emerged later in 1960s, and to connect that conflict to a dark turn in the culture. When Sharon Tate, played by Margot Robbie, drops the needle on an album and starts to dance, the tunes are from 1966: Paul Revere & the Raiders' "Hungry" and "Good Thing," both from the album, *The Spirit of '67*. (The bicentennial joke aside, the album was actually released November 28, 1966.) Later in the film, we glimpse the Raiders performing a different song, "Mr. Sun, Mr. Moon"—this one from 1969—on a blurry TV being watched by Manson Family members sitting around at the Spahn Movie Ranch. The different settings are significant. Tate's visceral pleasure belongs to 1966; the sullen zombie-watching by murderous girls belongs to 1969.

When Tate plays "Hungry," the scene provides the key for this interpretation of the soundtrack, and maybe the movie as a whole. Jay Sebring comes dancing into the room where Tate is already dancing to the album, then stops, embarrassed. She teases him: "Aw, what's the matter? Are you afraid I'll tell Jim *Morrison* you're dancing to Paul Revere & the Raiders? Are they not *cool* enough for you?" It's a commonplace 1960s conversation about what was cool and what was not. At a time when "bubblegum" and "commercial" were serious slurs, cultural credibility was a touchy subject. The reference to Morrison and the Doors foreshadows the coming darkness, but the script rewrites the Manson murders as a pulp-fiction revenge fantasy that vanquishes the murderous hippies and spares the beautiful Tate, along with Sebring and the other victims. Jim Morrison and the Doors actually did stints at the Whisky a Go Go in Los Angeles. We might have expected *that* band's dark psychodrama-rock to provide the soundtrack for the film's end-of-the-1960s moment. But one of the first times we glimpse the bearded Charlie Manson, through a window, he's skulking outside while sunny pop plays inside the house on Cielo Drive. Early on, one of the Manson girls had declared that all actors are "phony." Tarantino deliberately uses the uncool pop band Paul Revere & the Raiders, who dressed in gimmicky Revolutionary War costumes, as a metaphor for an alternate poptimistic universe, in which joy—and acting, and storytelling, and record producing—win out over darkness and violence. All of this is paradoxically argued in a hyperviolent Tarantino film.

There is an actual link between the house on Cielo Drive and Paul Revere & the Raiders, as Tarantino knows. Back in 1966, the band's producer, Terry Melcher, had lived in the same house that Tate would share with Roman Polanski in 1969. The Raiders' singer Mark Lindsay had stayed there with Melcher in 1966—in fact, he and Melcher wrote "Good Thing" in that very house. Manson was an aspiring musician known to Dennis Wilson of the Beach Boys and others, and the Tate murders have sometimes been seen, at least in part, as retaliation for Melcher's refusal to sign him to a record deal. Manson had reportedly visited the house looking for Melcher earlier that year. Whether or not Manson was directly motivated by the rejection, the producer was likely part of the mix. Melcher was a producer at Columbia Records during the same time period that Wilson was at the company. He played his own role in the birth of folk-rock by producing the Byrds' electric take on Dylan's folk music. Wilson later joked that, before Melcher came along, he thought of *himself* as "the folk-rock Czar," the implication being that Melcher had taken over that role.[44] Setting Manson's derangement aside, producers like Melcher and Wilson did wield immense power in the world of 1960s pop.

That Raiders' record from 1966—in the film, we see the album cover—is a deliberate choice by the director. To have that music still playing three years later, in 1969, still haunting the house that Melcher had rented, where Mark Lindsay had slept and composed and played the music, is to celebrate an alternative to the darkness of 1969. The lyric of "Good Thing" recites a positive charm against "bad vibrations," celebrating a willed "groovy world" to counter the actual world that has "got you down." As the song says, "They don't care if you live or die . . . . Girl, we're gonna have a good thing."

Tarantino's final revisionist anachronism in the film is about Batman, which makes sense because comic books often deal in alternative timelines and speculative parallel universes. During the closing credits of *Once Upon a Time in Hollywood*, we hear an actual 1966 AM radio promotional contest for the *Batman* TV show—which, in real life, had been off the air for a year before the 1969 story we've been watching. It's just one more counterfactual fantasy: what if *Batman* had stayed on the air through 1969? (The talent agent played by Al Pacino had earlier in the film suggested that Leonardo DiCaprio's character might end up with a part on the show, just as if it *were* still on the air.) The radio spot opens with the well-known "Batman Theme," followed by the voices of Adam West and Burt Ward as Batman and Robin. In an early example of transmedia marketing, radio listeners were given a series of clues and asked to guess the secret number of the red Batphone seen on the TV show. They were told to send their entries in on postcards, and the winning fan would get to visit the TV studio and have lunch with Batman and Robin. Then, as West's Batman continues, "you'll ride to the Batcave in the Batmobile, where Robin and I will present you with a 1966 color television set." Full circle, back to television.

THE NOSTALGIA TRAP

Tarantino's film is clearly nostalgic for the go-go innocence destroyed by the bad trip of 1969, epitomized in Manson's obsession with and apocalyptic interpretation of *The Beatles* (a.k.a. "The White Album" [1968]). But the conflicts of musical genres at the time—pop versus underground, bubblegum versus acid rock, folk and blues versus psychedelia—were not experienced as a straightforward succession of eras. The genre options overlapped in the mid-1960s and the conflicts were dynamic and shifting, connected to cultural anxieties around race, genre, and authenticity.

There is something admirable about Tarantino's stubborn insistence on the pleasures of music, comics, and fandom in the face of the harsh realities of history. But there's also something slightly creepy and escapist about it, maybe because it demonstrates how a fetish for go-go boots (or bare feet) and pop songs can serve as a mechanism of defense and denial, denial even of one's own implication in violent storytelling. An obsession with mid-1960s music is an especially seductive trap for the Boomer demographic, people whose childhood or youth took place to that soundtrack (raising my own hand here). It's a trap I probably can't altogether escape. But in this book, I try to remain self-conscious about it, to make it part of the story, a story that continues to resonate today.

So let me say: despite being inspired by some of my favorite albums and TV shows from the 1960s, including the first album I bought with my own money, this book is not an exercise in nostalgia. Instead, it's intended as a slice of pop music history. Like most history, it's about conflicts and complications. I've tried to keep those conflicts and complications—about race, for example, and about commercial exploitation—front and center. I obviously think the albums I've written about are important: I wrote a book about them! I even think they're pleasurable to listen to. But I've avoided tedious barstool debates (nowadays more likely to take place on the internet) over who or what was "the greatest" or "most underrated" whatever: song, album, guitarist, NFL quarterback, or superhero. I don't consider any of the albums in the chapters that follow a "lost" or "rediscovered" masterpiece. Most were never really lost; some are not masterpieces. But all of them are historically important. I hope this book can convince you that all of the albums are at least *interesting*, as cultural artifacts and as music, worth hearing or hearing again. At this late date, when the album as a form has almost been displaced by streaming and social media distribution, almost dissolved into tracks, clips, short-form videos, and memes—or, conversely, turned into a collectible analog fetish object, pressed in colored vinyl, reissued with new packaging—it takes an act of historical imagination to return to a time over half a century ago, when the album first emerged as the dominant material form for conveying recorded pop music. One key purpose of this book is to aid that act of imagination.

WHAT FOLLOWS

In that spirit, I've structured the book like a stack of albums we can flip through and talk about. A playlist of selections from the albums and songs discussed can be found here: https://music.apple.com/us/playlist/everything-is-everything/pl

.u-EdAVzvWT95bGK. One way or another, whether via a streaming service, on YouTube, or on vintage or reissued vinyl (or even CD), you should be able to find most of these records, listen to them, and follow for yourself this book's alternative route through 1966. All of the albums, with a few exceptions, were produced by Tom Wilson.

Here's the core list: *Batman and Robin* (1966), by "Dan & Dale"; *Live at the Cafe Au Go Go* (1966) and *Projections* (1966), by the Blues Project; *The Futuristic Sounds of Sun Ra* (1962), *The Magic City* (1966), and *Strange Strings* (1967), by Sun Ra and his Arkestra; *The Velvet Underground & Nico*, by the Velvet Underground and Nico (recorded 1966, released spring 1967); *Lou Reed, Words & Music*, by Lou Reed (recorded 1965); *Freak Out!* (1966) and *Absolutely Free* (1967), by Frank Zappa and the Mothers of Invention; *Grrr* (recorded 1965, released 1966), *The Americanization of Ooga Booga* (1966), and *Hugh Masekela's Next Album* (1966), by Hugh Masekela; *Animalism* (1966), *Eric Is Here* (1967), and *Winds of Change* (1967), by the Animals, Eric Burdon, and Eric Burdon & the Animals; *The Monkees* (1966), *More of the Monkees* (1967), and *Headquarters* (1967), by the Monkees. Sometimes I set these albums in the context of adjacent albums, or albums (or, occasionally, singles) that appeared just before or after 1966–1967, like the Monkees' *Head* (1968), for example, a milestone—or tombstone—in their career.

The final chapter is about the Monkees, the TV show, albums, and film. A made-for-TV band, as the story goes, they rebelled like four Pinocchios against their puppeteers with the goal of becoming a real band. Of the albums discussed in this book, only *The Monkees* and other Monkees albums—and those secondary albums on my list for purposes of context—were not produced by Tom Wilson. But, along with the TV show it was recorded to promote, *The Monkees* album was the culmination of the transformations pop music underwent that year, transformations Wilson's work helped bring about. It's almost as if the Monkees had to be invented to embody the shifts in genre and audience, the conflicts around issues of genre, and the search for an ever-elusive authenticity, that characterized pop in 1966. No one pursued eclectic and hybrid sounds more tirelessly than Wilson. In the end, that's what he meant by his oft-repeated catchphrase, everything is everything. But it can also refer to the fractal nature of music and pop culture history in 1966. Wider meanings are contained within each smaller moment of pop culture; every *thing* contains everything, when you look closely enough. This is true even in the case of a throwaway kids' record and tie-in for a popular TV show, based on a campy comic-book hero, as we see in the next chapter.

CHAPTER ONE

THE YEAR OF THE BAT

The Sensational Guitars of Dan & Dale, *Batman and Robin* (1966)

THIS CHAPTER IS ABOUT A MOSTLY INSTRUMENTAL *BATMAN AND ROBIN* album released at the beginning of 1966. I open this book with it for several reasons. To begin, it was the first album I bought with my own money in 1966, and it meant a lot to me. It meant even more years later, when I learned who played on it, listened with new ears, and came to appreciate its rich musical and cultural contexts.

Second, some truly amazing musicians played on the album. It's an example of the kind of work by later famous or significant artists that's worth considering for what it tells us about those artists: in this case, an eclectic combination of avant-garde jazz players and blues-rock musicians. Chapters 2 and 3 are about those players: Sun Ra and members of his Arkestra and the Blues Project. Their work on the album helps prepare us to understand their more significant work later that same year.

Finally, both sets of musicians shared a producer, Tom Wilson. Both he and the musicians were obviously overqualified for the job. The album ended up better than it had any right to be. And it exemplifies a key feature of pop in 1966: it aimed a double-voiced appeal at a multilayered audience. So these first three chapters are closely related. Chapter 1 is about an odd side project by an influential producer and a diverse group of session musicians, as if they were all moonlighting as superheroes. (Sometimes they even wore capes, as both Sun Ra and Al Kooper of the Blues Project did.) Then, chapters 2 and 3 are about the musicians' "true" identities—that is, their *public* identities as creative professionals.

IN DEFENSE OF EPHEMERA

A word about ephemera. The label certainly applies in this case. The *Batman and Robin* album was a commercial cash-grab meant to be consumed and forgotten quickly, and it appears to have been made mostly for children. These two qualities could make it easy to dismiss. But I think the album was meant for kids only on one level. That's the key to understanding its appeal. The fact that it *was* a cash-grab meant that it likely aimed to appeal to multiple demographic slices of the audience—like the TV show it was cashing in on. I also want to resist dismissing this album as "bad" just because it's a commercial piece of ephemera. That begs the question of the album's significance and its pleasures, both of which are considerable.

It has been a long time since a product of mass culture was deemed beneath our attention just because it wasn't serious, high art, a work of literature or film (rather than a mere movie). Mid-twentieth-century cultural studies included the work of Roland Barthes in *Mythologies* (1957), for example, in which he interpreted professional wrestling, popular movies, detergent ads, a French travel guide, a new-model Citroën automobile, the striptease, and plastic, among other apparently trivial, ephemeral things.[1] Since then, cultural studies has made serious use of ephemera as a kind of fleeting archive, evidence for the study of historically specific practices and products.[2] Ephemera can reveal important things about the (sub)cultures that produce and consume them, and about the historical moments in which they are produced and consumed.

So this chapter is about a bit of ephemera, a 99-cent bargain-bin album that I picked up one day that continues to mean a lot to me and, it turns out, to a lot of other people. This is no doubt thanks in part to its surprisingly rich musical and cultural associations—who was involved and what they went on to do. But for me, now, it also just sounds like its moment in pop music history. I hear echoes of 1966 every time I put *Batman and Robin* on the turntable, drop the needle, and am hit with that first rolling A7 chord on the Hammond organ.

BATMAN FROM THE BARGAIN BIN

Wilson produced *Batman and Robin* at the beginning of 1966 to cash in on the ABC TV show that premiered on January 12.[3] No doubt prompted by the news of the upcoming show, expecting it to fuel a craze (or at least to make for profitable tie-ins), Wilson booked a recording session on behalf of Tifton, a novelty and toy company in Newark, New Jersey, and quickly pulled together musicians to make a Batman album.[4] Its cover features three-color comic-book images of the dynamic duo, the bat logo, and action panels down the side showing the heroes and villains, the Batmobile, and sound-effect word bubbles ("ZAP," "POW," "EEYOW"). Its aesthetic is recognizable these days as "Batman '66," one specific universe within the caped superhero's multiverse of versions and retellings. The record is credited to a fictional musical duo "Dan & Dale," whose names were probably meant to invoke Jan & Dean (but who always make me think of Chip & Dale and, by power of cartoon association, Alvin & the Chipmunks). Headlining the fake duo and their "Sensational Guitars" suggests this is going to be a surf-rock dance record of the kind still popular at the time. A number of other records were credited to the same imaginary duo. Dan & Dale seem to have been pseudonyms for a roster of anonymous studio musicians who played on the different records.

But most of *Batman and Robin*'s anonymous studio musicians have by now been unmasked. They included, improbably enough, the great jazz composer and bandleader Sun Ra on the Hammond B-3 organ, with members of his avant-garde Arkestra: John Gilmore, Pat Patrick, Tom McIntosh, and Jimmy Owens; and some of the members of the newly formed rock band the Blues Project: guitarists Danny Kalb and (maybe) Steve Katz, with Andy Kulberg on bass and Roy Blumenfeld on drums (but not, it would seem, Al Kooper—there are conflicting accounts about his presence[5]). All of the songs were apparently arranged and conducted in the studio by the Black composer and filmmaker Edward Bland, known for his 1959 documentary *The Cry of Jazz*, and who may have helped Wilson recruit some of the studio players. Wilson and Bland had met in Chicago in the 1950s.[6]

Like the episodic TV show, the album is dependably repetitive: its twelve tracks have a unified sound. That is, it's all simple garage-band surf-rock with blues-based R&B grooves. There is some riffing on royalty-free public-domain melodies by classical composers, Tchaikovsky, Chopin, and Bach, plus one blatant theft from the Beatles, with the same chords, basic melody, and guitar riffs as "She Loves You" ("The Riddler's Retreat").[7] Probably after they were recorded, the tracks were given throwaway titles: "The Bat Cave," "Batmobile Wheels," and "Robin's Theme." There are tracks named "Batman and Robin over the Roofs" *and* "Flight of the Batman," as if someone ran out of names, and there's a "Batman's Batmorang" (technically, it should be "Batarang")—in the same way that everything on the TV show was called, tongue-in-cheek, Bat-this and Bat-that. In other words, the album was one of many that year and the following year like it, and it might never have attracted attention decades later if not for the weird eclectic group of musicians who played on it. But that list of personnel allows us to look a little more closely at an album that was produced not for the ages but for the moment. That very fact—that it *was* produced for the moment—means that the album might tell us interesting things about that moment.

NA-NA-NA-NA, NA-NA-NA-NA

The opening track, of course, is "Batman Theme." It takes an effort to imagine a time when we did not already know the soon-to-be immortalized double-time bass and vocal chorus ("NA-na-na-na, BAT-MANnn!"). The tune was written by jazz and pop composer Neal Hefti, who released his own version as a single that same January, followed by his own Batman-themed album. The Hefti single debuted on the Billboard charts on February 12, where it stayed for twenty-one weeks. In March 1967, Hefti's official Batman theme won a Grammy for Best Instrumental Theme. The theme was written for the show, and a version was included on the official Nelson Riddle–orchestrated soundtrack, also released at the beginning of the year. A flood of cover versions followed, by artists including the actual Jan & Dean but also the Marketts (another group of professional studio musicians, many of whom would become famous as the Wrecking Crew), the Ventures, even the Who. This tells you something about the hip-ironic appeal of Batman-related stuff in 1966. The Ventures' cover was more or less inevitable since the group's surf-guitar sound was likely an inspiration for the tune in the first place. The Ventures' "Batman Theme" appeared on an album containing several other Bat-related titles, as well as covers of other hit TV themes: *The Man from U.N.C.L.E.*, *Get Smart*, *The Green Hornet*, and *Secret Agent*. Another likely influence on Hefti's tune was the iconic James Bond theme, which in turn helped to inspire Johnny Rivers's hit "Secret Agent Man," a tune he played for people doing the twist and the frug along with go-go dancers at

L.A.'s Whisky a Go Go. Jan & Dean's Batman album is an elaborate novelty record,[8] with comedy skits that involve "Captain Jan & Dean the Boy Blunder" loosely tying together Batman-themed tracks, most of them straight-ahead surf-rock. The opening track is a mashup of "Batman Theme" and a standard Beach Boys or Jan & Dean hit, like "The Little Old Lady from Pasadena"—a song explicitly referenced in the first skit.

That's just a small sample of the cover versions of "Batman Theme." The song, like the TV show, was everywhere that year. By contrast with most versions, the Sun Ra and Blues Project "Batman Theme" is relatively straightforward rock music. The vocals are markedly less pretty than in most versions, a little funkier, even a little raunchier. The bass is heavier. And then there's that Hammond organ, which, in the hands of Sun Ra, drives the "Theme" in a way that sets it apart from other versions.

SICK SOUND EFFECTS

Like the TV show, the album is jokey, even corny, just in terms of how it sounds. One of the ways we know it was intended in part as a novelty record and in part as a kids' record is the prevalence of goofy sound effects. Some tracks on *Batman and Robin* use sound effects to suggest themes or actions, as if you were listening to stories on the old radio show *Batman*. What sounds like a combination of both a siren whistle *and* a manual slide whistle, bat squeaks, and manic laughter—invoking the Joker or the Riddler—mimic mad pursuit on "Flight of the Batman." A wailing harmonica riff and rhythmic jaw harp suggest jack-in-the box insanity on "The Joker Is Wild."

Sound effects like these have a long history in pop music, especially in novelty tunes, going back at least to Spike Jones in the big-band era and continuing in folk music and on many dance records in the early sixties. The Surfaris's 1963 hit "Wipeout," for example, opens with a crazy laugh, leading into its iconic drumroll. In July 1966, a novelty single charted that even had manic laughter in its title: "They're Coming to Take Me Away Again, Ha-Haaa!," by Napoleon XIV (Jerry Samuels). Just a chanted lyric over a marching snare drum, handclap, and tambourine, it uses echo, pitch distortion, and its own weird siren effect to suggest insanity.

Distortion and found sounds, sometimes borrowed from experiments in early twentieth-century avant-garde symphonic music or *musique concrète*, had been showing up in pop music for years by the mid-1960s. It's no surprise that such sounds became part of psychedelic rock when it emerged, including taped speech and nonverbal human sounds, loopy siren whistles, kazoos, weird analog synthesizers, Theremins, early Moogs, or even rarer electronic instruments like the Tubon played by Al Kooper with the Blues Project. You can hear sounds like this on records like *Psychedelic Moods* by the Deep (1966), for example. But more familiar examples are everywhere, including on songs by Bob Dylan (the famous siren whistle on "Highway 61 Revisited") and Frank Zappa (the zany kazoo on numbers like "Hungry Freaks, Daddy" and all the manic runs on xylophone or marimba). Kazoos, along with wrapped combs, washboards, and of course jugs, were also conventional jug-band instruments. Novelty song sounds overlap significantly with psychedelic sounds in the mid-1960s.

SURPRISINGLY RAUNCHY

A number of more conventional musical effects on the *Batman and Robin* tracks exist on the same audio spectrum as novelty sound effects but are used to create general mood or atmosphere. For example, in "The Bat Cave," heavy tom-toms, cymbal, and raw sax and glissando horns invoke 1950s rock 'n' roll dances, juke-joints, or striptease music. A musician who played on the TV show, Johnny Green, claimed that Hefti and others were explicitly looking for something "raunchy" for "Batman Theme," which would seem to put the tune in tension with the whole idea of making a kids' record.[9] Except that this was the 1960s, and double entendres and age-inappropriate humor were everywhere. Drum-heavy combos and bluesy riffs of this kind sounded like sex, audio cues even kids could pick up without fully understanding them. An instrumental pop album in millions of 1960s record collections, Herb Alpert's Tijuana Brass's *Whipped Cream & Other Delights* (1965) included a "striptease" tune (having one striptease track per album became a tradition for the band), a version of "Love Potion No. 9." The iconic slide-trombone song "The Stripper" by David Rose had already entered the pop vernacular after it topped the charts in 1962. In 1967, the tune was everywhere again, thanks to a suggestive Noxzema shaving cream commercial—itself maybe inspired by the Herb Alpert album thanks to the record's cover art, a photo of a "whipped cream"-covered "nude" model (in fact she was wearing a swimsuit and covered in shaving cream).

As a working musician, Sun Ra had played strip clubs in Calumet City, among his various gigs in the Chicago area, before coming to New York in 1961.

He would later ask drummers to reproduce that "burlesque sound" or "Calumet City sound," which was especially heavy on the snare drum.[10] Vamps like that, bump-and-grind numbers, were standard repertoire for *any* band playing backing music for dancers or filling out late-night sets in dive bars and clubs.

The overlapping contexts are complicated: on *Batman and Robin*, slightly sexually suggestive sounds and jokey or wacky sounds may have both been part of an attempt to create a funky "sick-humor" or "wild" feel, to use the language of the day. It was briefly a popular style. Think of Lenny Bruce's boundary-pushing standup comedy act and albums at the time or, closer to the putative kids' market, the humor of *Mad* magazine or the images from hot-rod culture of Ed "Big Daddy" Roth's Rat Fink cartoons. Different aesthetics, perhaps, but all adjacent to the kind of music you might hear on the street, in shady clubs or late-night radio, as opposed to a well-scrubbed national network TV-show soundtrack, much less a kids' record based on that kind of prime-time show. Despite the comic-book cover, calling *Batman and Robin* a kids' record misses the point of the marketing impetus ("strategy" is perhaps too strong a word) behind the album. Tifton Records and Tom Wilson may have simply been trying to hedge their bets on a potential crossover, putting out a record quickly that might reach at least some susceptible preteen listeners, but might also work as dance music for teens and smirking adults. The wackiness of the laughter or the jaws-harp bounce amount to an audio version of a tongue-in-cheek attitude, like the double coding of the campy *Batman* TV show itself—which was clearly designed to be experienced on two levels: sincerely by the kids in capes and ironically by the adults on the couch or in the bar.

A SESSION PLAYERS' RECORD

Although members of the Blues Project and Sun Ra and his Arkestra personnel are now regularly listed as playing on this album, the anonymity of session work of this kind means that, in fact, we can't really be sure who it is we're hearing. Despite Edward Bland's later reports, and the Sun Ra discography by Campbell and Trent, which is largely based on Bland's reports, with some additional expert listening, the full list of personnel on *Batman and Robin* is likely to remain mysterious around the edges—pretty much what we'd expect in a fast and anonymous production of this kind. Some adjustments to the list of the album's personnel have been made over time on discographies. Arkestra trumpeter Jimmy Owens did play on the record.[11] When he recounted the story for me, Owens was understandably a little uncertain about the specific details of a minor record from over fifty years ago, but he read to me over the phone from what he said were his own typed notes, attached to a copy of the album in his collection. (He wasn't sure when the notes were written, so they too may be memorial reconstructions.) Owens told me he thought guitarist Eric Gale was on the session. This is at least plausible and might help to explain why the Blues Project guitarists Steve Katz and Danny Kalb at different times equivocate or deny playing on the album. Maybe *Gale's* was in this case one of the "Sensational Guitars of Dan and *Dale*?" Gale was a highly regarded session guitarist and sideman who played with many well-known jazz, R&B, and pop musicians, including, just in the mid-1960s, Eric Andersen, Fats Domino, Herbie Mann, Hugh Masekela, and Clark Terry. Later, he played with Al Kooper. More to the point: Gale played on an even more blatantly commercial record—literally soundtrack tunes from TV commercials—called *Tune In, Turn On: To The Hippest Commercials of the Sixties*, by tenor sax player Benny Golson with, among others, Art Farmer on trumpet and flugelhorn (see chapter 3). With its swinging light jazz tracks from TV spots for products from Pepsi to Cool Whip to multiple brands of cigarettes, the album was released on Verve just over a year after *Batman and Robin*. It too was produced by Tom Wilson.

ORGAN BY SUN RA

As for that Hammond organ, it sounds exactly like Sun Ra. It opens the album with a bang, introducing "Batman Theme" with that swirling A7 chord, a more conventional version of what Sun Ra in his experimental music called a "space chord," that is, "a collectively improvised tone cluster at high volume which 'would suggest a new melody, maybe a rhythm.'"[12] Here the chord is held for a few seconds, then resolves into the key of G as the double-time shuffle beat of the theme begins, with a slightly different bass line than Hefti's chromatic hook. (Near the end, another held chord introduces a modulation to the key of A.) The bluesy R&B sound was different from the avant-garde jazz for which Sun Ra would become well known, but he had played plenty of pop music already in his career, including with swing and blues musicians in Chicago. He never lost touch with the power of jump blues and big-band swing. He always championed Fletcher Henderson, for example, with whom he had played, even after beginning to perform his own music in New York in the 1960s. On the other side of the genre mix, the members of the Blues Project were likely hired to provide the surf-guitar sound (maybe alongside Eric Gale). But Sun Ra's Hammond dominates the sonic texture of the record, building a foundation under the jangly surf and blues guitars of Dan & Dale—whoever they are.

FEATURING: ANONYMOUS VOCALS

One of the highlights of the album is the unattributed female vocals on some tracks, wailing, soulful, wordless (or one-word) scat-like improvisations. More than one singer, from the sound of it. Although the Arkestra's cosmic diva, June Tyson, would seem to be an obvious candidate, her participation is unlikely. She would not formally join the Arkestra until 1968, after which she went on to perform signature vocals on numbers like "Space Is the Place," and "Astro Black."[13] Whoever sang them, the vocals on *Batman and Robin* are impressive examples of the kind of riffing common in gospel-influenced backup singing ("Robin—hey! I said-ah-Robin!"). It's a stronger, less slick vocal performance than we hear on the official TV soundtrack, much better than we have a right to expect on a throwaway record like this one, brought to the front of the mix in what were essentially instrumental dance tracks.

A DANCE-PARTY DISC

One potential market for a record like this was as a DJ's disc—something people could play at dance parties (for kids or, with tongue-in cheek, for teens and adults). Compare, for example, another album that came out in the previous year (1965), *Ghoul Music*, by Frankie Stein and his Ghouls. It's a similar collection of blues-based go-go tunes, complete with organ and surf guitar parts and plenty of the same sound effects: siren whistles and manic laughter. The cover, however, spells it out: "Sounds and Dance Music: Twist. Frug. Fox Trot. Hully Gully. Swim." Goofy, cartoony rock 'n' roll filler to dance to. There was a flood of records like this at the time, including other albums from the budget label, Diplomat Records, by the same pseudonymous/fictional duo, Dan & Dale, and their "Sleepwalk GUITARS," played in the studio by other musicians, before the Blues Project members were slotted into the names in the following year. Take, for example, the ineloquently titled *Theme from 'Thunderball' and Other Themes.* A tuxedoed model playing James Bond is of course the hero on the cover of this one, looking down at a seated woman at his feet wearing a wetsuit and holding a spear. A small disclosure on the cover reads, "This is not the original soundtrack. The 10 additional tunes (other than Thunderball) are originals composed by Dan & Dale."

Craze-riding albums in the mid-1960s were often dance-party records. This was the height of the go-go era, when discothèques and clubs were filled with dancers in suits or minidresses, Beatle boots or tall white leather boots, doing the frug, the Watusi, or the swim. Sometimes, as in the case of L.A.'s Whisky a Go Go, girls were dancing elevated high above the floor in plexiglass boxes or barred cages. At the Whisky, a go-go dancer might also serve as DJ, spinning records for the club up in her booth while dancing along to them. The associated go-go craze was widespread. Motown superstars the Supremes released an album in 1966 titled *Supremes A' Go-Go*. Everything was for a brief time à go-go. Even the traditional Newport Folk Festival was jokingly described with the term in one 1965 review: given the trends, it said, Newport might have to be renamed "Folk Festival à Go Go."[14]

The *Batman* TV show rode that trend. The premiere episode on January 12 included a now-famous scene: Batman is dancing at a new Gotham City discothèque, the What a Way to Go-Go (underaged Robin has to remain outside). The cowled superhero makes a mask with his fingers in V-shapes around his eyes and swirls his cape while dancing, thus creating the Batusi (a play on the Watusi), a dance later nostalgically immortalized by John Travolta and Uma Thurman in the dance-contest scene in Quentin Tarantino's *Pulp Fiction*. Promoting the Batusi as a dance craze out in the world was part of the show's marketing campaign from the beginning: Nelson Riddle's soundtrack included "Batusi A-Go! Go! (I Shouldn't Wish to Attract Attention)"—that is, the verbal parenthetical remark from the script, one of the patently absurd lines the costumed Batman delivers during the scene. The Batusi shows up again in episode 28, when Batman and Nefertiti dance to "Batman Theme." The dance may have first been created as part of a promotional event to coincide with the premiere of the show, a "Cocktail and Frug Party," with a live band and an uninvited cosplaying Batman performing on the dance floor, held at Harlow's Discothèque on East 79th Street in New York City, January 12, 1966.[15] Andy Warhol was there, as the *New York Times* reported, and thus "Batman's Pop Art bona fides were established." Guests were later taken on buses up to the York Theater on 64th Street for a screening of the premiere episode, complete with TV commercials, while being served popcorn and champagne. As the *Times* says, the comic-book hero had been around since the 1930s, but the 1966 TV show aimed "to make him the caped crusader of high camp." The theater lobby displayed Batman stickers and drawings labeled "authentic pop art." In a typically deadpan remark, "one of the pop artists present commented that he thought his kids would love 'Batman' but he didn't know if adults would get it." That pop art *bon mot* sums it up. Similarly, the *Batman and Robin* album was a kids' record that was also not (only) for kids—not everyone would get it, but many would buy it. Just like the TV show, it could be experienced on multiple levels by a broad audience.

A CAMPY POP ART RECORD

Camp and pop art were always closely related, as the critic Susan Sontag acknowledged in her famous 1964 essay "Notes on 'Camp.'"[16] But Sontag goes out of her way to differentiate the two, saying that they are related but distinct, that the sensibility of pop art is relatively "more flat and more dry, more serious, more detached, ultimately nihilistic."[17] Pop art reframes the frivolous icons of mass culture, for example—advertising, comics panels, consumer products, and packaging (Campbell's Soup cans and Brillo Pad boxes)—as serious enough to count as art. For Sontag, the aesthetic of camp is based on a kind of radical acceptance, an appreciation of cultural detritus, of ephemeral cultural products. Note that she includes in her list of "canonical" camp objects "old Flash Gordon comics." And Sontag says that in the early sixties, the pop music genre known in French as yé-yé—akin to bubblegum, performed mostly by adolescent girl singers, its name derived from the Beatles' "yeah-yeah-yeahs"—was "annexed" by camp. The serious/not serious attitude of yé-yé music, and the oblique and vaguely kinky sexuality it invokes, overlap with camp. (Warhol released an underground film in 1965 titled *Camp*.) The *Batman* TV show—comics plus a mod pop art style—fits the pop art profile. Indeed, Roy Lichtenstein's well-known appropriations of comics helped to inspire the show, and he was commissioned to create a *TV Guide* cover featuring the show on March 26, 1966, showing Batman with the kind of big word bubble seen in his paintings ("POW!").

Sontag's descriptions of both camp and pop art sensibilities apply to Warhol in the mid-sixties: a detached, nonjudgmental taste, set against elevated seriousness, authenticity, and sincerity, instead celebrating examples of mass culture that are so banal they're good. But Warhol's dry, flat declarations of affection for trivial things ("I love it" he liked to say with his flattened affect, and "oh, wow") verge on performative nihilism. The *Batman* craze was right up his alley: no surprise, Warhol attended the *Batman* Frug party at Harlow's. Jon Savage connects the *Batman* TV show (and by implication the craze it inspired) to the trendy camp of its moment, also evident in Warhol's Exploding Plastic Inevitable.[18] In August 1966, Warhol posed for a photo shoot for *Esquire* magazine costumed as Robin the Boy Wonder; in one shot he stands over the Velvet Underground's female vocalist, Nico, who sits on the floor dressed as Batman. At one pop art party attended by Warhol and members of the Velvet Underground, there was a discotheque with a Bat Girl dancing in a cage.[19] The artist had made his own experimental silent film, *Batman Dracula*, in 1964, the same year as Sontag's "Notes on 'Camp'" and two years before the TV show premiered. The *Batman* show, with its "Pop Art bona fides," as the *New York Times* put it, later satirized pop art and Warhol directly in a set of episodes featuring the Joker as a charlatan artist.[20] The Joker's sidekick, Baby Jane Tower, is a reference to real-life Warhol superstar Baby Jane Holzer, who—not really coincidentally, once you understand the connections—had appeared in Warhol's film *Batman Dracula*.

It doesn't really matter if *Batman* counts as "authentic" pop art in any precise sense (whatever the oxymoron "authentic pop art" might mean) or even whether it was 100 percent camp according to the terms of Sontag's definition. The show was *perceived* at the time as both pop art and camp by critics and many average TV viewers. It's important to remember something obvious to just about everyone in 1966: a good deal of pop art (along with a good deal of camp culture) was closely bound up with contemporary fashion and music, especially styles inspired by underground or avant-garde art in the first place but repurposed in deliberately naive, sometimes brazenly commercial, ways. This included semi-sincere put-ons like go-go, yé-yé, and bubblegum. This context—the underground (however distorted) entering the pop mainstream in banal, obvious ways, in fashion, film, photography, music, and dance, intriguing members of the general public but also making them uneasy—best explains Warhol's work as the ringleader for the Exploding Plastic Inevitable, one component of which was the Velvet Underground (more about that in chapter 4).

POP MUSIC ON *BATMAN*

Meanwhile, back on TV: on February 5, 1966, Paul Revere & the Raiders appeared on ABC's *American Bandstand* with the host, Dick Clark, lip-synching to their bluesy song "Steppin' Out." "Well I had to leave town because of Uncle

Sam's deal," the lyric opens, referring to the always-looming Vietnam War draft. The band dances and clowns around in tricorn hats and ruffled shirts. (Their gimmicky outfits, as well as their name, were a satire on the latest "British Invasion.") At one point, Paul Revere leaves his stand-up keyboard and tiptoes over to open up the shirtfront of Drake Levin to reveal a Batman T-shirt. A little later, bassist Phil "Fang" Volk bounces across the stage behind the band holding up a big sign with the bat logo and the words "Batman is Coming." The sign had been seen hanging on the wall behind the dancers during an earlier episode of *Bandstand*, part of a cross-promotion for the new TV show airing on the same network. Season 2 of *Batman* premiered September 7, 1966, and it included a "window cameo" by Dick Clark himself. This was one of the recurring gags in which Batman and Robin climb the side of tall building with Bat-ropes (the camera was turned on its side to make this happen), and celebrities or actors popped out of open windows for a few lines of repartee. In this case, host Dick Clark sticks his head out of the window and asks, "Are you a vocal group?" and then explains, "I thought perhaps you might be a singing duo—you know, the outfits and all that?" The joke is a reminder that in 1966 heroes in camp costumes resembled pop musicians in camp costumes, and vice versa (as far as the general public could tell). It was a moment when psychedelic blues bands wore capes onstage and comic-book superheroes danced at the go-go.

Late in the first year of *Batman* (November 2, 1966), Paul Revere & the Raiders appeared on that show, too, playing themselves performing at a fundraiser dance for Penguin's mayoral campaign, a scene that included both white-booted go-go dancers singing a vote-for-Penguin jingle and, gratuitously, a lone belly dancer. The appearance by the Raiders was a rare example of a real-life rock band appearing on *Batman* as themselves. Pop singer Leslie Gore performed wearing pink cat ears in two later episodes, and the British folk-pop duo Chad & Jeremy played in an episode in season 2. They were announced with a wink using the collective sobriquet for Batman and Robin: "the music world's dynamic duo."

And then there's Johnny Green and the Greenmen. An actual garage/surf band out of California, they were hired by the show to perform as the Joker's green-haired henchmen (Green later said the Joker had orange hair before they showed up and gave the show runners the idea for the villain's green dye job). They appeared in season 3 as a villainous rock band playing on the beach, but with their real-life logo still legible on the bass drum. Even before *Batman*, they had green hair but sometimes wore spacesuits—like little green men. Beyond the *Batman* show, they were a backup band for Dick Clark's *Caravan of Stars*, and in 1966 they played gigs with—to come full circle—Paul Revere & the Raiders. Green also provided incidental music for the *Batman* TV show. As we've seen, he later took credit for the "raunchy" quality of "Batman Theme," saying he had helped Hefti come up with the song in the studio and played bass on the track. The strange professional mobility of the Greenmen, a real band with a garish gimmick, hired as bit-part actors while serving as soundtrack session musicians and playing a fictional band on a TV show, epitomizes the weird relationship of the *Batman* show to pop music of its moment, and the blurry boundaries the show crossed—between real and fake, serious and camp. As much as comics, pop music provided the *Batman* TV show with key references. The show was especially irreverent when it came to the music business. Season 3, episode 16, features "Little Louie Groovy," a "teenage tycoon who's never missed producing a million-seller record." He's a kind of proto-*Austin Powers*, a Carnaby Street mod in Hollywood, a temperamental producer surrounded by luxury collectibles, including an array of gold records on his bedroom wall. When we meet him, he's in the midst of recording a new group, the Gotham Boulevard Offramp. Another character who appears in the same episode owns a mod fashion boutique called Karnaby Katz.

THE *BATMAN AND ROBIN* SERIAL IN THE 1940S (ALREADY CAMP)

Nowadays, there's a multiverse of Batman stories and styles, comics and collectibles, one universe of which is designated "Batman '66," thanks to associations with the TV show and its wide cultural influence.[21] Especially in our own era, with its dark, existential Batman stories, the Batman of 1966 is disdained by many serious fans or treated with an ambivalent ironic distance as an aberration, mere kid stuff. That ironic distance is actually (ironically) perfectly in keeping with the tone of the original TV show. One version of the show's origin story says that it was inspired by the re-release of old 1943 and 1949 live-action serials from Columbia Pictures, *Batman and Robin*, versions of which were screened in theaters in 1965, just before the TV hit, including at the Playboy Theater in Chicago. One 1965 poster for a New York feature showing of all fifteen episodes of the 1943 serial calls it "the In-tertainment scoop of the year"—presumably meaning "In" as in the "in"-thing to see—and tellingly adds: "Come to Jeer—Stay to Cheer . . . and Vice Versa!" (Whatever. Just buy a ticket, it means.) The TV show had already been in development for several years by then, but the successful screenings of the corny old films, reframed in this way, show that versions of Batman were already being watched knowingly and ironically, with a camp eye to their absurdity and kinkiness, before the 1966 TV series premiered. The *Batman and Robin* album was surely made in something of the same spirit.

POP MUSIC PROMOTING THE *BATMAN* TV SHOW

Music and dance were always part of the show in 1966 and the craze it aimed to inspire. On Saturday, June 25, 1966, a promotional concert was staged in Shea Stadium in Queens—where the Beatles had famously performed for a screaming audience in August of the previous year.[22] (In just a couple of months after the Batman show at Shea, on August 29, 1966, the Beatles would play their final live show—before the famous London rooftop concert in 1969—at another stadium, Candlestick Park in San Francisco.) There were two Batman shows at Shea Stadium that day, a matinee and an evening performance, featuring Adam West as Batman and Frank Gorshin as the Riddler, along with (or so it was planned and billed) seven musical groups—including the Young Rascals, the Chiffons, Jr. Walker & the Allstars, and the Temptations—as well as an orchestra and, inevitably, a troupe of go-go dancers named "the Batusi Girls." Batman T-shirts and helmets (for some reason) were handed out to the estimated three thousand fans. The event got caught up in a near scandal over its finances and, in the end, suffered a loss; a number of the planned acts were canceled. The TV stars themselves arrived at the climax of the show, driven across the field in a Cadillac convertible. The *New York Times* review remarked that the Batmobile must have been in the shop. The event was billed as a "pop concert." It was one of a planned but doomed series that summer meant to culminate in a performance by Peter, Paul & Mary and Bob Dylan in August. But if Dylan ever actually meant to play this show, it was among the bookings he canceled after having his infamous motorcycle wreck on July 29, 1966, and subsequently withdrawing from the public eye for a time. That planned show—though it was canceled—was, in its roster of acts and genres, a sign of the times, with a first half to be dominated by folk singers, followed by a second half featuring Dylan with his notorious electric band.

The Batman concert and revue at Shea Stadium included a variety of dance routines, comedy skits, and music. The headliner, Adam West, out of costume, sang a few songs at the very end. Tie-in, cross-promotion, epiphenomenon, a "pop concert" like this was part of producing and exploiting any media craze at the time. In this case, that also included a new technicolor *Batman* feature film released in theaters that same summer of 1966. A media object like *Batman* is a tangled knot of promotional and spinoff products, in a range of genres, at various degrees of separation from the TV show itself. Just in terms of music, we can start at the center, with Nelson Riddle's *Exclusive Official Television Soundtrack Album*, as it was labeled. It was pretty typical for TV in its day, mostly orchestral easy-listening jazz or swing, mostly upbeat. Riddle's "Batman Theme" includes syncopated woodwind and brass solos and lots of scat-singing vocals, but more "doo-do-doos" than "na-na-na-nas." The single of "Theme" was backed with "Nelson's Riddler," an even jazzier tune, with even more scat singing. One track on the album was titled "Batman's Blues," but it's a slow and sultry swing-band style blues, with a slinky rhythm and brushes on the drums. Bits of dialogue are sampled as skits between numbers. At the end, we get a reprise of "Batman Theme."

That soundtrack was just the tip of the iceberg. A little further out from the show itself, we find authorized tie-ins like Hefti's album *Batman Theme and 11 Hefti Bat Songs: From the Original Score of the Greenway Production 20th Century Fox Television Series on ABC TV*, where "Theme," which Hefti had composed, is instructive. It's slower than Riddle's version, and, more important, in terms of genre-signaling, it keeps a steady 4/4 rock 'n' roll beat. Though it includes the same solos on organ and trumpet after the first chorus, Hefti's version doesn't shift into the syncopated jazzy bounce the way Riddle's TV soundtrack does. The other tunes on the Hefti album are even more recognizably rock or pop in feel. There are some weird keyboard parts and sound effects (like popping bubbles), harmonica, twangy guitars, and some jokey tunes, like a graduation march played with organ and brass titled "Holy Diploma, Batman . . . Straight A's." Hefti's take on "the Batusi" is not "Theme" but a mid-tempo dance tune with an organ solo and lots of tambourine—and wing-flapping and high-squeaking bat sound effects. On the back cover, Hefti's signed liner note refers to himself as a "composer for hire," and he later said that RCA Records pushed for the album after the single of "Batman Theme" was so successful he had to compose the additional tracks in one weekend. All of the tunes (including more than one version of "Theme") sound like radio-ready, or dance-party ready, pop music, in contrast to Riddle's orchestral smooth jazz.

Two more examples, a little farther out from the show (in every sense): novelty tunes released in 1966 featuring vocals by Adam West ("Miranda") and Burt Ward ("Boy Wonder I Love You"). Both combine spoken-word skits and music. West croons a love song about refusing to take off his mask, until he finally does and, in the slapstick punchline, Miranda tells him to "please put it back." A high Farfisa organ riff sounds the "Theme." In the middle of the song, a supervillain (Mr. AC/DC) turns off the power and the song stops for a couple of seconds. Ward's single is even stranger, if that's possible. It was composed and produced by none other than Frank Zappa, and it sounds like one of his own sarcastic doo-wop songs. Ward reads from fan letters, mocking teen girls as a stereotype. The song was reportedly pulled from some radio playlists because of the sexual innuendo—shockingly enough, a fangirl wants to have Robin over for a "sleepover" and to serve him breakfast in bed. *True* cash-in novelty records that were also long-shot promotional efforts, these two singles make the Tom Wilson album project seem, by contrast, like a relatively straightforward musical effort.

There were multiple layers of exploitation and marketing involved in all of the music related to *Batman* in 1966, from the authorized soundtrack, to various tie-ins and promotions, to blatant cash-ins, covers, rip-offs, serious and ironic homages. As a former literature professor, I find it tempting to explain these layers in terms of the theory of *paratext* as articulated by French literary theorist Gérard Genette.[23] It's a way of accounting for the effect on interpretation of various materials that are not the main text but that frame or shape our experience of the main text—for example, introductions, prefaces, author interviews, blurbs printed on the book jacket. If we think of the *Batman* TV show as the main text, then all the other Bat-products can be considered paratexts, related texts that serve as "thresholds" or frames for our experience of *Batman* twice a week on national television. In literary theory, paratext is sometimes further divided into *peritext*, any up-close, attached element, like a book's foreword or introduction, for example; and the further-removed *epitext*, like an author's book-tour interview or blog post, or a publisher's advertisement—or that big promotional pop concert at Shea Stadium.

TAKEOFFS ALL THE WAY DOWN

The idea of related concentric layers radiating out from a cultural thing, whether a book or TV show or record, all of which affect not only the marketing but the interpretation of the main thing, is useful. But in the end, the specifics of the theory apply only in a limited way in this case. Such distinctions as "main" text and paratext are blurred when it comes to trans-media pop culture, in which everything is always already promoting and taking off on everything else, flowing back and forth in feedback and feedforward loops.[24] The TV show itself was a takeoff on the comic books in the first place. More immediately, it was a takeoff on the 1949 black-and-white film serial, which, as we've seen, was already being revived in camp quotation marks in those 1965 showings in Chicago and New York. Then, on January 12, 1966, animated heroes in capes ran toward the "camera" in the opening titles sequence for the live-action TV show and started a pop culture craze, one for which viewers were primed. After that, any single contribution to the craze could stand alone as its own expression and act of commerce, whatever its direct (or legal) link to the production companies or intellectual properties being marketed, exploited, ridden like a wave for various purposes, to different ends.

Take, for example, just one unauthorized R&B single, "Batman at the Go Go" (backed with an instrumental, "Robin at the Go Go"), by Butch Baker, as the label says, "12 Yrs. Old." It was recorded and released in Chicago without permission and was promptly pulled from the market. But it was then re-released under the hopefully more legal title of "Fat Man at the Go Go"—which sounds like a joke from the show. Intended as a simple cash-in, the song tried to ride the wave, and succeeded to some degree. It's impossible to say how many listeners would have been clear on the legalistic distinction, hearing "Batman at the Go Go" in the words "Fat Man at the Go Go." The traditional opacity of rock vocals going back to "Louie, Louie" may have worked to the benefit of the pirates in this case. At any rate, the song made its own small contribution to the craze.

That 7-inch single is just one weird example from among the flood of Batman records that were released that year. A legal notice appeared in *Billboard* magazine for January 29, 1966, by the Licensing Corporation of America, exclusive agents for National Periodical Publications, the comic-book company that owned the Batman and Robin copyright and trademark: "it has come to our attention," it begins, "that a number of companies are currently manufacturing and playing unauthorized records illegally using the name BATMAN and/or BATMAN AND ROBIN." The notice goes on to threaten to pursue legal enforcement "against all infringers"—and notes that the theme song of the TV series is the *only* authorized Batman music. The same issue of *Billboard* contained an ad for the "runaway smash" hit version of the theme performed by the Marketts. The following week (February 5, 1966), an article titled "Labels Bat Out 'Batman' Disks" reported that twenty labels, to that point, had already released Batman singles. The number continued to increase for months, though recordings and radio airplay were surely slowed by the published threat of legal action.

A TIN-FOIL GOLD RECORD

The Sun Ra and Blues Project *Batman and Robin* album was just a drop in the ocean. The flood of Bat-stuff rose rapidly in 1966. This is the environment in which Tom Wilson's *Batman and Robin* album was made, released, consumed, and heard. For his part, Wilson was a big fan of the campy TV show. According to one source who worked with him at TTG Studios in Los Angeles, he scheduled recording sessions to end in time to get home to watch *Batman*, and he would come to work the next day talking and laughing about the show.[25] His fandom of the show, of course, developed after the album was made. It was obviously an attempt to cash in on the expected craze. But it's noteworthy that the supposed kids' record was a spin-off of a show Wilson would come to love. The album was made with legal rights secured for the images and characters from National Periodicals Publications, as the cover declares. It was not *only* a kids' record. That the hip Wilson was glued to his TV set as the album was being distributed and sold reminds us of the larger context and of the potential appeal of both the album and the show to adult listeners/viewers. The album stands on its own, I think, as a particularly interesting take on the source material, in part because of the combination of jazz and rock musicians involved, thanks to Wilson and Ed Bland. The more serious and influential projects later pursued by those same musicians inevitably color how we view an obscure project like this. This was one of many such records, most of which may be lost to history. This one almost was, until interested listeners, fans, and musicologists rediscovered (or reconstructed) it. I'm not the only original listener to the album who responded to it with enthusiasm. Something about it sets it apart from most of the Bat-stuff of 1966.

It's not clear exactly how many of those Dan & Dale *Batman and Robin* records were actually sold, how many unsuspecting parents bought or allowed their kids to buy the brightly colored album, like my mom did, from discount bins in supermarkets, only later to discover that it was not the official TV show soundtrack they'd expected. It's difficult to fully believe Wilson's story in 1967 about getting a gold record for it from Tifton: "they did it in tinfoil, which they cut with scissors. We sold a million Batman albums [laughs], and, uh, they said 'we're a budget company, this is all we could afford.' They sold the records for 99 cents each. We all have a reason to sing the blues" (*The Music Factory*, program 13). It's always possible he made up the whole story about the gold record, just as he invented the fictional barbecue out behind *The Music Factory* studio. On the 1967 episode of the radio show in which he mentions the *Batman* album, his guests are two members of the Lovin' Spoonful, Jerry Yester and Joe Butler, and the three of them have fun mocking the music business. Wilson first jokes about having the blues because he narrowly missed producing the Spoonful and making lots of money as a result. They all laugh and then the subject turns to having gold records on your wall: "I've still got space for those in my house," Wilson laughs. "Have you ever played them?," one of the guests asks, and Wilson jokes that he's waiting until he wins a diamond needle (more laughter). "They're never the records they say they are," the young musician reveals, and then goes into the process of how old records (actually it was often metal stamps for earlier records) were just gilded, coated in a gold finish, to make the trophies. The Spoonful say they ripped apart a couple of theirs and found old country records covered with the gold. Wilson responds that if he ever gets another gold record, he's going to make sure it's made out of something "of value," for example, an Ink Spots record. That's when he mentions the *Batman and Robin* album. After commenting wryly, "we all have a reason to sing the blues," he adds as a record intro, "James Cotton will do my singing"—then plays Cotton's "Off the Wall," a blues stomp with heavy harmonica.

It's a joke. But this anecdote about the *Batman and Robin* album also tells us something about how its producer saw the side project. It was indeed a cash-grab, one that succeeded pretty well in terms of sales, though maybe not in terms of profit for Wilson. As a symbol, the tinfoil gold record is almost too obvious: all that glitters is not gold; the award itself is patently inauthentic, fake, just a facade covering the sordid truth that what you take as "your" music is actually not what it appears to be. As a commodity, it's ultimately just "plastic ware" to be sold by the record company. Chart-based popularity, at any rate, is an inauthentic measure of success. But that is precisely how the music business works, through a kind of illusory alchemy: it turns the ineffable magic of music into fool's gold—tinfoil trophies, as well as actual money. Sometimes underneath it all there is good music (the gold record can contain music by the Ink

Spots or Hank Williams). Bringing together the strange-bedfellows personnel for the *Batman and Robin* record was one of Wilson's many attempts to produce a hit, some degree of monetary success, through a quirky combination of very different skilled musicians, like one of those nights in a club when seemingly incommensurate players happen to sit in on the bandstand and improvise something momentarily great—or at least groovy (to use one of Wilson's favorite descriptors).

Batman and Robin, the album, was released in a moment of cultural conflict. Pop culture had its signals crossed, its codes confused—sometimes on purpose, sometimes productively enough for interesting things to happen. That ephemeral record is still being collected, mostly over the internet, bootlegged and talked about, partly because of its novelty and its association with the fan-favorite dark superhero franchise. But sometimes it's because of its oblique association with another underground hero, Sun Ra. I find it appealing in part because its personnel—avant-garde jazz players jamming with the young Jewish blues-rockers, arranged and produced by two influential Black impresarios, Ed Bland and Tom Wilson—represent that historical moment's eclectic and hybrid-fueled pop culture, and its often-productive conflicts. We can't really understand the conflicts or tune in to those complicated mixed signals if we pay attention to only the strongest, most canonical sounds, the Beatles, the Beach Boys, Dylan, or Donovan. It's necessary sometimes to shift the dial or to switch media, adjust the cinematic lens away from those stars and focus on the players beside or behind them, to pay closer attention, say, to the band that was half-jokingly referred to as the Jewish Beatles but also as "New York's favorite underground band"—the Blues Project. Their part in this story picks up at around the same time they went into that Newark, New Jersey, studio as mere session musicians, behind the cartoon masks of Dan & Dale with their "Sensational Guitars." But it actually begins over in Manhattan, at the daily Washington Square hootenanny and in the guitar shops and folk clubs of Greenwich Village. So in the next chapter, that's where we go: downtown.

CHAPTER TWO

THE AUTHENTICITY BLUES (AND THE PSYCHEDELIC SOLUTION)

The Blues Project, *Live at the Cafe Au Go Go* (1966); *Projections* (1966)

IN THE EARLY 1960S, THE BATTLE OVER MUSICAL AUTHENTICITY WAS fought in the clubs and coffeehouses of Greenwich Village, a folk-music scene vividly fictionalized in Joel and Ethan Coen's film *Inside Llewyn Davis* (2013). The title character is based on Dave Van Ronk, a guitarist and folk singer known as the Mayor of MacDougal Street. In the film, young Llewyn Davis resists selling out, even when he's down and out. He watches other folk singers making silly novelty records for money and suffers the condescension of uptown patrons, burnishing their own authenticity through contact with the struggling musician. Though it all, Davis remains devoted to the music. The final scene returns full circle to the opening of the film in the Gaslight Cafe. Davis has just finished a solo set and is standing near the bar talking to the owner as the next performer begins to play in the background. We recognize the new singer, out of focus in the dim spotlight, by his unique nasal voice. It's the young Bob Dylan, a harmonica rack around his neck, doing a traditional-sounding song titled "Farewell." It's actually a typical folk-music variation on a traditional song, "The Leaving of Liverpool," in real life recorded by the Clancy Brothers, among others. But it has a family resemblance, shared musical DNA, with the tune Llewyn Davis has just performed in the movie, "Dink's Song"—named by a folklorist for the Black woman he heard singing it in a migrant workers' camp. Davis is leaving the club, having been kicked out, and briefly notices the new singer with the nasal voice. He hesitates for a minute. The camera's focus shifts dramatically: the background comes sharply into focus and we see the new singer clearly, the unmistakable halo of hair and slumped shoulders. To Llewyn Davis, it's just another Village folk singer with a guitar, but as we watch, we know that in just a few years the scruffy singer will become a famous genre-crossing poet and international star—and will get booed for playing electric guitar with a rock band.

The scene demonstrates with a basic cinematic device—that shifting depth of field—the importance of *framing* when it comes to historical events, and the use of out-of-focus areas to represent "background" in a metaphorical as well as literal sense. There's always something beyond the lens that might change our perspective if we were to shift our focus just a little. In the story of the fictional Llewyn Davis, Dylan is in the blurry background. Davis is in focus. But at that moment, in that room, they're both just working musicians. Davis is actually the more typical participant in the Village scene, more like all the countless other aspiring folk singers. To see *him*, and all of the singers like him, we have to adjust the lens to put Dylan and other canonical figures in the blurry background for a moment, so the primary focus can shift to the busy foreground, where the everyday stuff was happening that made the scene what it was.

FOLK ROOTS

Joel and Ethan Coen read Dave Van Ronk's autobiography for an insider's point of view.[1] The fictional Llewyn Davis is (bathetically) much more obscure than the real-life Van Ronk, who was well connected to everybody in the Greenwich Village folk scene. In his own book, Van Ronk spends a good deal of time describing the collective gatherings in Washington Square Park, spontaneous urban hootenannies broken down into clusters of affinity groups: bluegrass players in one corner of the park, blues guitarists around the fountain, and so on. He explains that most of the "urban folk singers" who were part of the "revival"—many of them political leftists—"made their commitment to folk music consciously, for political and aesthetic reasons."[2] Some were purists or "neo-ethnics," who adopted the precise styles and even the accents of the rural singers they admired. They sought an elusive (and illusory) authenticity by imitating traditions they knew only secondhand, at best. This was ultimately a hopeless pursuit. Worse, from Van Ronk's point of view, it was an act of appropriation that led to a state of cognitive dissonance in the face of "internal contradictions."[3] These contradictions were intensified when it came to race since traditional styles of so-called folk music came from Black blues and gospel and most of the revivalists were white students, hipsters, or academic folklorists. This appropriative, sometimes condescending fandom limited the general understanding of the music, even changed it. As Hugh Barker and Yuval Taylor argue, "the quest for authenticity did tremendous damage to the blues by codifying certain traditions and limiting innovation."[4]

By the mid-1960s Van Ronk was himself already highly influential and a sought-after guitar teacher. Among his pupils were two Jewish high school kids from New York, Steve Katz and Danny Kalb, who rode the train down to the Village whenever they could to be part of the scene, including joining in on the jam sessions in Washington Square Park. They both took flat-picking blues lessons from Van Ronk. Before long, Kalb was playing lead guitar as a session musician, and in 1963 he played guitar and harmonica in Van Ronk's Ragtime Jug Stompers. Van Ronk referred Katz to another guitar teacher up in the Bronx, the Reverend Gary Davis, for further lessons. Katz ended up playing with a different folk group, the Even Dozen Jug Band. Jug-band music was a form of traditional blues and early jazz played on acoustic folk-music instruments—guitars, banjos, fiddles, and harmonicas, but also homemade instruments like the wrapped comb kazoo, washboard, washtub bass made from a broomstick, and of course the jug itself, which could provide rhythm and carry the bass line. The most well-known jug band on the East Coast at the time was the Jim Kweskin Jug Band, out of the Boston area, which included Geoff and Maria Muldaur, both of whom had come to Kweskin from the Even Dozen Jug Band. Playing with the Even Dozen Jug Band was one of Kalb's first professional gigs.

THE BLUES AS A PROJECT

In 1965, Kalb formed a new rock group, with Roy Blumenfeld on drums, Andy Kulberg on bass, and Artie Traum on guitar. Later that summer, Katz replaced Traum and, as Katz says, had his first experience playing electric guitar.[5] Tommy Flanders was added as a frontman-vocalist. The band was named after the title of an earlier album, oddly enough, a 1964 multi-artist anthology that Kalb had contributed to, *The Blues Project*. So, the new band defined *itself* as a project, which, when you think about it, is a little abstract for rock 'n' roll. The original album, which Steve Katz later called "Elektra's anthology LP of white-boy blues,"[6] collected songs to serve as specimens of traditional blues. It made a project of the blues, in the same revivalist spirit as the field recordings by Alan and John Lomax for the Library of Congress or Harry Smith's influential multidisc *Anthology of American Folk Music*. As a name for a white, mostly Jewish rock band, the Blues *Project* offered some wiggle room, implying a degree of self-consciousness on the part of the musicians about their secondary, appropriative relationship to the folk-music genre they thought of as truly authentic only when created by Black musicians. Historically, Black and white jazz musicians often made a point of playing together and of defying segregated venues when on tour. Still, given the facts of racism and segregation in the Jim Crow era, and given who benefited financially from gigs and records sold, the question of who had a "right" to sing (and claim) the blues was always in the air. The Blues Project expressed an awkward mixture of veneration and embarrassment about this, especially when they were in the presence of Black performers who had inspired them.[7] More than inspired them: in many cases, provided guitar licks, tricks of style, and sometimes even hired them to join their tours. As their own music shifted from jug-band, to folk-rock, to electric blues, and finally to blues-based psychedelic rock, the Blues Project remained anxious and sometimes defensive about their own identity.

AUTHENTICITY BLUES, PSYCHEDELIC ROCK

Consider, for example, the traditional song "Two Trains Running" (also known as "Still a Fool"). Writing collectively in 1967, the Blues Project said, "We are aware of that tradition and draw on it. But as a group we aren't imitative. If we do a *Two Trains Running*, it's a 1967 *Two Trains Running*, never a 1947 version."[8] In the early sixties, Van Ronk had covered Muddy Waters's version of the song on acoustic guitar in a fingerpicking style. But even earlier—back in 1951—Waters himself had recorded a version with electric guitars, bass, and harmonica for Chess Records, over a decade before the Blues Project began to play their electric version. At one Blues Project performance, the man himself showed up and, and when the band asked Waters how he liked the number, he reportedly said, "you really got to me"—a relatively understated approval that nonetheless meant the world to Kalb, as he later admitted.[9] The song became a signature tune for the band. They didn't "turn it electric"—Waters had already done that—but in their own minds, they believed they added *something* new, something that made their version a 1967 version.

That something new was psychedelia. The Blues Project claimed a kind of authenticity because they adapted the song to fit into that emerging genre hybrid or meta-genre. Their version, they believed, was true to their own identities in their own historical moment, not in terms of the purism of Van Ronk's "neo-ethnics" or Paul Butterfield's technically faithful imitations. In their minds, they were more pop oriented than the folkies and more eclectic than the blues revivalists. They were authentically psychedelic, cosmic and sincere—sometimes, as was common at the time, pretentiously so. Simon Frith has written insightfully about the question of authenticity when it came to the shift from folk music to folk-rock in the sixties, concluding that "folk-rockers individualized the folk concept of authenticity."[10] Individualized is right. More specifically, they *internalized the search* for authenticity. What had been a troubled quest for an organic connection to a folk community became, in psychedelic folk-rock and psychedelic blues, an inner voyage of radical self-discovery and self-expression. The twelve-bar song structure often remained the same. This had the double advantage of allowing the musicians to claim a new *kind* of authenticity and—since it involved playing jangly electric guitars and drums and organ—to make music that was more commercially marketable, more pop-sounding.

When Al Kooper joined the Blues Project in 1965, he later joked, he "had to be initiated into the Mystic White Knights of Da Blooze."[11] He characterized the band as "the New York Jews for Electric Blues Crusade,"[12] the word "crusade" a sarcastic synonym for "project," a way of mocking the earnestness, and maybe defusing the internal contradictions, behind the whole idea of a blues "revival." More seriously, Kooper also differentiated the Blues Project from the Paul Butterfield Blues Band and their faithful "ethnic" imitations of the Chicago style. They were not "a traditional blues band" like Butterfield: "We'd change *all* the arrangements, never doing a tune like someone else had done it. . . . We also did folk-rockier things than Butterfield's scope allowed for, like Donovan's 'Catch the Wind' and Bob Lind's 'Cheryl's Goin' Home.'"[13]

OUR SOUND

In 1968, an odd book aimed at young-adult readers was published, *The Sound: The Blues Project*, a kind of group autobiography, with chapters written by the band members. (I read it myself at the time and had to track it down again while researching this book.) I've already quoted from it earlier in this chapter. *The Sound* was written just before the band broke up in 1967. Because it was intended for young readers and uses simple language, it's particularly revealing, giving us the band's perspective on the essential qualities of their sound and on music in general in 1967. In one chapter, Kalb describes his dissatisfaction with the "sort of whitened, weakened blues" he had played back in his folk days.

> In the modern sense, the electric band and the Negro changed folk blues into a tremendous external expression of love, protest, and anger. . . . This is why the folk revival has gone from folk to rhythm-and-blues to rock 'n' roll, and finally, to our sound. . . . as a group we aren't imitative. . . . We may assimilate the vitality but never the complete thing.[14]

Whatever it means to "assimilate the vitality" (it sounds vaguely vampiric), we can't help but hear some anxiety expressed between the lines. The now-dated phrase "the Negro" was of course meant respectfully, an attempt to pay tribute to the band's Black musical heroes—Muddy Waters, Jimmy Reed, Blind Willie Johnson, and others—many of whom had been playing electric blues for a generation. Kalb makes it clear that their own trajectory from folk to psychedelic rock was seen by the Blues Project as a quest for musical authenticity. Starting from folk and blues and then "going electric"—Dylan, with Wilson (and Kooper), had led the way just a year earlier—was not only a way to succeed in the pop market. It was also a way to play more authentically, paradoxically by doing your "own thing" within a Black musical tradition you would otherwise be in danger of merely appropriating.

Kooper later said that he and Kalb used to get on each other's cases about trying to sound Black when singing the blues, gospel, or R&B.[15] This confirms that they *did* try to sound Black, but also shows that they were self-conscious enough about it to try to police one another's attempts. Today, it's called adopting a "blaccent" and is widely seen as an offensive act of appropriation. On social media, people are sometimes admonished to "act [their] race." It's the original sin of American popular music: exploiting Black creativity for white profit. From minstrelsy, to swing, to Elvis, and countless others since—Vanilla

Ice, the Beastie Boys, Eminem, Miley Cyrus, Justin Timberlake, and so on—white performers have adopted the voice or style of Black performers and thereby claimed the cachet (and record sales) associated with that voice. But these crossings, by musicians and fans, however heartfelt, can't erase the systemic inequalities and persistent divisions in the music business.[16]

In the end, the troubled conscience of white players in the 1960s is less important than the economic and cultural consequences of continued segregation for Black musicians. Searching for "authentic" blues was always a lopsided game. Skip James tells the story of being asked by white fans to play acoustic country blues at Newport Folk Festival workshops, a common experience for a number of Black performers: "Sometimes they would just look at me like I was . . . I don't know what—a bear, or something."[17] Speaking of white performers, Wilson said that he just wasn't "interested in hearing . . . singers who were copying 1937 Negro singers like Robert Johnson. Robert Johnson had his thing and I exhort everybody to develop their own."[18]

THE PSYCHEDELIC FILTER

When it came to pop music in 1966, one solution to developing their own thing for young white musicians like the Blues Project—at least for a brief moment—was to push the blues through the overdriven amps of rock and, conceptually, through a colorful psychedelic filter. Katz later said the Blues Project had "dissected and psychedelically interpreted" a tune by Waters.[19] Psychedelic interpretation became a conscious part of the band's mission. In 1965, the newly formed Blues Project auditioned for Wilson, then a staff producer at Columbia Records. He arranged for them to make a demo tape, tellingly comprised of two very different cuts: one a classic blues tune by Willie Dixon, "Back Door Man," and one a psychedelic folk-rock ballad by Greenwich Village musician Eric Andersen, "Violets of Dawn." The trippy lyrics of the latter include poetic phrases like "shadows bursting into mist" and "no colors fade blazing / Into petaled sprays of violets of dawn." The two demo tracks, taken together, are data points that allow us to plot the trajectory the band was soon to follow in their repertoire and self-presentation, from blues to psychedelia. But note: both tracks already have that electric sound that made them assimilable into the trends of the moment. They were released in January 1966 as the A and B sides of the Blues Project's first single. For that demo session, Wilson brought in his session player from the Dylan recordings, Kooper, to play keyboards (including a Farfisa organ), thus filling out the band's sound. At lunch the next day, Kooper was asked to join the group. When Wilson moved to MGM/Verve shortly thereafter, the Blues Project moved with him.

LIVE PROJECT(IONS)

In the fall of 1965, the band was hired to play at the Cafe Au Go Go at 152 Bleecker Street, and at the end of November they recorded the first tracks for their debut album, *Live at the Cafe Au Go Go*. The tapes were made during a four-day concert series there, created by Wilson through Verve/Folkways, called "the Blues Bag." (The plan was to record the whole series, but in the end, only the Blues Project tracks were released.) The shows featured traditional artists like Big Joe Williams, Son House, Bukka White, Skip James, and John Lee Hooker; but also an electric raga-rock band, the Seventh Sons (the name comes from a Willie Dixon song); and various folk musicians, including Eric Andersen and, from the Jim Kweskin Jug Band, Geoff Muldaur. Although he self-deprecatingly jokes that they relied on sheer volume, relative to the blues masters on the bill, Kooper also emphasizes the Blues Project's authenticity: "We were *real in our own way*. . . . We may have borrowed our music, but our demeanor was strictly our own" (my emphasis).[20]

After the Blues Bag, they were given a residence at the club. Their mostly positive reception had included a review by *New York Times* critic Robert Shelton (the first album's liner notes would later quote from the review).[21] After noting the recent trend of folk-music fans developing a "near-obsession with the blues, in general, and electrified instruments, in particular," and connecting this trend—the blues + electrification—to Dylan's earlier appearance at Newport, Shelton goes on to review a range of concerts that had taken place over the Thanksgiving holiday, including the big Blues Bag at the Cafe Au Go Go, which he calls "perhaps the most unusual and rewarding program of the weekend." Among the "electric" bands in the series, he says, "none impressed more than the Blues Project, possibly the most incandescent group in folk-rock today." He calls Kalb's guitar playing "imaginative" and Kooper's keyboard "volatile," and praises Flanders for his "vocal sky-rocketing." He also mentions that members of the Project played "background for a parade of folk performers who have rarely sounded so liberated and swinging." Folk-rock on the fly, the Blues Bag shows illustrate how organic-feeling and spontaneous the genre blending of the time could be, given a receptive scene.

The Blues Project's debut album recorded during those shows was completed a couple of months later, in January 1966—possibly around the same time the musicians recorded the *Batman and Robin* record with Sun Ra. By that point, Flanders was no longer with the band, so Kooper and Katz took on the vocals for *Live at the Cafe Au Go Go*. With Wilson, they began right away to work on a second album, a studio release to be titled *Projections*. That second album was not a hit—it peaked on the charts at number 58—but it enhanced the band's reputation. The members complained for years thereafter about the brief studio time they were given by Verve to make the record, about not getting to hear the final mixes before the album was released, and about the back cover—which contains typical candid photos of the band members in the studio, a track listing of the nine songs, and some oddly under-enthusiastic, even unintentionally comic, liner notes by their relatively new manager, Sid Bernstein: he calls them "a work of determination!" who have "made it" despite not having had a hit single on the charts. But neither front nor back cover lists the names of the musicians. One name *is* prominently displayed on the back, in large print just under the title: "Produced By: Tom Wilson."

ATTITUDE MUSIC

The band later groused that Wilson squeezed them into the studio schedule only when Eric Burdon & the Animals weren't recording. But the album represents the Project's strengths and the excitement they generated in 1965–1966, and it showcases their eclecticism,[22] the transformation of various genres—blues, but also folk, light jazz, gospel—into what was becoming recognized as psychedelic rock. This was not pop, the band said (pop had become "easy listening"). Using a vague term adopted from the DJ and impresario Murray the K, they called it "attitude music."[23] Murray the K published a book of his own in 1966, in which he explained teenage pop culture and offered insights into the contemporary scene. In a footnote about Dylan, he rejects the term "folk-rock" to describe Dylan's sound. Instead, Murray declares: "I call it what it is—'Attitude Music'!"[24] The phrase is typical DJ hype, like "the latest sound" or "what's happening" (the book is full of such phrases), but it's interesting that both he and the Blues Project agreed on the descriptor, if perhaps with different nuances. Murray used it to refer to Dylan's post-electric music. Katz and the Blues Project associated "attitude music" with the social and emotional "realism" of the Black traditions they were drawing on (as in "keeping it real").

In that sense, Katz said, the "best example" of attitude music was "still the blues."[25] Remember, the blues was often treated at the time as falling under the umbrella of folk music, which helps to explain how Murray's folk-rock and Katz's blues might both be celebrated as expressions of a similarly "authentic" attitude, an attitude of authenticity.

The Blues Project were often received with an ironic distance. Take their nickname, the Jewish Beatles, for example. A cultural cognitive dissonance they embodied was both a little embarrassing and part of their appeal, like the Beatles' self-deprecating ironic attitude about playing R&B. Irony was necessary protection for the band of shaggy-haired, white, Jewish guys wailing away at the blues; the problem of who they were and how they approached the blues was part of their "project." We hear a desire to revalue their ambiguities in this way in the retrospective 1973 review (already cited above).[26] Surveying recent releases from 1972, the reviewer takes a moment to look back to the Project's heyday in the Village. He quotes Kalb saying in liner notes: "I play the blues because it is my most natural form of expression. I love the blues because . . . they're real," an explanation he calls out as "silly" and a sign of "hypocrisy."[27] And yet he also praises the band and claims that at its peak the Project "was downright subversive." Recalling a show at the Cafe Au Go Go when they "ripped the place apart," the reviewer adds, "the Project made it impossible to play it cool anymore."

> What The Project did was take a blues and pretend to play it. . . . The Blues Project . . . was the first band to realize how ridiculous it was for middle-class whites, especially if they were Jewish, to try to play the blues. So they caricatured and melodramatized it, distorting it into rock frenzy.[28]

The reviewer has it both ways, both honoring and execrating the Blues Project for their ironic meta-blues (which they "pretend to play"). It's important, here, to avoid the condescension of posterity, as a cultural historian once put it, to assume that we can see through an earlier era's illusions and naive enthusiasms.[29] Starting with the band itself, many listeners at the time fully understood the appropriative nature of the Project's "project," how ambiguities around questions of irony, sincerity, and authenticity were built in—the knowingness being part of the band's appeal. That's perhaps the real sense in which the Blues Project were like the Beatles: they were similarly self-conscious and ambivalent about their relation to their sources.

THE MIXED BAG OF *PROJECTIONS*

Looked at one way, the blues was just part of the "everything" in Wilson's "everything is everything" worldview. Kooper seems to echo Wilson when he describes the music scene around 1967: "It seems that there is a great deal of fragmentation, and because of it more good things are happening," and the record from the previous year embraced that ideal of eclecticism.[30] Kooper left the Blues Project soon thereafter, and with Katz formed a new jazz-rock band centered on an R&B horn section: Blood, Sweat & Tears. But without the horns, *Projections* already includes a similar mix of genres, the Project's own version of everything is everything. Some tracks are identifiably folk-rock ("Steve's Song," "Cheryl's Going Home") or rock 'n' roll ("You Can't Catch Me"), gospel ("Wake Me, Shake Me"), pop ("Fly Away"), or jazz fusion ("Flute Thing"), along with covers of traditional blues ("I Can't Keep from Crying," "Two Trains Running," "Caress Me Baby").

Even the straight-ahead blues tunes are qualified in interesting ways. The opening track, for example, "I Can't Keep from Crying," incorporates a noisy psychedelic rave-up at about the two-minute mark, featuring Kooper playing glissandos up and down with the heel of his hand on the keyboard of a kind of ondioline called a Tubon. The ondioline was a vacuum tube–based early synthesizer, an electronic instrument later associated with the French pop musician Jean-Jacques Perrey. (In 1993, the band Stereolab would name a song for it: "Jenny Ondioline.") Kooper also played a full-sized ondioline for years. You can hear it on the *Super Session* album in 1968, for example. But at the time of *Projections*, he had just acquired a Tubon, the cylindrical tube-shaped version. It had a keyboard cut into the tube, and he wore it on a strap, making it look something like a keytar or a saxophone. Battery-powered, it made a croaky electronic sound. It was given to him by the Guild guitar company, which had imported it from Sweden. Kooper came to be so closely identified with the instrument that it became known in music circles as the Kooperfone. The first time Kooper played it on a recording was on the opening track, "I Can't Keep from Crying." Unlike the Hammond organ or an electric piano, the Tubon was monophonic, which meant that each note in a fast run sounded separately, discretely, one at a time.

The second track on the album is a folk-rock, proto-prog rock, tune, "Steve's Song." Katz's own title was "September Fifth," but the rush to produce the record led to using the placeholder. It opens with a baroque dance tune on fingerpicked guitar, flute, mallets on the drum, and a clavioline keyboard part, before the folk-rock ballad proper begins. Katz complained that Wilson wouldn't allow him to rerecord the vocal because Eric Burdon & the Animals (their studio-time nemeses) needed the studio. Maintaining the genre alternation of blues/R&B and folk-rock, track 3 is a cover of Chuck Berry's "You Can't Catch Me," a 4:17-minute long version with impressive guitar parts by Kalb and Katz. Roy Blumenfeld said that he thought Kalb sang it "with sincerity" and a "sense of connective, organic meaning to the lyrics and to the words. So . . . it's very authentic in that sense"—which tells us a lot about what the band was going for when they covered blues and R&B songs.[31]

Track 4 is Kalb's tribute to his great hero, Muddy Waters, a cover of "Two Trains Running." Kalb said their very slow arrangement was like a short rock opera and, somewhat cryptically, that it was Waters but it was also "us," the Blues Project.[32] At just after the 9-minute mark in the 11:29-minute track, one of Kalb's guitar strings sounds a note a half-step flat during an otherwise silent pause. In the moment, on tape, he twists the tuning key while plucking and brings the string into tune, making it sound like an intentional improvisation.[33] The combination of Kooper's Hammond organ and Kalb's high-register solos in this slow jam, with a heavy downbeat and a triplet rhythm that shifts into a syncopated swing, sounds like the style of blues later heard by the Allman Brothers, for example. Kalb recalled that when they played on the same bill as Waters, he asked the blues great what he thought of their version of "Two Trains" (a story I alluded to above). The account reveals how significant the question was to him. When the show was over, he says, Waters was leaving the venue: "and I had to find out, in my deepest part, what he thought of our version of this tune that started out in the South many years ago, before he recorded it with any electric band. And these strange white people were doing this song." So, he asks the blues musician what he thought, and Waters replies, "You really got to me." Kalb says he could have died after hearing this, and it "would have been enough."[34] Notice how Kalb's distinctions frame the story: it's about a song from the South, that dates from a country-blues, pre-electric era. In seeking validation, he's deeply moved to hear that their version, however appropriative, had moved the Black creator, had affected *him*. In that way, Kalb and the Project achieved what he believed was a valid, if paradoxically derivative, kind of authenticity.

The appropriation of a Black musical tradition is even more pronounced in track 5, "Wake Me, Shake Me," a song Kooper had heard performed by a group called the Golden Chords at a strange theme nightclub on 46th Street in midtown Manhattan, the Sweet Chariot. There was even a picket line on the sidewalk out front protesting the blasphemy and decadence, organized by a group of Black ministers (which eventually succeeded in shutting down the club). To encourage audience participation, guests could rent tambourines for $5 as they came in, the doormen wore choir robes, and the cocktail waitresses were called "Angels" and wore outfits with halos and sparkly wings. The bathrooms were labeled "Brothers" and "Sisters." A cynical article in *Time* magazine appeared when the club first opened, noting (historical accuracy aside) that gospel music was "the last remaining unpackaged expression of Negro culture."[35] It turns out that none other than Tom Wilson produced three compilation albums for Columbia Records in 1963 recorded live at the club, starting with *Introducing the Sweet Chariot (The Sensational New Pop Gospel Club with "Soul")*.[36] Before the band had formed, Katz recalls, he had sometimes attended a Black gospel church in Berkeley, California, where he joined in the music and even played a tambourine.[37]

The Blues Project played "Wake Me, Shake Me" with the kind of R&B-style enthusiasm they were known for, making it their closing number when playing live because it allowed for free improvisation and built to an ecstatic climax at the end. After Kooper left the group in 1967, the song was sung by his replacement in the Blues Project, the Black organist John McDuffy. Kooper performed it himself with other musicians, including at Monterey in the summer of 1967. A few months later, the Blues Project performed a psychedelic version, complete with a go-go dancer and light show and video-filter effects, for *Steve Paul's The Scene* TV show. (The show aired in September 1967. It includes Aretha Franklin and the Staple Singers, but also, in a telling combination, the psychedelic rock band Moby Grape.)[38]

Just in terms of genre, the inclusion of a traditional gospel song on *Projections* shouldn't be surprising. Gospel and blues have always been closely related, both in terms of musical structure and cultural contexts. The blues was cast as the devil's music by the pious (for good reason), the bad cousin to church-based gospel. But in the fifties and early sixties, gospel and the blues were recognized as closely related forms. Gospel groups and soloists were often featured at the Newport Folk Festival, and other shows aimed at a rock audience. Take the Chambers Brothers, known today as a psychedelic soul band, as exemplified in their 1968 hit "Time Has Come Today," maybe the most famous example of that hybrid genre.[39] But just a few years earlier, the group was performing the kind of gospel they had sung in their childhood Baptist church in Mississippi. A little later, they played a gospel-inflected folk music in coffeehouses and clubs, like the Ash Grove in Los Angeles. Then, in 1965, they performed the traditional gospel number "I Got It," at Newport—the same year as Dylan's notorious electric performance with members of the Butterfield Blues Band. The Chambers Brothers' gospel song was included on the Newport compilation LP for that year. In 1966, they released an album with political folk singer Barbara Dane on Folkways. And in 1967 they released a live LP on Vault Records: *Now! The Chambers Brothers! Live*, its cover image showing through a psychedelic fish-eye-lens a spiraling block-letter title, set against a backdrop of colorful daisies. The album includes traditional rock 'n' roll ("High Heel Sneakers" and "Long Tall Sally"), R&B ("What'd I Say"), and blues ("C.C. Rider," "You Don't Have to Go," and "It's Groovin' Time"). "Time Has Come Today" also appeared on a different live album in 1966. With its spacey echo and reverb, fuzz-tone guitar, tick-tock cowbell, and rhythmic shifts—not to mention the immortal line: "And my soul has been *psychedelicized*"—it's the paradigmatic psychedelic soul song. Indeed, it's possible to hear that line as an expression about the fusion of two genres: his soul [music] has been psychedelicized. An 11-minute version was included a year later on *The Time Has Come* (1967). That long version has a raga freak-out section in the middle, complete with manic laughter and ecstatic screams over a persistent beat. Chambers Brothers records of 1966–1967 exhibit a familiar genre diversity, even suggest a trajectory from folk to blues, to electrification, to full-blown psychedelia.[40] The genres overlap at each stage rather than following one another in strict sequence. We might think of them as more like alternative concentric musical universes, through which musicians and listeners could travel.

Projections by the Blues Project aspires to represent that kind of mixed-genre multiverse on one disc. But the psychedelic culmination was undoubtedly privileged at the time by musicians and fans, (inaccurately) valorized as the ultimate result of some kind of musical evolution. By the summer of 1966, psychedelic music seemed to many like it was the "everything" that could contain everything. The other tracks on the album continue the eclecticism, from the folk-pop/folk-rock of "Cheryl's Going Home" and "Fly Away" (tracks 6 and 9) to the slow blues by Jimmy Reed, "Caress Me Baby" (track 8), which features a prominent acoustic piano played by Kooper and a harmonica solo by Katz, along with Kalb's improvisations on guitar.

THE "FLUTE THING" EPITOME

Track 7, "Flute Thing," stands out from the mix as a kind of anomaly that somehow also sums up the Blues Project's quirks and contradictions. It's a pop-jazz tune put together by Kooper to showcase Andy Kulberg's flute, titled, as if in an afterthought, "Flute Thing." (Kooper admitted that the opening piano cadenza came from a tune by jazz guitarist Barney Kessell, who, incidentally, often played arrangements that included flute.[41]) The opening melody owes something to Bach. Whatever its DNA, the song is an effective earworm: it would show up again in 1994, sampled on the Beastie Boys' "Flute Loop." On *Projections*, the flute was recorded straight through the mic, but shortly after making the album Kulberg installed a pickup, and in later performances he used effects boxes and pedals to further psychedelicize the tune. In the era of Herbie Mann's Afro-Caribbean exotica-adjacent jazz, and bachelor-pad lounge music, the sonic texture and timbre of the flute with a beat behind it would for many listeners have signaled "jazz."

D. A. Pennebaker's 1968 documentary about the 1967 Monterey International Pop Festival includes among its outtakes the Blues Project's performance of "Flute Thing" on Sunday, June 18, 1967, the last day of the event. The band was edited out of the final film and mainstream music history to make room for full sets by acts like Jefferson Airplane, Jimi Hendrix, and Ravi Shankar. But the outtake is available in the video release.[42] Paul Simon introduces the band, the bass and drums (mallets on a cymbal) start, and Kulberg's flute kicks in, the pickup attached with a trailing cord. Kalb plays guitar solos with raga and jazz-influenced runs on a gold-top Les Paul, and Blumenfeld at one point takes an extended drum solo. The keyboardist, John McDuffy, has replaced Kooper on the organ. (Kooper, who had just left the band, was working at the festival as stage manager and performed a solo set of his own.) Kooper's piano cadence from the album version is played at the festival by Katz on bass. About five minutes in, Kulberg reaches over and switches on one of the latest effects, a magnetic drum-based Binson Echorec machine. The band drops away to a background volume as the flute sound expands exponentially, turning into a reverberant sonic collage of free-jazz improvisation with elements of baroque folk dances. It's Kulberg's way of recreating something of the echo-heavy multitracked solo on the album. As the live solo starts, the camera cuts to a close-up shot of a spellbound Mike Bloomfield. In fact, almost the whole festival audience seems to be sitting still and listening closely, either high or entranced by the music (or both), as the camera zooms in on various individual faces. As the song ends, we see Kooper standing in the wings, applauding his former bandmates, and then the camera briefly cuts to the audience for another glimpse of his old fellow Brill Building songwriter, Paul Simon. A reminder of the ubiquity of politics during the Vietnam conflict, Katz says, just as the performance ends, "that last song . . . as always, we dedicate to peace and to the end of this dirty and dishonest war."

Listening to the Monterey performance now, we can now hear a foretaste of Ian Andersen's flute in Jethro Tull and a whole range of prog-rock and jazz-fusion sounds of the 1970s. We may even hear an anticipation of more recent examples, like André 3000's neo-psychedelic/ambient album *New Blue Sun* (2023); or the similar turn to flute by André's collaborator, saxophonist Shabaka Hutchings. Or, in pop, singer and rapper Lizzo's skilled flute solos. Back in the mid-twentieth century, we can count flautists like James Moody or the extremely popular Herbie Mann (another artist Wilson produced in the 1960s). Avant-garde jazz multi-instrumentalist Rahsaan Roland Kirk, for example, included flute in his performances. Rock bands like Canned Heat and Traffic, to name just two, but also Love (e.g., "Orange Skies") featured flute. So did Van Morrison's hybrid folk-jazz album *Astral Weeks* (1968) and the 1970 eclectic soul band Eric Burdon & War. Nico, of the Velvet Underground, famously hated the flute that Wilson added to her solo record *Chelsea Girl*. But it can be argued that in Nico's case it gave the tunes a baroque-pop sound that enhanced her aura as a Euro-cabaret singer.[43] Of course, Sun Ra's music included flute parts. And jazzy R&B in the 1970s often featured flute (sometimes over congas or bongos), for example, the spoken-word and sung tracks by Gil Scott-Heron (who would turn out to be the last artist Wilson produced, in 1977).

For most listeners in 1966–1967, the Blues Project's "Flute Thing" would have sounded both jazzy *and psychedelic*: the two were not mutually exclusive. In a 2016 interview, Blues Project drummer Roy Blumenfeld said the song "became the Muzak to a lot of folks' acid trips out there on the West Coast. It was, so to speak, their metaphoric elevator." The governing genre term was "psychedelic." In the same set of interviews, guitarist Danny Kalb described "I Can't Keep from Crying" as "a psychedelic adventure and a gospel song together" (note the unexpected genre fusion); and Steve Katz said his own "Steve's Song" was "like a psychedelic love song."[44]

PSYCHEDELICIZED

It's worth taking seriously the band's repeated use of the term "psychedelic." For them, and for much of their contemporary audience, it was clearly more than just a marketing label. Music critic Jim DeRogatis says, "to the extent that it can be pinned down at all, the birth date of psychedelic rock is best listed as 1966."[45] What did the term and the music mean at the time, in the year of its birth? What makes the gospel, jazz, pop, and blues tunes in the Blues Project's repertoire come across as psychedelic for the musicians and many in their listening audience? Flute music, according to widely adopted clichés, is ethereal, otherworldly. It's sometimes heard as "primitive" when associated with traditional bamboo and tin instruments. All of these associations would have contributed to the perception that the flute was an apt instrument for psychedelic music.

There are a few other sonic cues in Kulberg's performance for psychedelia, including heavy reverb and echo, and fast improvised runs in the solos. But I think an important part of the answer is social and contextual, a matter of both (mind)set and setting, to use the terms of researchers studying psychedelic drug experiences. DeRogatis acknowledges that "LSD had captured the popular imagination by 1966 to the point where people who never had a psychedelic experience *thought* they had a fairly good idea of what one was like."[46] Likewise, with psychedelic music, expectations shaped the popular reception as more and more people thought they had an idea of what it *sounded* like—and were in the right frame of mind, in the right context, to experience it as such. In context, "the word 'psychedelic' came to signal a set of sonic clues."[47] These included

> circular, mandala-like song structures; sustained or droning melodies; altered and effected instrumental sounds; reverb, echoes, and tape delays that created a sense of space, and layered mixes that rewarded repeated listening by revealing new and mysterious elements.[48]

Interestingly, DeRogatis finds the ancestor for psychedelic rock in the deliberately strange R&B single from 1956, Screamin' Jay Hawkins's "I Put a Spell on You."[49] Indeed, blues already contained a number of the same sonic clues, from droning, to circular structure, to the use of (acoustic as well as electrically generated) echo or reverb. This is no accident; it's the result of the defining role played by blues in blues-rock, and by blues-rock in psychedelia as a whole.

WARM SAN FRANCISCAN NIGHTS

Jon Savage opens his book *1966* by citing an experimental magazine from December of that year, issue 3 of *Aspen*, designed and edited by Andy Warhol and David Dalton.[50] Like previous issues, number 3 was a 9 ½ by 12 ½-inch hinged cardboard box, in this case printed to look like a shiny container of Fab brand laundry detergent. In the tradition of surrealist books in boxes and Fluxus kits in boxes, the multimedia magazine had serious artistic pretensions. It contained various loose materials curated by Warhol, from a set of postcard-sized reproductions of pop art paintings in a private collection (including one of his own Campbell's Soup prints) to a playable 7-inch plastic flexidisc record, the B side of which contained a droning-feedback guitar track ("Loop") by John Cale of the Velvet Underground—the band Warhol was sponsoring. Along with LSD, rock music is the common theme running throughout the issue. The flexidisc came in a packet labeled "Music, Man, That's Where It's At." Savage is primarily interested in the essays on music that were included in that packet. But the issue as a whole also contains interesting music ephemera, like an ad from Verve/Folkways Records pasted inside the back cover of the box: a full-page black and white photograph of the members of the Blues Project (label mates of the Velvet Underground, both produced by Wilson), shaggy hair, ostentatiously "loud" ties, corduroys, standing on a sidewalk in San Francisco. The title above the photo—all caps in a "military"-style stenciled font—reads "The Blues Project/Projections," the band name and the title of their new album. "You are earwitness to the most explosive music event of our era," the copy announces, calling this second album from the band "the high-trajectory Phase Two"—comparing with hopeful hype the arc of their career to a multistage rocket.

That same photo, but in full color, became the album cover for *Projections*. It was taken by legendary rock photographer Jim Marshall at 1541 Haight Street and shows the five musicians standing beside a parked car, with a partially obscured bystander behind them further down the street. Katz later recalled, "You can't see it in the photo, but there were hippies all around us—white hippies, black hippies, Chinese hippies, teen runaway hippies—with flowers in their hair, joints in their mouths, patchouli oil in their clothes, and LSD on their brains"; he adds, "It was glorious."[51] Like the fisheye-lens shots of bands that caught on around that time for album cover illustrations—for example, for the Byrds' *Mr. Tambourine Man* (1965), among many others—the composition creates a sense of tunnel vision: the band is foregrounded, in your face, but everything recedes backwards from the perspective of the lens. All that framed-out context, the noisy and smelly Haight, is implied in the warped and limited vision; it's there, just peripheral. That spring and summer was a psychedelic moment, first as a subculture, then as a musical genre, finally as a fad and mass marketing term. The Blues Project were at home in the moment, were in fact a force in emergent psychedelia, and they began to identify themselves as a psychedelic blues band.

As evidenced in that very first album, live performances made the Blues Project's reputation. Not counting later reunions, the band released only three albums: *Live at the Cafe Au Go Go* (1966), *Projections* (1966), and *Live at Town Hall* (1967). They disbanded in 1967. *Projections* was the only studio album of the three, sandwiched between those two live records; another set of tapes resulted in a later-released live album, *The Blues Project Live at the Matrix September 1966*, recorded at the club in San Francisco. The New York band traveled to California more than once in 1966, including in April.

EMMARETTA

For that April tour, the band hired a young Black female vocalist, Emmaretta Marks, to replace Tommy Flanders. They may have met her through Wilson. Beginning when she was a freshman at Howard University, she was in a relationship with Eric Burdon of the Animals while Wilson was producing the British band. She sang background vocals with the Blues Project for their West Coast gigs and then for a brief time afterwards. Her time with the band came between albums, for the most part, but she can be heard on the single "Where There's Smoke, There's Fire."[52] She also introduced the band members to her friend Gail Sloatman, who would go on to marry Frank Zappa. Marks appears as a full member of the Blues Project in a photo taken in a San Francisco park by Alice Ochs in 1966, everyone standing among big rocks with a blue-sky backdrop.[53] She was technically a background vocalist, but a series of photos of the band's performance at the San Francisco State College Folk Festival, April 15–17, 1966, show her standing right up front on the stage, playing tambourine and sharing a microphone with Katz.[54] After leaving the band, she would go on to become a cast member in the original production of the Broadway musical *Hair*, in which one of the songs was "Electric Blues" ("Rock . . . folk rock . . . rhythm and blues / Electronics explodin'"). Marks also sang "White Boys" in the show, dressed as a member of a girl group based on the Supremes. She was a background singer for Jimi Hendrix, with whom she was in a relationship and for whom she acted as copyeditor/amanuensis. Deep Purple knew her well enough to write a song about her ("Emmaretta"). One brief, haunting scene in the never-released documentary film about the Rolling Stones' 1972 tour, *Cocksucker Blues*, features an uncredited Marks in a floppy-brimmed hat, sitting backstage in the locker room at an arena. Everyone's smoking and talking in the echoey improvised green room. She's laughing and gossiping; someone says something about the locker room, and she says she *loves* a locker room (for its acoustics), and then she demonstrates, throwing her head back and belting out a powerful high C with a strong but natural-sounding vibrato, holding the note, showing off. Then someone puts a piece of bagel or pastry in her mouth to stop the singing. Like Hendrix, Marks serves as a reminder that Black musicians in the 1960s didn't always fit the strict, genre-segregated stereotypes. Many played prominent roles in rock, Broadway, and mainstream pop, never mind what the separate charts and emergent specialized radio formats might suggest. We encounter her again in chapter 4, as she crosses paths (and metaphorical swords) with Nico of the Velvet Underground at the end of the 1960s.

ALL YOU LYSERGIC PEOPLE

As far as I can tell, Marks would have been singing with the Blues Project when they headlined two nights at the Avalon Ballroom in San Francisco, April 22–23, 1966, as the first act at the venue for opening night shows produced by Chet Helms and the Family Dog commune. That *Aspen* magazine-in-a-box issue (#3) that I discuss above, published at the end of 1966, included among the music essays a piece of participatory new journalism about one of those Blues Project concerts at the Avalon, "The View from the Dance Floor," by Bob Chamberlain. Like a stream-of-consciousness trip journal, it says more about the author's own perceptions, including of the light show's "giant amoeba surging back and forth all over the rhythm," than about the band's music. Chamberlain seems, at least, to have drunk the Kool-Aid (or, in this case, the 7-UP, spiked with pure Owsley acid):

> And under the ultraviolet lights people dance with their fluorescent clothes, or with their waving hands and bare feet painted with fluorescent paint, or splashed in their hair or all over everything and eyes and teeth that glow naturally.

Then, he reports, Kalb steps up to the mic and greets the crowd: "hello, all you, uh, lysergic people"—

> and suddenly it's exploding all over us, a thundering shock wave of sound, so strong, but oh so crisp, so clean so clear so electric and the colors are working and the kid is digging it and IT'S ALL OKAY.

Chamberlain also describes Kooper's look as he's setting up the organ: "his new brown velour cape with the yellow polka dot lining and one of his 40 new L.A. shirts . . . [. . .] he's some kind of mystic prince of the black arts . . ." (ellipses in the original). During their cover version of Donovan's folk song "Catch the Wind," he says that "a high piercing single electric organ note held on and on and on breaks loose the words into music."

We have to make an effort, now, to imagine a time when such experiences would have seemed fresh, even shocking, when this kind of Tom Wolfe–style gonzo reportage combined with beatnik poetry was new and unusual. It's an odd, yet also typical, document of the times, and it gives us a sense of what it felt like to attend a Blues Project *show* in 1966, however traditional or roots-oriented their music may sound on the records, and however often they mention the traditional blues that inspired them. The scene in clubs like the Avalon or the Fillmore, even cabarets in New York like the Cafe Au Go Go, just *became* psychedelic at some point in 1966, and were suddenly perceived as trippy happenings. Besides the strobes, black lights, movie and slide projections, and liquid light show blobs—the producers of which were credited on the gig posters—there was the participatory carnivalesque atmosphere. (Those multimedia "projections," using overhead, slide, or movie projectors and sometimes colored blobs of liquid, may be one source of the Blues Project's album title.) All of this—plus high volume, feedback and distortion, heavy reverb, and other electronic effects—altered the way blues or folk-rock music sounded to the audience, changed the way it was perceived, received, and given meaning. Members of the crowd danced with tambourines; some painted their bodies or wrote in notebooks in the midst of the chaos; some carried transistor radios, presumably listening to their different drummers; and one reveler carried a small device that just emitted "electronic beeps."[55] The show was an extension of Ken Kesey's Acid Tests held in the previous year, which had culminated in the famous three-day multimedia Trips Festival in San Francisco in January 1966. The Avalon was only one venue for what was becoming an increasingly distributed scene. The Blues Project also played numerous college campuses, for example, and were at first surprised when some of those campus events resembled Acid Tests, with theaters full of zonked-out students.

THE PSYCHEDELIC BLUES

Not all psychedelic music was the blues, of course. There were plenty of other psychedelic genres, including pseudo-baroque chamber pop, and some of Zappa's modernist experimentation. But if not all psychedelic music was the blues, by late 1966 most electric blues would have been perceived as psychedelic. Like the set and setting of an LSD or psilocybin trip, expectations and context changed the way the music was heard. It's worth remembering that, over in England, the psychedelic band Pink Floyd first called itself the Pink Floyd Blues Band, named after two American blues musicians, Pink Anderson and Floyd Council. And their twelve-bar roots show beneath the sound effects of their cover of "I'm a King Bee" from 1965. Once the blues became intertwined with psychedelia, it changed the way even a good deal of electric Chicago blues was heard. Some musicians, like Buddy Guy, were already straddling the two categories anyway. The Paul Butterfield Blues Band, the most faithful exponent of the Chicago tradition in rock at the time, released *East-West* in 1966, recorded in Chicago (the cover image shows the band posed like statues between the caryatid statues of Chicago's Museum of Science and Industry), with long jams by Michael Bloomfield that frequently cross into psychedelia, especially on the title track, which features jazz and raga elements. *East-West* also includes its own up-tempo cover of "Two Trains Running" and a funky rendering of newly minted Monkee Michael Nesmith's original tune, "Mary, Mary."

We can even see the effect of this trend from folk-music blues to psychedelic blues in the work of Muddy Waters. A 1968 album at Chess Records, *Electric Mud*, was put together with backing by Rotary Connection, a psychedelic band formed in Chicago in 1966. In 1964, Waters had come out with *Folk Singer*, an album of acoustic blues intended to ride the wave of the folk craze. But by then Waters had already long been electric. He bought his first electric guitar in 1944 after moving to Chicago, where he helped to create the electric blues sound at Chess Records in the 1950s. And he recorded a live album *with an electric band* at Newport Jazz Festival in 1960—he played a Fender Telecaster—five years before Dylan's mythic performance at the Newport Folk Festival, with Waters's acolyte Bloomfield on guitar. *Electric Mud* can be seen as a return to the electric blues sound he had helped to pioneer. He just turned up the volume, increased the distortion, and added effects and filters to produce a recognizably psychedelic sound. Indeed, *Electric Mud* might have more accurately been titled "Psychedelic Mud." Photos of the Rolling Stones hang at Chess Records today, commemorating the British band's recording there in 1964. But the Waters cover track of "Let's Spend the Night Together" on *Electric Mud* is not based on the Stones' version but on an overdriven bass-string lead-guitar riff taken from Eric Clapton's part on "Sunshine of Your Love." When it was released, *Electric Mud* was predictably criticized by some listeners as inauthentic, a sellout by the venerated blues musician. Waters later distanced himself from it. But it has quietly gathered fans since 1968, among them hip-hop pioneer and rapper Chuck D of Public Enemy, who said that *Electric Mud* was the album that introduced him to the blues! In 2003, Chuck D was part of a project for a film series produced by Martin Scorsese, *The Blues: Godfathers and Sons*, joining an ad-hoc band called the Elektrik Mud Cats. The group brought together musicians who had played on the original 1968 album, along with rapper Common, Chuck D, and a DJ/turntablist. They recorded a tribute version of "Mannish Boy," a weird cross-generational remix of blues in a multilayer cake of musical and cultural contexts.

In an episode of his radio program, Wilson mocks the solemnity of folk-music knowledge and folk authenticity: "this fellow called me up and he says, 'hey, man, you don't know anything about folk music.' I said, 'what makes you say that? I'm just plain folk'" (*The Music Factory*, program 2). The implication is that being Black did not disqualify him from producing folk music because, as he jokes, he is "just . . . folk." The joke conceals a serious point about his interest in actual folk music produced ca. 1966. But it also reveals his skepticism about "ethnic" pretensions on the part of white folk singers, and that included blues musicians. In another episode of his radio show (*The Music Factory*, program 18), he interviewed Dave Van Ronk, whom he calls "one of the most famous blues and ethnic singers of them all." Van Ronk is there to promote his new album with his band, the Hudson Dusters, in which the folk singer goes electric—sort of. Wilson is interested in discussing this move, but Van Ronk confesses that on the album he actually plays an acoustic guitar with a pickup installed (he says it's better for playing rhythm). It turns out the record includes two songs by a new Canadian folk singer, Joni Mitchell, as well as a heartfelt semi-amplified version (with strings in the background) of "Dink's Song"—that same traditional tune we hear in the opening and final scenes of *Inside Llewyn Davis*.

Van Ronk and Wilson talk about the Greenwich Village scene in recent years, leading into Wilson's playing Donovan's "Catch the Wind" as performed by the Blues Project. As he introduces the track, the producer tries to talk to Van Ronk about the occasion of the recording, which he says was made "live at the Cafe Au Go Go," at the "first big Blues Bash [Bag] back in 1965." Wilson thinks he remembers Van Ronk playing there. When Van Ronk demurs, Wilson insists, "I *saw* you there!" Van Ronk mutters a reply: "Oh—I was—everybody was hanging out." With this exchange, Wilson performs a verbal trick like the cinematic trick in *Inside Llewyn Davis*. His focus on Van Ronk is actually a way to shift attention to the Blues Project. The folk singer's folk singer, the Mayor of MacDougal Street—who had given guitar lessons to Katz and Kalb and played in a jug band with Kalb—goes out of focus and becomes just another Greenwich Village busker in the background, who might or might not have joined a jam session, or may have just been part of the audience, hanging out on the scene. In that same moment, at the Blues Bag in late 1965, the Blues Project first came into sharp focus as the up-and-coming thing. Crowded together on a tiny stage in that low-ceilinged dark club, playing overdriven electric blues as well as some folk-rock and pop songs, they would soon attempt to dissolve the blues—with a mixture of other genres—in a psychedelic solution. Thus, they believed, they were redefining the problematic "ethnic" blues as a new thing they called "attitude music," a music of personal expression and inner exploration. In that way, they performed their sometimes-anguished quest out in public, onstage and on their records. A lot of people in the audience and among those who bought the records, were, for a couple of years at least, on the same trip.

CHAPTER THREE

ASTRO-INFINITY MUSIC AT SLUGS' SALOON

Sun Ra and His Arkestra, *The Futuristic Sounds of Sun Ra* (1962); *The Magic City* (1966); *Strange Strings* (1967)

SLUGS' IN THE FAR EAST

In the summer of 1966, if you were to leave the Cafe Au Go Go after hearing a set by the Blues Project and make your way through the Village crowd out in the streets, then walk a block uptown to West 3rd Street, then east across town for a bit, you'd arrive at Slugs' Saloon, between Avenues B and C. Nowadays it's occupied by a bakery/coffee shop. It takes some imagination to picture the seedy, dark, shotgun bar that used to be there behind grated windows, with exposed brick walls inside, dim lights, sawdust and peanut shells on the floor, nylon parachutes hanging above the tables.[1] Drugs were dealt and musicians got in free. It was called Slugs' "in the Far East" because, for many, getting to the dive bar required some pretty exotic travel to the Lower East Side, where taxis often refused to go.

As advertised, Slugs' was "comfortably air conditioned," and it was a hotbed of avant-garde jazz, featuring musicians like Albert Ayler, Art Farmer, Archie Shepp, and Ornette Coleman. Starting in March 1966, every Monday night you could witness a "special attraction," Sun Ra and his Astro-Infinity Music, a ten- to twelve-piece big band, the Arkestra, led by the great keyboardist and composer who always said he was not of this world. He and the Arkestra members lived in a building nearby on 3rd Street, in the neighborhood that would become hip-famous as the Lower East Side. Their building was occupied by artists, poets, activists, and musicians, among others. One contemporary account of Sun Ra's residence published in *Newsweek* called it "a broken-down apartment near the Bowery embellished with 'cosmic' paintings, plastic spheres and rubber balls suspended by string. He has created an entire universe out of Woolworth leftovers in which he is the sun god."[2] Onstage, the band wore found-material homemade costumes that crossed comic-book superhero outfits with space-suits with African and Egyptian ceremonial dress; with accessories made from foil, fabric, beads, and glitter; capes and gilded headdresses (more "Woolworth leftovers"). Traditional jazz instruments were played—often with virtuosic skill—but sometimes combined with homemade percussion instruments like hand-carved African drums, as well as electric or electronic keyboards of various kinds.

In the tradition of the big bands, the music was carefully orchestrated. But its performance depended on improvisation—in this case, often group improvisation that sometimes crossed into free-jazz territory—within the framework provided by the score, the whole thing conducted by the composer, Sun Ra. In this way it differed both from more traditionally fully notated music and from some of the free jazz that was starting to flourish at the time. The props and lighting, including projections superimposed on the players onstage and on the house, were integral to the show. That same magazine article with the remark about "Woolworth leftovers" described one of the five-hour shows at Slugs':

> The sun god [Sun Ra] unleashed the full fury of his art and anarchy before a small, spellbound, sober audience of some 100 devotees. Boxed in on a tiny stage, Sun sat kingly at the piano, his head crowned by a cap of gold, his drummer backed against the backdrop curtains, his bassist hunched over his instrument. The rest of the Solar Arkestra . . . were forced to crouch along the edge of the stage, hardware in hand—trumpets, French horn, trombone. The program included everything from lush pastoral hymns to solid jazz and wildly improvisatory numbers. A motion-picture projector bathed the musicians in rotating orbs of light and they became African astronauts playing to the cosmos.[3]

That last sentence is a reminder that a recognizably "psychedelic" light show was part of Sun Ra's staging. As for the music, it was structured on (collective) improvisation, not "anarchy." Sun Ra was known as a stickler for discipline, and he always touted the need for structure. Like Frank Zappa, he composed music that incorporated passages of often atonal improvisation as an element in the composition. But, also like Zappa, he was always the conductor, even of the Arkestra's collective improvisations.

ASTRO-AFRO INFINITY MUSIC

While it's fair to assume that everyone in the audience at Slugs' was not entirely "sober," as the review claims, they were no doubt "spellbound" by the music and spectacle, immersed in what they were hearing and seeing. The reviewer's most significant observation may be that the Arkestra was transformed during the performance into "African astronauts." In terms of style, performance, mythology, and music, Sun Ra was a key creative source of what we now recognize as Afrofuturism.[4] Early on, the poet, critic, playwright, and activist LeRoi Jones (who would soon thereafter convert to Islam and change his name to Amiri Baraka) was among the earliest to see Sun Ra in this way, long before the term "Afrofuturism" was coined. In one essay, Jones noted that "Sun Ra wants a music that will reflect a life-sense lost in the West, a music full of Africa."[5] Jones/Baraka was also a downtown resident for a time, a key player in the Lower East Side arts scene, which included performances and readings in lofts and coffee shops by poets, painters, and free jazz experimentalists, many of whom were to help form the Black Arts movement that Baraka spearheaded, based uptown in Harlem.[6] Sun Ra was involved from the beginning in the emergent movement, if from a bit out of left field. In May 1966, the Arkestra even provided music for Baraka's stage play, *A Black Mass*. Baraka developed the idea that "space" is a way of imagining freedom. Sun Ra, he said, "understands 'the future' as an ever widening comprehension of what space is, even to the 'physical' travel between the planets as we do anyway in the long human chain of progress. . . . It is science-fact that Sun-Ra is interested in, not science-fiction."[7] Over twenty-five years later, Mark Dery would coin the term "Afrofuturism,"[8] but here in 1967 the concept was already laid out by Baraka in everything but the name, with Sun Ra as its chief avatar.

The meta-genre or movement known as Afrofuturism—especially in Sun Ra's deep-historical version—clearly influenced Tom Wilson too. Near the end of his life in 1978, he was working collaboratively on an R&B opera, *Mind Flyers of Gondwana*, with fellow producer and arranger Larry Fallon, Danny Sims (who managed Johnny Nash and first signed Bob Marley to a record contract), and composer and arranger Larry Willis. It was left unfinished when Wilson died.[9] But he and others talked about it at the time in terms we now recognize as Afrofuturistic. In this case, the futurism in Sun Ra's Egyptology and the Black Panther comics, for example (the Black Panther character, T'Challa of Wakanda, first appeared in a *Fantastic Four* comic in 1966), is embedded in a deep-historical or prehistorical context. If ancient Blackness can be thoroughly reimagined, then it becomes possible to imagine Black futures in other worlds. This is how Wilson's opera was framed: from an ancient Afrocentric Egypt one can extrapolate to far-flung interplanetary possibilities. Gondwana was a prehistoric supercontinent, a landmass that included what is now Africa, as well as South America, India, Antarctica, and Australia. It was part of the later supercontinent of Pangaea. In 1976, Miles Davis released a live double album titled *Pangaea*. It includes two full side-long tracks titled "Gondwana" (parts 1 and 2), featuring overdriven electric guitars, a prominent flute solo, and Miles's trumpet through a wah-wah pedal. Around that same time, near the end of his life, Wilson was planning his Afrofuturist R&B opera.

Wilson's public remarks about the opera suggested that *Mind Flyers of Gondwana* was intended to "[weave] together the story of Atlantis and the story of the black man in America from his roots in Africa."[10] The cast was meant to include Gladys Knight, LaBelle, the Righteous Brothers, Gil Scott-Heron (whom Wilson produced), Minnie Riperton, and Johnny Nash—and it was hoped there might be music by Bob Marley. As we've seen, as early as his radio show in the late 1960s, Wilson had said that the eclectic music of the times was trending toward something "operatic." *Hair* and *Godspell* had proven that Broadway musicals could be based on rock and gospel music, and the Who had tested the concept of the rock opera with *Tommy*. In 1966, Wilson produced an original-cast album from the Broadway musical *A Hand Is on the Gate*, with music-backed poetry by Black authors. Closer to the time when Wilson was developing his project, Charlie Smalls wrote the score (and William F. Brown the book) for the "Super Soul Musical," *The Wiz*. It opened in 1974, then opened on Broadway to general acclaim the following year. For the *Mind Flyers of Gondwana*, the inclusion of reggae musicians Nash and Marley indicates that Wilson was thinking of the broadly eclectic music of the African diaspora. The musical-theatrical opera has traditionally been seen as a multimedia form, combining instrumental and vocal music, design, acting, myth, and storytelling. It's a form conceptually compatible with Wilson's ideal of everything is everything. He may even have returned to the general inspiration of his former label artist Sun Ra for the kind of Afrocentric science fiction on which to base what became his final, unfinished creative project.

Half a century later, examples of Afrofuturism are everywhere, and Sun Ra's founding influence on Afrofuturism is everywhere acknowledged. I have seen hand-painted album covers for Sun Ra records displayed in the same gallery as Parliament/Funkadelic's shiny life-sized stage-prop, the iconic Mothership (along with an artist's take on it in the form of a Gemini-style space capsule), at the African American History Museum in Washington, D.C.[11] Photos of Sun Ra's costumes, and those still worn by Marshall Allen and the continuing incarnations of the Arkestra, bring to mind the recent "Soundsuits" by the artist Nick Cave, elaborate constructions made of found materials that make sounds invoking African and Indigenous ceremonial garb. Sun Ra is an acknowledged source of inspiration for Janelle Monae's music, costumes, and films. Underground hip-hop duo Madvillain sampled Sun Ra's poetic speech from the film *Space Is the Place* for their "Shadows of Tomorrow" track (2004).[12] It sounds right at home in the mix, partly because the mix itself—not to mention the wrestling masks the artists favor and their dark comics villain vibe—was likely inspired in part by Sun Ra's musical and theatrical examples. A whole range of imagined Black futures and alternate ways of being in the present can be traced back to the innovative bandleader.

DOWN IN THE VILLAGE

Many call Sun Ra unprecedented, a true original. Much has been written about his leading place in avant-garde jazz and Afrofuturism. But in fact, as original and as groundbreaking as his music and performance (both onstage and in daily life) were in the mid-1960s, they were not entirely *sui generis*, not truly without any precedent or lacking any context. My purpose is definitely *not* to debunk the mystique of Sun Ra's originality—far from it. But his creativity was socially connected, contextual, embedded in multiple layers of other interesting examples of music and cultural expressions, linked to adjacent genres, related styles, and scenes, both avant-garde and popular, some rigorously artistic but some that are usually treated as trivial, vulgar, or commercial. In fact, Sun Ra was part of a new *kind* of avant-garde that emerged in the mid- to late 1960s, one drawing directly on "actually existing and close-to-home popular culture," exemplified in Amiri Baraka and the Black Arts movement and seen as well in the connection between free jazz and underground rock.[13]

For his part, Sun Ra said that, indeed, he was "underground," but deliberately so—"self-underground, that is, out of the music industry"—which he associated with his music's being "primitive, natural and pure."[14] His esoteric ideas were of the underground, as well. He had been part of a community of Black intellectuals in Chicago in the 1950s that included the Thmei Research Society, formed with his collaborator and business partner, Alton Abraham. The two of them produced and handed out broadsheets in Washington Square Park, and Abraham remained involved with the music and the El Saturn label after the Arkestra moved to New York.[15] In New York, Slugs' Saloon was itself an underground kind of place. It was opened in 1964 by two men who had met at a Gurdjieff reading group. The slugs in the name allude to alien creatures, "three-brained beings," in mystic and composer George Gurdjieff's allegorical science fiction, which combined extraterrestrial and ancient Egyptian elements and was titled *All and Everything* (which is not far from "everything is everything"). Esoterica, mysticism, spiritualism, and out-there science fiction were everywhere downtown in those days. In 1966 you could buy folk-music magazines in the Village that included science-fiction stories and articles on occult schools of mysticism, and you could be handed smeared mimeographed pamphlets on the streets that expounded on aliens, Theosophy or other systems, and radical politics. This feature of bohemian life predates psychedelia, even predates the Beats, but it reached a kind of peak in the mid-1960s when combined with psychedelic language and graphics. Indeed, this is an important context for understanding another famous visionary Black musician, Jimi Hendrix. He left the world of R&B, traveled downtown, first as Jimmy James, and began to showcase his own outrageous electric guitar sounds, wearing far-out clothes in Village clubs in the summer of 1966. In his case, electronic distortion, feedback, and febrile poetic lyrics connected the blues with cosmic exploration, sometimes employing the kind of outer-space imagery found in avant-garde and psychedelic culture in general.

Sun Ra didn't need downtown New York to inspire his own explorations of cosmic resonances. These had begun during his last years in Chicago.[16] But the downtown scene spurred him on to a more intense involvement with the avant-garde and—though not under that name—with burgeoning psychedelic culture. When Sun Ra and his band came to Greenwich Village in 1962, it was "in a state of readiness for anyone who shared their views."[17] From the moment of his arrival, Sun Ra influenced the underground scene in the Village as much as he was influenced by it. He was what one musician (invoking the Romantic poet Percy Shelley) called "one of the unacknowledged legislators of the world."[18] Shelley's term, "unacknowledged," can be interpreted as a synonym for "unconscious"—the idea being that poets often define the leading edge just by exploring it, without consciously trying to be in the vanguard. For Sun Ra, it had started when he had changed his name from Herman "Sonny" Blount to Le Sony'r Ra in 1952 and began to tell people he came from Saturn. A decade later, he found the East Village a fertile field, discovering a network of roots and nodes to which he could join his own experiments. The experimentation accelerated in the first years of the 1960s as his connections increased, especially when it came to the rise of the New Thing, free jazz, in the context of which Sun Ra explored his post-jazz space music.

PSYCHEDELIC BIG-BAND MUSIC

In 1966, Slugs' was the mothership. The Arkestra's shows at Slugs'—which were long, sometimes running from 9:00 p.m. to 4:00 a.m.—were multimedia happenings, events many at the time interpreted as psychedelic: "within only a few years reviewers would speak of his performances in LSD-color terms, as total experiences, as freak-outs."[19] This wasn't really Sun Ra's intention. But we'd do well to take seriously those contemporary interpretations, some of which came from fellow denizens of the underground. For example, avant-garde saxophonist Marion Brown, in a review of Sun Ra's 1965 album *Secrets of the Sun*, shares that listening to the album or attending a live performance by Sun Ra was "like a psychedelic experience induced by sound."[20] In another review, James Semark writes that he for one would like to see a "total experience," a kind of Sun Ra Happening, in which "all those fascinating elements fuse together into a mighty SUPERNOVA THAT WOULD BLOW EVERYONE'S MINDS CLEAR OUT OF THE GALAXY!"[21]

Adjacent contemporary examples abound. A hand-lettered ad in the *East Village Other* promoted a series of concerts at the Astor Place Playhouse on Lafayette Street for February 15–March 1, 1966, featuring a variety of acts on the ESP-Disk record label: "Hear the psychedelic sounds of esp [ESP] Get knocked out of your skull with the FUGS, Albert Ayler, Sun Ra, Paul Bless, THE FUGS, Burton Greene, Marion Brown." The underground folk-rock band the Fugs were the headliners of these ESP shows, but note that avant-garde jazz artists like Albert Ayler, Marion Brown, and Sun Ra himself were grouped right alongside the Fugs as part of the label's "psychedelic sounds." Of *course* Sun Ra shows and albums were interpreted as psychedelic at the time, given the overlapping scenes in New York at that moment.

Spring 1966: if you were to leave Slugs' in the wee hours and walk back West and uptown for a few minutes, then cut through Tompkins Square Park over to St. Marks Place, you'd arrive at the Dom. This had been a Polish dance hall and social-event venue. In 1966, Andy Warhol made it into a club with a dance hall and a bar. During the month of April 1966, the house band was Warhol's adopted project, the Velvet Underground, whose music was briefly part of a swirling, overwhelming multimedia experience called the Exploding Plastic Inevitable (EPI). In the mix were Warhol's films, strobe lights, projected liquid blobs and other immersive light show effects, dancers, drugs—and loud and distorted rock music. (More about the Dom and the EPI in the next chapter.) Now, zoom out on that imagined map: in that spring of 1966, the Cafe Au Go Go, Slugs', and the Dom, all walking distance apart, briefly formed a triangle of micro-scenes in downtown Manhattan.

Each subscene was dominated by a group of musicians then in residence—the Blues Project, Sun Ra and his Solar Arkestra, the Velvet Underground and Nico. All of them had recently been produced or were still being produced by Tom Wilson. On any given night, the dapper and lanky Wilson might be seen in the crowd at one of those venues. One scene grew beyond pure folk and blues into folk-rock and electric blues; one emerged from free jazz and avant-garde improvisation into Space Music; one came out of pop art, doo-wop, garage rock, and experimental minimalism, mixing up a dark underground art-rock. The point is, they all overlapped, in terms of personnel and participants, but also in some of their aims and aesthetics. They had more in common than their immediate genre differences might lead us to believe. Accepted genre distinctions, the categories that allow us to sort records into bins and streaming channels, can get in the way of seeing what would have been obvious at the time: the lights flashing, the electric instruments, the costumes, and the deliberate genre-crossings of the music—it was all part of a shared context, however diversely constituted.

ALL HAPPENING

Happenings and total-experience environments were trendy that year. But they were often serious art projects, experiments in boundary crossing and practical demonstrations of what inclusivity of form might look like in practice, combining audio, visual, static, and kinetic art forms.[22] An article by John Wilcock for Andy Warhol's *The Plastic Exploding Inevitable*, a "one-shot underground newspaper" included in the box that was *Aspen* magazine issue 3 (December 1966), explains the "underground" scene downtown at the time:

> All the traditional forms have been and are being changed. In music, pioneers such as the late Edgar [sic] Varèse and time-space experimenters such as John Cage have taught us that the mechanical sounds of this electronic age, and even silence, possess musical content. Currently such "farout" jazz exponents as Albert Ayler, Ornette Coleman, Sun Ra, are mystifying the traditional jazz buffs with their cacophonous sounds although, once again, it is mainly the unfamiliarity that bothers traditionalists whose Western ears tag Oriental music with the same farout indictment.

Forget for a moment the specifics of the claim to absolute newness. It's clear that Wilcock takes for granted that avant-garde classical music, experimental conceptual music, and free jazz make up a shared context for both Sun Ra and the Velvet Underground.[23] And he presents this context in a discussion of the underground as a disputed term defined by the struggle between authentic creativity on the one hand and "selling out" for commercial gain on the other.

Wilcock goes on to connect pop art and multimedia happenings like the EPI to the underground's explosion of *forms*—the context for appreciating Sun Ra's "cacophonous sounds." The term "happening" itself, Wilcock insists, is just a "convenient label, but it should always be understood to mean everything rather than something." Music and sound, dancing, performance and visual art, immersive effects of projected lights, influences from John Cage to Ornette Coleman. This is an everything that overwhelms petty distinctions.

That same issue of *Aspen* (#3) contained that ad for the Blues Project's album *Projections* discussed in the previous chapter. Think again of the rock band's album title. The word "projections" had a range of associations at the time—Sun Ra apparently used the term abstractly, to refer to mental exercises in imagining possible futures, akin to the out-of-body experiences (astral projections) that were common to various esoteric spiritualities and in psychic as well as psychedelic experiments.[24] But in a more literal sense, projections would have referred to light show effects using overhead, slide, or film *projectors*. "Everything rather than something" was a lot to expect from a night in the discotheque or club, but that was 1966. These spaces shared the cultural DNA of the moment via traveling bicoastal personnel and borrowed or stolen ideas with the Acid Tests and ballroom shows out in California, as we've seen, total experiences linking otherwise disparate bands like the Velvet Underground and the Blues Project. Later, in 1969, Sun Ra and the Arkestra joined an eclectic bill at that year's Newport Jazz Festival, which included Zappa and the Mothers of Invention, as well as Kooper's Blood, Sweat & Tears, with Art Blakey, Miles Davis, and other jazz musicians. Much of the program was what we might call psychedelic-adjacent. The performance by Sun Ra's Arkestra included the visuals of the Joshua Light Show, famous for their contributions to psychedelic shows in California ballrooms and elsewhere from 1966 on, shows likely influenced in turn by Warhol's EPI.[25]

FUTURISTIC SOUNDS

To understand what Sun Ra produced in 1966, I want to look first at an important earlier album. Four years earlier, in 1962, the Arkestra, recently arrived in New York, had begun to play gigs in Greenwich Village. That year, Sun Ra released what many consider his last truly accessible album, *The Futuristic Sounds of Sun Ra*, on Savoy Records.[26] This was also the last Sun Ra record to be produced by Wilson, who had brought out Sun Ra's first album, *Jazz by Sun Ra* (2 vols.), on his Transition label in 1957–1958. Wilson would stay in touch with Sun Ra for years and continued to find work for him and members of the Arkestra, as we've seen in the example of the *Batman and Robin* session in 1966. But in 1961 (released 1962), *The Futuristic Sounds of Sun Ra* was clearly an attempt to market the visionary composer and bandleader to a broader audience. It would be easy to see it as evidence of yet another attempted cash-grab on the part of the producer, who was still working with the avant-garde musician after Wilson had begun to move into the more commercial forms of rock and pop. But that would be an oversimplification. I think it's clear that Wilson cared about the music on this record. He seems to have thought of it as a kind of diplomatic overture to Sun Ra's potential Earthly listeners.

Wilson was not above trying to make a commercial success out of serious jazz music or music made by serious jazz artists. In 1967, he produced an album by the saxophonist Benny Golson, *Tune In, Turn On: To The Hippest Commercials of the Sixties*, containing Golson's light jazz arrangements of TV themes from commercials for Wink and Diet Pepsi sodas, several brands of cigarettes, and Alka-Seltzer, among other products. The album cover shows a psychedelically decorated TV set sitting in a parched desert (no doubt the infamous "vast wasteland"). Wilson knew Benny Golson and respected his music. He was known for his work with Art Farmer in the bebop Jazztet from 1959–1962. In 1962, Wilson tried another experiment. He produced an audio-demonstration album arranged and conducted by Golson, *Pop + Jazz = Swing*, on the Audio Fidelity label (more about that record in chapter 4). And he produced an Eric Burdon album with Golson as arranger and player, *Eric Is Here* (1967; more on that album in chapter 7). The TV commercials album was an attempt at selling records, no doubt, but it also seems likely it was a bit of a lark on Wilson's part, maybe in the spirit of Warhol's use of "commercial" objects in his art. Most of all, Wilson would likely have viewed the album as another opportunity to bring a real jazz musician over into a more broadly commercial space, to reach new listeners by reframing the music, crossing yet another boundary.

As far as commercialization goes, Sun Ra himself once said "I don't object to commercial success; in fact you have to be successful at every level. If you aren't you're at the mercy of someone who is."[27] That fits with Wilson's pitch in his liner notes to *The Futuristic Sounds of Sun Ra*, declaring that "Sun Ra is a man of many paradoxes. . . . at one and the same time an avowed modern jazz purist *and* an unabashedly commercial showman." Interestingly enough, Wilson assumes that the Arkestra's far-out aesthetic, including its outer-space "costumes," would have a commercial appeal. But he insists that the visionary bandleader is "sincerely dedicated to the belief that the dawning of the Space Age offers mankind one last chance to achieve harmony, unity, and peace." Wilson's note glosses over what we now see as the crucial African/Egyptian elements of the band's music and performance. But his remarks provide a useful reminder of the culture into which the album emerged, a moment when space-age costumes and a futuristic style were all the rage, popular and potentially commercial. Wilson wasn't trying to conceal Sun Ra's essential characteristics to market his music. For a long time Sun Ra would remain more *recherché* than popular, but Wilson thought he saw an opportunity to bring Sun Ra before a wider audience, one already primed for visions—and maybe sounds—of the future.

THE MIDCENTURY FUTURE

The aesthetic is well known: popular midcentury space-age futurism looked like swooping, dramatic "Googie" architecture, big-finned cars, and other aerodynamic and otherworldly designs. Disneyland's Tomorrowland opened in 1955. Sputnik was launched in 1957. *The Jetsons*, a popular TV cartoon about a modern space-age family living in modernist apartments in the sky, premiered in September 1962. The Century 21 Expo was held in Seattle in 1962. Its theme was "Living in the Space Age," and the fair included the debut of the famous monorail and the Space Needle. The Tornados' instrumental hit single "Telstar" came out in 1962 and ascended to the top of the charts.

It wasn't the idea of space music or extraterrestrial origins that made Sun Ra's self-presentation original. It was his Afrocentric approach to those things, and how his alien identity—always also a Black identity—figured in a productive tension between the popular and the *recherché*. Sun Ra engaged with the most vulgar (in the literal sense: popular) enthusiasms of the space-age moment while also exploring serious avant-garde ideas when it came to soundscapes and musical composition. He took those tensions seriously. Behind the advertising-pitch tone of Wilson's liner note ("Get set to blast off with SUN RA into a new adventure in musical sound") lies a truthful acknowledgment of the tension as Sun Ra understood it, as the productive relationship between contradictory things, "where rhythms have become super-rhythms, where trite arrangements and instrumentation have given way to exotic sound pictures combining distant rumblings from the primeval past of all music with strange strains from the future. Be ready to experience something on the other side of 'something else': the futuristic sound of SUN RA . . . ." Oddly, Wilson also mentions the fact that the Arkestra "has enthralled teen-age audiences in the rock 'n' roll palaces of Chicago," presumably meant as reassuring proof of its visceral appeal and midcentury pop potential, despite being as out there as one could be, "on the other side of 'something else.'"

EXOTICA

It's clear Wilson wanted to tie the *Futuristic Sounds* album to the exotica trend. Just notice the key words: "super-rhythms," "exotic," and "primeval." The album's first track, "Bassism," is built on Ronnie Boykins's bass and Sun Ra's acoustic piano, before settling into a soft-bop horn groove with a trombone solo. It could have appeared on any number of late fifties modal jazz records (e.g., Miles Davis's *Kind of Blue*). But for Sun Ra, this is space jazz. Framed in that way, Marshall Allen's flute solo, with harmonically oblique arpeggios, sounds at once "primeval" and otherworldly. After a brief Latin-rhythm section, the tune quickly concludes at just over four minutes. The whole album is like this, eminently listenable. The brevity of most of the tracks stands out in contrast to other Sun Ra records from the time, which had extended arrangements that might take up a whole side of an LP. All of the tracks on *The Futuristic Sounds of Sun Ra* range from around two to six minutes. And yet there are glimmerings of that "something else." For example, the first full solo in "Where Is Tomorrow"—a freeform duet, a flute accompanied with piccolo—involves the kind of high-pitched atonality we might expect to hear from a Theremin or a keyboard synthesizer. On this album, however, Sun Ra sticks to acoustic piano. Even a track like "Space Jazz Reverie," with a traditional swing arrangement featuring piano and reminiscent of Sun Ra's time with Fletcher Henderson and his orchestra in Chicago, supports layered improvised solos.

Critics tend to forget what most album listeners take for granted—that context, that is, set and setting, matters. It starts with an album's packaging and presentation, as well as the cultural contexts within which it's heard. These form thresholds into the music, part of the overall experience of hearing a vinyl LP. "Listening" often involves poring over album art, notes, and a track list while the record plays. Consider the hand-painted cover art for *The Futuristic Sounds of Sun Ra*, by an elusive "primitive" artist known as "Harvey," who became legendary for his cover art for gospel albums on Savoy. It shows a melted, stretched-out, twisted, conga drum flying above a warped keyboard, the black keys looking vaguely like tusks or a rib cage, all set against an eerie orange sky. Primitivist surrealism or proto-psychedelia, this image for an album titled "futuristic" made for a cover that would have looked at home on any shelf of exotica in 1962. Paul Youngquist notes the close connections between Sun Ra and space-age exotica of the late 1950s and early 1960s, including popular albums by Les Baxter and Martin Denny, and records like Russ Garcia's *Fantastica: Music from Outer Space.*[28] The Garcia album includes tracks like "Lost Souls of Saturn" and "Red Sands of Mars" and credits the chief engineer on the sessions for creating "unusual electronic effects." Exotica traded in the "oriental" and the "primitive," and offered only an "ersatz otherness" via "easy listening."[29] Sun Ra was clearly interested in lounge music and exotica, though his own Afrocentrism went deeper than the primitivism of those records.[30] His juxtaposition of Egyptian/African motifs with space-age speculation was in part a response to racial and musical segregation, a way of "opening up wider vistas, new horizons," where Black people might imagine a greater freedom.[31] The desire for other worlds worked as an implicit critique of the world as it was.

Irwin Chusid has explored the connection between Sun Ra and exotica in a practical way, by compiling and producing a three-LP/two-CD album, *Sun Ra—Exotica* (2017), with tracks selected from across the catalog and archives (some previously unreleased) that fit the genre. Chusid admits this is not an album Sun Ra actually made or intended to make. It's an act of revisionism, a kind of speculative scholarly edition of Sun Ra music. It makes an implicit argument, just by existing, about musical and cultural contexts, through the cumulative effect of the tracks framed in these terms. The titles of the tracks suggest the aptness of the genre category: "Cha Cha in Outer Space," "Brazilian Sun," and "Tiny Pyramids," for example.

Although Chusid doesn't include any tracks from *The Futuristic Sounds of Sun Ra*, he could well have done so. "China Gates," for example, though not an original Sun Ra composition, has a stereotypically "oriental" melody, using parallel fifths and lyrics full of clichés. It was composed by Victor Young and Harold Adamson for a 1957 film titled *China Gate*, and the Arkestra vocal was clearly modeled on Nat "King" Cole's version of the song from the film score. "Tapestry from an Asteroid," to take another example, includes a lounge-style piano with brushed snare drum under a soothing horn melody. "Jet Flight," a multi-voiced bebop tune, even without the title would have registered as contemporary/futuristic, just in terms of its "modern" sound. Then there are percussion-based tracks like "The Beginning," and "New Day," which feature a guest percussionist and a variety of instruments listed on the back cover—"Bells from India, Chinese Wind Chimes, Wood Blocks, Maracas, Claves, Scratchers, Gongs, Cow Bells, Turkish Cymbals, Castanets"—the list itself signaling the kind of percussion-heavy primitivism often featured on exotica compilations of conga and bongo music, with Latin beats, or vaguely tribal or Tiki themes.

When we take *The Futuristic Sounds of Sun Ra* as a whole, its song titles, presentation, cover art and notes, the link to exotica is obvious. Wilson's liner notes confirm the link by referring to Sun Ra's "exotic sound pictures combining distant rumblings from the primeval past of all music with strange strains from the future." Sun Ra's musical taste was always closer to pop than his avant-garde recordings might suggest. His playing the strip clubs of Calumet City starting in 1949 actually required him to perform "Tin Pan Alley standards and even light classical tunes" that the dancers wanted as their accompaniment.[32] And even before his work with bandleader Fletcher Henderson, Sun Ra had played with the jump blues "shouter" Wynonie Harris. His own music retained traces of these experiences, borrowings from a range of genres. It was no great stretch for Sun Ra to make the music for *The Futuristic Sounds of Sun Ra* relatively accessible, even conventionally melodic. Still, again there are signs of a characteristic strangeness, a truly (not superficially) alien quality that would be foregrounded in the records made in 1966–1967. Even that alliterative term used by Wilson in the liner note, "strange strains," perhaps coincidentally, chimes with the title of one of the most experimental records Sun Ra ever made: *Strange Strings* (1965; released 1967). More on that remarkable album below.

THE MAGIC CITY

But first, *The Magic City*. If *The Futuristic Sounds of Sun Ra* in 1962 was the last album by the composer that could easily be filed under "jazz" (as Chusid says in his liner note), then 1966's *The Magic City* is one of those records that "prove the categorical futility" of all such genre bins when it comes to Sun Ra's albums:

> When assessing the post-Chicago (1960–) work of Ra, "jazz" turns out to be less a genre than a journalistic and marketing convenience. Jazz has a glorious tradition. Sun Ra was schooled in it, emerged from it, and grew to transcend it (though he never abandoned it). Even the flippant "Space jazz" cannot frame the extremes to which Ra pushed his art in the mid-1960s. In this regard, *The Magic City* was a pinnacle.[33]

Many who would formerly have been recognized as jazz musicians were challenging the genre "filing system" at that time. A good deal of experimentation took place in the post-bebop environment. Other freeform experimental music had emerged from the downtown scene, such as free jazz, often referred to simply as the New Thing, and Sun Ra was frequently included in this development, along with Ornette Coleman, Albert Ayler, and Cecil Taylor (all of whom, interestingly, had been produced by Wilson). Everywhere you looked, jazz musicians were extending their sound beyond anything easily recognizable, easily sortable. Some even declared the death of jazz. Some experimented at the intersection of jazz and modern-classical minimalism. Sometimes free jazz was deliberately spiritual, chant-based, inspired by Indian ragas and other Eastern music, or by a continuity with African music and music of the African diaspora.

Similar formal and sonic experiments were happening in rock at the time, and Sun Ra was recognized by rock musicians as a kindred spirit and inspiration. On Sunday, June 18, 1967—the year *Strange Strings* came out—Sun Ra and His Myth Science Arkestra performed on the same bill at the Community Arts Auditorium in Detroit with the proto-punk band the MC5.[34] Guitarist Wayne Kramer of the MC5 was inspired by free jazz in general and Sun Ra in particular. His song "Starship" went so far as to list Sun Ra as a coauthor since it incorporated his poetry into the lyrics. The psychedelic op-art poster for the show features a small image of Sun Ra's head, as if it were the pupil of an open eye, lines radiating from it. "The Magic Veil" is credited with creating the light show.

That concert came at the culmination of Sun Ra's creative emergence, 1965–1967. A whole flood of albums was released in those years, including many on his own Saturn Records out of Chicago, most recorded much earlier. But one album, critics agree, marked an aesthetic and conceptual turning point, the "clearest signal of change" in Sun Ra's overall direction.[35] This was 1966's *The Magic City*. Robert L. Campbell canonizes the album this way: "[if] any one piece was intended to be Sun Ra's monument, it is *The Magic City*."[36] Youngquist calls it "a miracle of musical invention," and "quite simply the most moving, evocative, and sustained group improvisation to come out of the sixties."[37] *The Magic City* breaks from the apparent attempt to reach a broad audience we saw in *The Futuristic Sounds of Sun Ra* with its future-imagining, no longer merely *futuristic*, sounds. It's also clearly different from the session work Sun Ra continued to do at the time, a truly convincing expression of "something on the other side of 'something else,'" to use Wilson's words.

The Magic City appeared on the Saturn label. A dense black and white pen and ink drawing by William White on the cover combines hieroglyphics and Egyptian symbols, abstract squiggles, and evocative lines. The central shape is ambiguous: it may be the domed train station terminal in Sonny/Herman Blount's birthplace, Birmingham, Alabama. A giant sign at the actual station read: "Birmingham: The Magic City." But if you shift your perspective by zooming in or out, Magic-Eye style, the image can flicker into a sketch of the turbaned head of a mysterious bearded man waving darkly scribbled hands. It looks like something in a flyer you might have been handed on the street by a blanket-on-the-sidewalk vendor in Chicago's Washington Square Park or New York's Greenwich Village.

The over twenty-six-minute title track, "The Magic City," takes up all of side

A. It's one long group improvisation, within the structure of the score and controlled by Sun Ra by pointing and making hand gestures or sending audible keyboard signals. This is the kind of piece the Arkestra performed live all the time, but in this case, it defines the form of the *album. The Magic City* was recorded in 1965. Sun Ra plays the vacuum-tube-based Selmer Clavioline as well as acoustic piano, and the combination of keyboards contributes to the uncanny feel of the album as a whole. The title track opens with a brief rolled piano chord, which is repeated/echoed, accompanied by drums and cymbal, before morphing into a rippling solo. Then, the space-age Clavioline floats in from high above, sliding between notes with heavy vibrato, like the theremin in a sci-fi movie soundtrack. The Clavioline trades lines with drums for a bit before a fuller free-style wind ensemble joins in. The contrast of relatively traditional-timbre jazz piano, tenor sax, or alto flute with that blatantly experimental-sounding—but increasingly, also, contemporary pop-sounding—electronic warble sums up the track and the way it feels. It's a jazz or jazz-like musical soundscape superimposed with some very out-there sounds, layered like an audio version of a multiple-exposure screen print. An "in" sound from way out.

At about 12:40, Sun Ra comes back in on the Clavioline in a lower register. With the earlier high solo, this lower passage has the effect of seeming to surround the core bass and percussion. The flutes and horns are defamiliarized in such a soundscape, rendered strange and otherworldly by juxtaposition with the weird electronic sounds. In the very middle of the track, Sun Ra makes the Clavioline sound almost like a human voice, giving it a sort of syntactic rhythm, with clipped phrases that rise and fall, stop and restart like sentences spoken in an alien language, in excited dialog with its counterpart (played by Sun Ra with his other hand) on the piano. The productive tensions in that central musical dialogue epitomize the feel of the track and the album as a whole. The tensions are powerful because they express a tension at the heart of that wider cultural moment: everywhere you looked and listened, but especially downtown in New York City, experiments were testing the musical limits of found forms and sounds.

About fifteen seconds in, a burst of cacophonous group noise gives way to a saxophone solo, and on the original release, at the end, the whole thing fades abruptly during a final Clavioline part. Chusid's 2017 reissue includes as a bonus track the lopped-off ending, treating it as a coda found among the tapes. In it, yet one more massive, bursting space-chord gives way to a fading Clavioline solo. "The Magic City" title track makes for a powerful side. At almost half an hour, it passes surprisingly quickly once you're immersed in its soundscape.

The album was among that mass of recordings released by Sun Ra ca. 1966. As we've seen, by that time, the Arkestra was playing the weekly gig at Slugs' and was getting other work as well, collectively and individually. They were becoming a key part of the downtown avant-garde scene as well as the emergent Black Arts movement. The recording continued apace. The Monday night performances at Slugs' were treated as onstage rehearsals. Other rehearsals and recording sessions were treated as performances and happenings. It was all of a piece, music being made from scratch and from surrounding found sounds.

STRANGE STRINGS EVERYWHERE

Found sounds from found objects was the idea behind *Strange Strings*, recorded in 1965 and released on the Saturn label in 1967.[38] The album opens with Sun Ra on timpani, which he sometimes called "thunder drums," along with Ronnie Boykins bowing the bass, a track called "World's Approaching." The rhythm continues with free improvisations throughout the ten-minute track. "Strange Strings" follows. The B side was taken up with a track apparently titled "Strange Strange" (labels on the tapes vary, and this may have been a printing error). The title track, "Strange Strings," opens with drums and cymbal but is quickly awash in dissonant cacophony. Members of the Arkestra noisily bow, hammer, pluck, and strum an unknown (but large) number of stringed instruments. A kind of call-and-response sets in, walls of sounds alternating with percussion—including on homemade instruments like a piece of sheet metal, for example, being struck and perhaps bent (an age-old theatrical sound effect for thunder). At about 3:27, we hear Thlan Aldridge's weird, unintelligible "space-voice" vocal, filtered through a megaphone (?), with heavy reverb.

SONGS OF INNOCENCE, TONE SCIENCE

The album was "a study in ignorance," Sun Ra said. None of the Arkestra members knew how to play the various stringed instruments he had handed out. That was the idea: radical musical innocence. Expert musicians and improvisers, the players make something powerful happen. John Szwed calls it "perhaps the most completely improvised but organic piece in the history of jazz, with no prepared rhythmic, melodic, or harmonic material, performed by players on instruments foreign to them."[39] But presumably, as usual, the bandleader controlled the mix by pointing to musicians or giving hand signals.

Sun Ra often referred to the Arkestra as a team of "tone scientists" experimenting with sound.[40] Although this may lead us to expect high-tech synthesizers, the mundane ukuleles, lutes, guitars, etc. on *Strange Strings* produced what may be the most experimental sound the Arkestra ever made. It was akin to any number of musical experiments undertaken at the time in avant-garde circles, music made with everyday objects, kitchen utensils, typewriters, and, in the case of Frank Zappa, bicycles or other unlikely objects. It's also kin to the explorations inspired by John Cage and others in ambient music—the discovery of the musical sounds in the everyday environment: city traffic, crickets, or even the blood rushing in one's ears as the pianist sits silently at the keyboard.

I once played a building in downtown New York City. David Byrne of Talking Heads had created a sound installation by wiring an organ's keyboard to various actuators located in different spots in a giant empty warehouse in the Battery.[41] A depressed key would cause a hammer to strike a heating pipe forty feet in the air, up under the skylights, for example. Another key would make an overhead beam vibrate, another would make a hammer bang on a pipe near the ceiling, while yet another would activate a pump, blowing air through a conduit in a distant corner so that it whistled. Byrne had essentially "treated" the building, turned the whole thing into a giant musical instrument, one that visitors could play and hear. As I played, I was made acutely aware of the physical space occupied by the building, an air-filled metal and glass box of potential vibrations and sounds, an environment Byrne had found and treated so that it became a massive multiply strung instrument.

The Byrne installation provides a useful analogy for what Sun Ra was up to with the *Strange Strings* project. In effect, Sun Ra had the Arkestra play the city's vast storehouse of varied stringed instruments. We don't know precisely where he located and collected all of them. Some may have been found on tour, in other cities. But we do know that downtown Manhattan in the mid-1960s was cluttered with thousands of stringed instruments, including some pretty strange ones. Thanks to the folk-music and jug-band craze, then in the process of mutating into folk-rock and psychedelic rock, downtown pawn shops, guitar shops, and some head shops and boutiques had guitars and ukuleles and mandolins and lutes and banjos and violins—and more exotic instruments, like koras and kotos and sitars—displayed in windows or hanging from walls and ceilings everywhere you went. Not to mention all the street buskers on the sidewalks and jammers in the parks who would have been playing those same kinds of stringed instruments. Strings were anything *but* strange in downtown New York in 1965. Or rather, strange strings were everywhere, all around.

Sun Ra's album was a project that treated stringed instruments as found objects, as if an alien from outer space (Saturn, say) had landed in Greenwich Village. One way or another, he found them, whether in pawn shops and music shops or who knows where, and then *rendered* them "strange" by putting them in the hands of flute and trumpet and sax players. Some, like the so-called oriental lute or the Japanese koto, were strange in the sense of being foreign to Sun Ra and his players (and much of their imagined audience), but all of them were *made* strange by the project, *estranged* or *defamiliarized*, as twentieth-century Russian Formalist literary theorists might say, familiar objects made fresh by being recontextualized and productively alienated from the audience's expectations. Indeed, this is precisely the way Sun Ra's whole artistic self-presentation, as a being from another planet making sounds from beyond, worked to defamiliarize music for his audiences.

But even the relatively untutored playing on *Strange Strings* was hardly anomalous. It was common practice in rock bands for musicians to swap instruments to produce a new sound through deliberate de-skilling (an attitude punk would later take to an extreme—nobody had to know how to play anything). And, to cite one example from one of Sun Ra's jazz contemporaries, on one track of his album *The Empty Foxhole* (1966), avant-garde saxophonist Ornette Coleman played free improvisations on a violin, an instrument he was not formally trained to play. And he played trumpet on a couple of tracks, for which he was similarly technically untrained. Of course, he was a genius and multi-instrumentalist nonetheless (but note that he also featured his ten-year-old son on drums). For that matter, some rock guitarists were trying out violin bows on electric guitars at the time, among them the Velvet Underground, a band that featured John Cale's electric viola. And Cale sometimes deliberately strung his instrument with guitar or mandolin strings. The Velvet Undergroud's drummer, Maureen Tucker, sometimes played metal garbage cans, the most basic kind of found instrument. Just a few years earlier, jug bands—like those from which members of the Blues Project emerged—were everywhere in Greenwich Village. Their collections included homemade or found instruments like the washtub bass (with a broomstick for a neck), washboard and thimble, paper-covered combs, and of course the jug itself as a readymade wind and rhythm instrument.

More generally, a found-art approach was in the air ca. 1965–1966, in both avant-garde and pop circles. With this particular "study in ignorance" Sun Ra directed his musicians to do something musical with what they found in New York (and maybe elsewhere), and in this way he in effect played the city, played songs of innocence, or at least played some of the ambient possibilities to be found everywhere all around him in downtown Manhattan. When you think about it, that approach was not unlike one of the Arkestra member's playing a horn from inside the phone booth inside Slugs', turning it into an interesting found-object isolation booth/echo chamber.

Sun Ra was no pop musician. I've included him in this book about pop music because of his link to Tom Wilson, but also because his adjacency helps us to understand the issues pop faced in 1966, from musical classifications to race. Sun Ra always asserted his own creative genius, just as part of his self-expression, and many listeners and critics have followed suit by focusing on his extreme originality. But his music, which emerged in the 1950s, reached a creative peak in the mid-1960s amid a layered set of contexts—psychedelic multimedia happenings, free jazz experimentation, Afrocentric cultural expression. We should understand these as overlapping categories, from space-age exotica to avant-garde experiments in atonality and found-instrument music. The center of this imagined Venn diagram, where the circles overlap to form the orbital paths of an eccentric solar system, could represent the collective genius of the downtown scene at that moment—what Brian Eno has called "scenius."[42] Eno stresses the role of community in this phenomenon, but in this case, the communities (and it *was* plural—there were in fact some strict borderlines, including when it came to race) can be described as scenes or micro-scenes that were attached to specific neighborhoods and venues—clubs, bars, lofts—as well as to available tools and materials, including readily available or symbolically resonant instruments, like new synthesizer keyboards, overhead projectors, strobe lights, foil balloons, and African drums. Sun Ra's music that year, so often treated as *sui generis*, as out of this world, was in fact a product of *a* world. It was the result of his own biography (traveling from the Magic City of Birmingham to the blues clubs and big bands and public parks of Chicago, then to Canada and the lofts and bars of avant-garde New York). His genius was catalyzed in the crucible of the overlapping downtown scenes of lower Manhattan ca. 1965–1966. His inventive music cuts across genres and forms and seems to transcend the classification system of record bins, not because he was from Saturn but because his genius flourished in the East Village at that particular historical moment, a moment of intense and eclectic creativity.

CHAPTER FOUR

UNDERGROUND AUTHENTICITY (NOT FOLK, NOT BLUES)

Lou Reed, *Words & Music, May 1965* (recorded 1965; released 2022);
The Velvet Underground, *The Velvet Underground & Nico* (recorded 1966; released 1967)

THE VELVET UNDERGROUND RECORDED THEIR FIRST ALBUM IN 1966 and released it in March 1967 as *The Velvet Underground & Nico*, with a banana print signed by Andy Warhol on the cover. (Starting with the members of the band themselves, people have come to refer to it as the banana album.) It grew out of a collaboration between the band and the pop artist, who liked to say he "sponsored" them, as if they were a worthy art project or a found object he could frame and sign. The album is now considered a classic of underground rock, but in the context of 1966, it provided a snapshot of the band's identity at its inception. At that moment, the Velvet Underground was in effect the house band for Warhol's pop-art revue/Happening/multimedia art project, the Exploding Plastic Inevitable (EPI). *The Velvet Underground & Nico* was actually the product of a three-way collaboration among the band's music, Warhol's art, and Tom Wilson's production. But without Wilson, it might never have been made. This chapter looks at that collaboration, including the framing provided by Warhol's Exploding Plastic Inevitable and the timely intervention by Wilson. The goal is not to reduce the aura surrounding the beloved album but to show how it *was* a collaborative product, how it emerged from a particular scene. And it emerged against the backdrop of a promiscuous diversity of pop music, was created through a process of selective eclecticism, the pursuit of hybrid genres defined against other genres. The album defined its own underground art-rock negatively, as *not* folk and *not* blues.

"SPONSORED" BY ANDY WARHOL, PRODUCED BY TOM WILSON

Warhol is credited as producer of the Velvet Underground, but it was Wilson, the music business professional, who actually got the studio work done that made the album a reality. Wilson got involved with the band at a crucial moment, after their own initial tapes had been made. Then he brought the Velvet Underground with him when he moved to MGM/Verve from Columbia Records. He oversaw the editing and remixing of the tapes, made "Sunday Morning" as a potential single and added it to the album, thus completing *The Velvet Underground & Nico* and bringing it out into the world. John Cale, recounting the history of the album, casually remarks that the band "met Tom Wilson . . . and we were getting somewhere. We could make a record."[1] Faint praise, you might at first think, which makes Wilson sound like someone useful mainly for his connections, a mere facilitator. But I don't think that's what Cale means. Although Lou Reed says that it was Warhol who "made it possible to make a record," he also says sardonically that "Andy produced our first record, in the sense that he was there, breathing, in the studio."[2] The pop artist's imprimatur certainly opened doors. But I think Cale is actually giving Wilson a kind of top-line credit. Notice that he does not say they had made an album that Wilson merely came in and finished or got released. Wilson is named as the key reason *The Velvet Underground & Nico* got made in the first place. Although "Sunday Morning" is the only track separately credited as produced by Wilson, the original notes also read: "Edited and Remixed under the Supervision of Tom Wilson by Gene Radice & David Greene [sound engineers]." For the Velvet Underground, Wilson was the key to the band's "getting somewhere" and being able to actually "make a record"—to make the album they more or less wanted to make.

Cale is more specific about Wilson's role in another interview. He suggests that the producer helped the band achieve one of their key artistic goals, to create a kind of Phil Spector–style wall of sound using just a few rock instruments: "On some tracks it worked. 'Venus in Furs' is the best, and 'All Tomorrow's Parties' and 'Sunday Morning.' The band never again had as good a producer as Tom Wilson. He did those songs, plus 'Heroin' and 'Waiting for [the] Man.'"[3] Cale credits Wilson for the tracks on which the band's sonic ideal, their own version of the wall of sound, was achieved, where "it worked." Another musician who benefited from Wilson's production, Frank Zappa, described *The Velvet Underground & Nico* differently, in terms of genre. He said, "I like that album. I think that Tom Wilson deserves a lot of credit for making that album, because it's folk music. It's electric folk music, in the sense that what they're saying comes right out of their environment."[4] Zappa puts his finger on the key to understanding the album, generically and historically, as "electric folk music"—something Wilson understood better than anyone. As Zappa says, it had a sound that emerged from a particular "environment," but not just the streets of New York, I'd add, but a specific, eclectic, Greenwich Village and East Village scene.

UNDERGROUND CREDIBILITY

Brian Eno is often quoted as saying that *The Velvet Underground & Nico* sold only a limited number of copies at first (30,000), but everyone who bought one started their own band. It seems that Eno got the sales figure from Lou Reed but added the part about spawning new bands himself.[5] He means the album went viral, but stealthily, in an underground way. It was generative—it made 30,000 new bands bloom, but these were mostly not popular bands that went on to produce hits (the rare exceptions are the ones we notice, among the tens of thousands). Its lyrics about street life, drugs, BDSM sexuality, colorful gender-fluid characters, along with its minimalist experimental sound, offered aspiring musicians a kind of wormhole, a passage to an alternative universe in which a band could define itself against the dominant expectations of the music industry and the mass audience and still make a difference. For fans, as well, the record sounded like a forty-eight-minute act of opposition: to radio music, bubblegum pop, California psychedelia, and (a little later on) stadium rock and prog-rock pretensions, as well as middle-class morality and respectability in general. This was how the Velvet Underground presented itself, with a New York sneer for whatever might be merely popular. We see it in photos of the band on their May 1966 tour of California, for example, the vampiric pasty skin, dark shades, and black leather (or, in Nico's case, sometimes a fashion model's white suit), standing uncomfortably on the streets or in the airy modernist houses of Los Angeles, surrounded by tie-dye and sunlight. The Velvets hated the hippies, as they liked to say, but they also clearly resented that they weren't embraced by the Los Angeles and San Francisco scenes, performance venues, audiences, and critics. After their show at the Trip in L.A., May 1966, where they followed Frank Zappa and the Mothers of Invention on the bill, Cher (still then of Sonny and Cher) quipped, "The Velvet Underground won't replace anything. Except maybe suicide."[6] (This was perhaps not as bad a blurb as she intended.) Mary Woronov, who danced in the show as part of the EPI, said that the Velvets and Californians "spoke two different languages," and characterized the difference between them in terms of their preferences for amphetamines (New York and the Velvets) versus acid (the West Coast).[7] The drugs analogy is not as interesting as what she says just after that: the West Coast hippies were into "trying to be some kind of 'true, authentic' person; we could not have cared less about that."[8] Authenticity—pursuing it versus rejecting the pursuit—was at the heart of the bicoastal culture clash. The Velvet Underground presented themselves as bored by the whole thing, as seeing through any earnest quest to be "some kind of 'true, authentic' person."

That's also how the banana album was defined by those who discovered it in the 1970s: punks, art-rockers, and goths. But despite what Woronov said, the Velvets did seek a *kind* of authenticity: an underground kind. They and their first album were cool, authentic, real, precisely because of what they were *not*. Nico's first solo album, *Chelsea Girl*, includes a Bob Dylan song, "I'll Keep It with Mine" (which she claimed was written for her, even though Judy Collins recorded it first), that sums up the attitude: "I'm not loving you for what you are / But for what you're not."

NO FOLK-ROCK, NO BLUES LICKS

The first thing the Velvet Underground was *not* was a folk-rock group. God knows plenty of those were around in 1965. The full extent of the band's rejection of that hybrid genre identity only became clear in 2022, with the release of *Words & Music, May 1965*. Because the original tape was made in part to establish copyright, Reed declared his authorship before playing each song (hence the album title), and he sealed and mailed the tape to himself. A few months after these bedroom recordings were made, the new band worked up several of the songs for demo recordings, but in different arrangements. The new band was trying *not* to be folk or folk-rock. In effect, it wanted to play *not*-folk rock. But, like most oppositional identities, this one retained within it a kernel of the thing against which it was constructed. Cale and Reed needed the specter of folk music to measure their distance from it, to create something else in opposition. In fact, Cale later said it outright: he was "excited" when he heard Reed's songs played "on an acoustic guitar as if they were folk songs," thinking about "combining" his experimental minimalism with these songs.[9] This inevitably left a trace of the conflict, that hybridity, a bit of folk song DNA spliced onto minimalism. That hybridity gives the album its sense of urgency—you can hear the weird, bluesy folk song underneath "I'm Waiting for the Man," and that gives its achieved sound that much more of a punch.

Many of the songs on the original recordings that became *Words & Music, May 1965* sound like early Dylan. Cale sings harmonies and sings lead on one track, but he doesn't yet provide the arrangements or instruments that would become his signature contribution to the sound of the Velvets. No electric viola strung with guitar strings, no hypnotic bass drum used as a tom-tom, no feedback noise or repetitive overdriven electric guitar drone. The demos reveal the bones of the songs—their basic structure as just "words and music." But their core identity as folk songs also comes through from time to time. Even a tune that might at first seem an exception, "Wrap Your Troubles in Dreams," written by Reed and here sung by Cale (two years later Nico would record it for *Chelsea Girl*), is folk music of a different sort, a kind of second-order European troubadour tune. It has a Welsh Celtic feel, like an art-song version of a medieval bardic song—or, more accurately, as if it were a classical variation on such a song, ancient conventions self-consciously repurposed in a new frame. Cale accompanies his own chant-like vocal with a slow, improvised beat (ironically) made in the traditional blues and spiritual way, by hammering on the body of his guitar so that the strings ring with each blow. The result has the benefit of sounding like a tabor or tambourine. As sung in Cale's accent, "Wrap Your Troubles in Dreams" could almost pass for centuries-old European source material. That is, it might, if you were able to look past the modern clichés of the lyrics ("Life's really funny that way"). It sounds like distant kin to the Child Ballads, which in turn lie behind many of the "American" songs on Harry Smith's famous *Anthology*, a collection that everyone in the downtown folk scene in the 1960s carried around with them.

Understood in that context, "Wrap Your Troubles in Dreams" isn't all that different from the modernized versions of traditional songs and spirituals that were everywhere at the time, in Village basket houses, at hootenannies, and on records, from singalongs like "Michael, Row the Boat Ashore"—a version of which Reed recorded at home just a couple of years before making the tapes for *Words & Music*—to folk-pop on the radio, like Simon & Garfunkel's "Scarborough Fair" (1966), for example, or some of the material on Donovan's *Sunshine Superman*—"Legend of a Girl Child Linda," "Three King Fishers," or "Guinevere," just to name three—an album released a bit later in 1966. Everything on the *Words & Music* tapes could conceivably be put in the "folk" bin. This includes the novelty tune "Buttercup Song," which would have been at home in the repertoire of the early Fugs, and "Walk Alone," written by Reed with some of his fellow songwriters at Pickwick Records. "Buzz Buzz Buzz" and "Stockpile" are perfunctory R&B-based rock 'n' roll, but here they're performed acoustically, in a style that suggests country-blues roots. It's no surprise that, in a letter to his mentor, poet Delmore Schwartz, Reed seems to have referred to the demo tape as "a folk album."[10]

It's true that we find on the same tape "I'm Waiting for the Man" and "Heroin," songs that would become core Velvet Underground repertoire. But here even they sound a bit like coffeehouse numbers with darker-than-usual lyrics, for example, the matter-of-fact self-expression of an addict. William Burroughs and the Beats are obvious influences on that lyric, but the truth is there are also any number of traditional blues songs written from a similarly dark perspective about the depths of addiction and street life (though more likely to be about cocaine and whisky, knife fights and juke joints). The turnaround seventh chord at the end of each line of "I'm Waiting for the Man," which Reed plucks on an acoustic, along with the simple harmonica part, adds a Village vibe to the tale of going uptown to Harlem ("Lexington 1-2-5") to score. It's not really about Harlem; it's about the "white boy" who goes uptown to get his fix. Music critic Joe Harvard has said that this version of the song sounds "like Bob Dylan doing Leadbelly," which hits the nail on the head.[11]

The demo version of "Heroin" also sounds a little country, like a rolling, two-chord delta-blues. It opens with the gospel-sounding lyric, "I know just where I'm goin'" (instead of with the negative version that would appear on *The Velvet Underground & Nico* the following year: "I *don't* know where I'm going'"). The wistful verse about wanting to be a sailor on a clipper ship "a hundred years ago" (later, this would be upped to "a thousand years ago") would sound perfectly at home in any number of folk songs. The freight train–accelerating tempo emphasizes the obsessive repetition of the lyric as well as the rush after shooting up, just as it will on the album version of "Heroin," but the *Words & Music* demo tape adds a bit more detail, and in the folk-like setting, the catalog of social ills reads as a protest convention, much like Dylan's visionary catalog in "A Hard Rain": "When that smack bud's startin' to flow / Then I really don't care no more," Reed sings. Then he catalogs "people selling people pound-by-pound / And the politicians and the clowns / And the do-gooders with their frowns / Dead bodies piling down." "Thank God I'm not aware," he concludes. "And thank God that I don't care." It's true that the album version adds a more specific political/topical reference, revealing that the bodies are "piled up in 'Nam." But it's the folk version on the earlier tape that really *sounds* like a "protest song." By the time it's rearranged, the album version shifts the focus further inward, to the subjective mental state of the singer and the narcotic haze that releases him from caring, rather than the external social evils he needs to escape. The singer in the demo is aware, and he does care. Right before he isn't, and doesn't.

GONE ELECTRIC

Given their folk roots, we should probably say that *The Velvet Underground & Nico* is the *album* on which Reed and Cale, with Morrison and Tucker, "went electric." We'd have to qualify this with "in a recording." The band had already been performing loud electric live sets for months. That doesn't mean they just picked up electric guitars and turned up the amps. It was more a matter of exploiting the unique sounds provided by electric instruments, which opened up a whole new kind of immersive soundscape. Reed's own experiments with using electric guitars to produce a driving ambient music, which would lead eventually to the release of *Metal Machine Music* in 1975, were already underway in 1966—just months after recording the *Words & Music* tape in May 1965. But *The Velvet Underground & Nico* is indeed the album on which Reed and Cale committed to electric instruments used in particular experimental ways and thus made the Velvets into an underground art-rock band. As Jimmy Page observed, "It was really [an] arts lab, as opposed to pop music."[12] As opposed to pop music. At that point, the *Words & Music* tape was retroactively turned into a weird but milder precursor, a "folk album" from before the flood. This is the sense in which Reed and Cale "went electric" with the formation of the Velvet Underground: they differentiated their sound from its roots in folk. In doing so, they produced a new-sounding hybrid form of art rock or underground rock.

As was the case with Dylan at Newport, the shift from "folk" to "electric" music was for the Velvet Underground a matter of genre. As strange as it now seems, genres, and what were often very personal identifications with them, seemed to many fans at the time a matter of grave importance. The audience members who booed Dylan were accusing him of failing to be "sincere" or "authentic" in *folkloric* terms, of betraying folk music's supposedly pure roots and playing instead musical genres meant to court a commercial radio-listening and record-buying audience—that's what the fuss was about.[13] The disturbing thing for the Newport audience (and others later chimed in to help solidify the myth) was how Dylan's jangly folk-rock sound signified a recognizable inauthenticity, like the polka-dot shirt and pair of Wayfarers, it sounded like a pose, a performance of the *attitude* of rock 'n' roll or pop musicians.

Tom Wilson expressed the same idea from the other side when it came to white musicians performing supposedly authentic blues or supposedly authentic folk music or country music. He just wasn't interested in "singers who were copying 1937 Negro singers like Robert Johnson. . . . Robert Johnson had this thing and I exhort everybody to develop their own"; and he also "wasn't interested in hearing 'Sweet Betsy from Pike' . . . in hearing a bunch of middle-class kids singing about being coal miners, which they never had—just insults my intelligence, what little I've got."[14] In contrast, he said, Dylan was the first folk singer to "really reach" him.[15] This, too, was a matter of genre. Wilson's alternative, with Dylan and others, involved the pursuit of openly constructed, impure, *hybrid* genres, not just changing instruments or just turning up the volume but recombining sounds and traditions in different ways. The Newport arrangement of "Maggie's Farm" feels like a one-chord (D7 in this case) Chicago blues—"Smokestack Lightning," for example—but spliced together with rock rhythm and poetic lyrics. "Like a Rolling Stone" sounds like a mix of gospel- or country-tinged R&B + pop, epitomized in those descending organ riffs by Al Kooper and the twangy, tinny sound of the band. What Wilson admired about Dylan was that his own constructed musical identity by then was flouting demands for folk singer authenticity. If Wilson helped bring about a folk-rock sound for Dylan, it was in keeping with Dylan's already having forged a hybrid persona.

ART ROCKIN'

The same month as Dylan's epochal performance at Newport, July 1965, John Cale, Lou Reed, and Sterling Morrison recorded a few songs in a shotgun apartment in downtown New York. Cale later said the recordings "combined the music of Erik Satie, John Cage, Phil Spector, Hank Williams and Bob Dylan. The result was a new form of rock—more about art than commerce."[16] Cale's list of combined ingredients is revealing when it comes to the band's hybrid aspirations. But the Velvet Underground's earliest construction of their avant-garde minimalist art-rock worked as much by swerving away from the styles and genres it was not as by combining styles and genres. No folk. No blues, but also no folk-rock or blues-rock per se because those were already commercially viable combinations. With multiple influences, they still said no to merely adopting any recognizable style or hybrid of styles. In this way, they thought, they could claim to be making "a new form of rock." The resultant underground art-rock was symbolized by Cale's unusual instrument, the electric viola, which he often played like a found-noise object, rejecting its traditional associations and resonances. The music sounded deceptively simple. Like other forms of minimalism, it worked through a subtractive magic. But it was clearly meant to be art not pop. No doubt the band hoped to sell some records. But this was not the driving force in the creation of their music. They certainly did not want to sell recognizably commercial records, according to what was in at that moment in 1965–1966.

The timeline is compressed, just a matter of months crowded with significant events, so it's worth reminding ourselves that only a couple of months before, Reed and Cale had recorded some of those same songs on their "folk album" tape (which became *Words & Music, May 1965*). A little later, the Ludlow Street apartment tapes, including Morrison, marked the coalescence of the art-rock band. Later that year, Moe Tucker was added on drums, and by the end of 1965, they had taken the name the Velvet Underground, from the title of a book on unconventional sexualities. Around that same time, portentously, they fell under the mentorship of Andy Warhol.

In 1966, the band continued to set itself apart from all musical trends of its moment, blues and folk in particular. No blues licks! was reportedly a rule during band rehearsals—it was said they had a jar you had to drop a coin in if you were caught resorting to blues or rock clichés.[17] Morrison and Reed did play blues licks from time to time (see "Run, Run, Run"). Guitar parts based on rock 'n' roll riffs and pentatonic blues scales would have been hard to avoid. "European Son," for example, as it appeared on the first album, is built on an underlying blues riff. Its codename on some VU set lists was "Hooker"—presumably for the great blues musician John Lee Hooker.[18] Writer Joe Harvard says that the song comes in two parts, that the bluesy but conventional beginning is shattered by the loud crash at just before the one-minute mark (made by Cale scraping [and dropping?] a metal chair on the floor), then followed by a noisy montage of sound textures, which together serve to undermine or deconstruct the more conventional tune underneath.[19] I like that description of the abrupt shift or musical hinge as being almost like (though Harvard doesn't use this term) an imaginary bit of *musique concréte*. It's as if "assassin dervishes" suddenly take control of the song's "tinny radio," is how Harvard puts it, and then flip through channels to make the listener experience a series of strange alternative stations.[20] I would add that the limited, selective eclecticism implied therein, and the *particular* combination selected—blues-rock + avant-garde experiment—was the whole point of the song, musically.

The arrangements on *The Velvet Underground & Nico* produce an amplified minimalist wall of sound, built on droning electric guitar, often in an open tuning that makes for unpredictable harmonics and overtones, along with the chance results of amplifier feedback. The trance-inducing drone was famously inspired by Cale's experience with La Monte Young's Theatre of Eternal Music, where many pieces were based on a single note played for very extended periods. In a 1967 interview by Wilson with both Reed and Cale together, Cale conceptualizes, perhaps tongue-in-cheek, the idea of using pure sound to affect the weather—to heat up the air in a local environment, for example. In the same interview, Reed imagines custom-recorded personalized tapes that would play continuously for a full year, reflecting the listener's life and personality, a kind of ambient audio wallpaper for each person's individual environment.[21]

In that interview, Wilson laughs at these far-out ideas that he had solicited and helped to develop. In fact, he had long been interested in sonic experiments. Just a few years before his work with the Velvet Underground, in 1962, he had produced *Pop + Jazz = Swing*—interestingly, the same year as *The Futuristic Sounds of Sun Ra*. The *Pop + Jazz* album was arranged, conducted, and played by tenor saxophonist Benny Golson (who would later play with Hugh Masekela, among others). Besides the genre hybrid in the title, *Pop + Jazz*, the album exploited the then-new technology of stereo recording to create a literal sonic fusion: on the left channel, big-band or swing style "pop" arrangements played by an eleven-piece orchestra; on the right channel, simultaneously, improvisational, sometimes bebop-inspired jazz arrangements of either the same tunes or their basic musical structures, or different tunes that worked when overlaid with the tune on the opposing channel of the same track. Either way, the result was a series of listener-controlled stereophonic mashups. But these were designed to demonstrate different genres, pop and jazz, and they were fused into an interactive and experimental musical object, based on the affordances of the vinyl stereo album as a form.[22] As the directions printed right on the cover explain: "Each Triple Play Stereodisc in engineered to be played 3 different ways[. . . .] The Triple Play miracle . . . Using regular stereo controls you can create infinitely variable blends of lilting pop music with spicy jazz or you can create separate pop and jazz concerts."

The Velvet Underground and Warhol parted ways in 1967, but Wilson was hired again to produce their second album, *White Light/White Heat* (1968), which became another cult classic, a harbinger of punk, an album full of dark, loud noise rock. One of the more recognizably avant-garde tracks on that album, however, is the relatively quiet song "The Gift." Over eight minutes long, its spoken-word lyric is from a short story Reed had written about a man who mails himself to his distant and faithless beloved—and is killed by her as she tries to open the package. The short story was read matter-of-factly by Cale in his Welsh accent, recorded on the left stereo channel. An ominously repetitive musical accompaniment by the Velvets was recorded on the right channel. The combination is akin to beatnik poetry readings over jazz-band accompaniments, for example, and anticipates spoken-word performances by Patti Smith and others. But the stereo separation allows for the same kind of audio experiment touted in *Pop + Jazz = Swing*—as Wilson himself made clear in the interview with Reed and Cale on *The Music Factory* radio show. Referring to "The Gift," Wilson explains how you can listen to the story by itself, or just listen to "some very groovy music," or, "if you're a mad fiend like we are, you listen to them both together"—and the three of them burst out laughing. "That's where we're at. We've got stereo prefrontal lobes, here, so . . ."[23] Then, Reed and Cale offer those speculative conceptual scenarios for sound-art they'd like to create. The takeaway from this exchange is clear: Wilson appears to have been more than just a pragmatic facilitator of two Velvet Underground albums—he very likely contributed *ideas* to the band's avant-garde sonic experimentation, as well, through his production work and the general atmosphere created around the recording projects.

The Velvet Underground was intentionally primitive. Moe Tucker sometimes played the bass drum, turned on its head like a giant tom-tom, using mallets, and, as we've seen, she even played found-object trash cans. One of her key inspirations was Bo Diddley's signature repetitive beat. For some songs, Cale attacked the viola with percussive, amplified sawing, like an unhinged bluegrass fiddler. Nico, once she joined the band, would often play a tambourine, sometimes hitting it with a single maraca. Her voice was in effect a kind of natural drone. Months later, after she was pushed out of the band, Nico was performing solo at Stanley's, the bar downstairs at the Dom. When Reed and Cale felt obligated to accompany her, they nonetheless insisted: no acoustic guitars! Only electric. The last thing they wanted was to be mistaken for *folk singers*. The young Jackson Browne had to borrow an electric guitar to comply when he accompanied Nico in Stanley's.[24] The idea was to avoid playing folk—but also to avoid playing rock 'n' roll unless it was stripped down to its bare bones.

THE AUTHENTIC NO

By the mid-1970s, this general attitude of refusal and back-to-basics would be the hallmark of punk. Street-corner doo-wop or garage-rock two-chord repetition back in the 1950s and early 1960s provided readymade ancestors for Reed and Cale's strategic minimalism. It's significant that Reed used the same drone-ready open-D tuning with the Velvet Underground that he had come up with for his own pre-Velvets novelty-tune rock 'n' roll dance number, "The Ostrich," which was recorded at Pickwick Records and briefly performed live by a manufactured band with a telling name, the Primitives. Cale and Reed agreed to fuse rock 'n' roll primitivism with avant-garde minimalism. In this way, they laid claim to a new *kind* of authenticity—a new kind of primal energy and street credibility that avoided the obsession with authenticity per se.

This move exemplifies a strategy common in 1966: to assert authenticity by rejecting accepted forms of authenticity. Despite Zappa's remark about the album's being a kind of Wilson-produced "folk music" because it reflected the street life that Reed saw around him, what the Velvet Underground rejected *musically* was their own recent folk sound—that was too much like what they *heard* all around them in 1965–1966. This was not as simple as evolving from one style to another. It was not a matter of genre code switching to appeal to different audiences. It was more like genre overlay, the creation of a sonic collage in pursuit of a power greater than individual genres could provide. As we've seen, the Blues Project worried about their own authenticity in relation to the blues, self-consciously trying not to sing in the styles of Black artists who had inspired them, always distancing themselves from the imitative ethnic-music approach of Paul Butterfield's band, for example. The Velvet Underground rejected the earnest search for authenticity in *any* form, folk, blues, psychedelic, because contemporary examples of all of these, and the earnestness of the search itself, they saw as unsophisticated and phony. This is what Reed meant when he later said that what the Velvets were doing was "the *real* thing. . . . It wasn't slick or a lie in *any conceivable way*" (my emphases).[25] To keep it real, the band rejected any show of sincerity as inevitably *in*sincere. Some of this they may have picked up from Warhol's Factory scene. Warhol was often accused of being fake, his art a "con" or a hoax on the public, "and that therefore he was fundamentally insincere."[26] In that way, the whole question of sincerity and authenticity was central to his public persona. *The Velvet Underground & Nico* emerged out of a kind of three-way encounter: Warhol's pop-art scene, the Velvet Underground's discovery of an avant-garde art-rock hybrid, and the backdrop against which they refined that hybrid: Wilson's radical eclecticism. For Wilson's part, that eclecticism went back to his days at Transition Records, in combination with a pragmatic market-facing professionalism.

FROM THE UNDERGROUND TO THE DOM

The Velvet Underground & Nico was surely understood by some hip contemporary listeners as providing a tantalizing glimpse of the underground, a sample of what was essentially a live act, and a snapshot of a scene it was part of and had helped to create. The back cover of the album played to this, with a photograph of the band in performance—dancers, lights, projections, and all. Despite its musical power, everything about the album said: you had to be there. Around the same time Wilson was rounding up Sun Ra, members of his Arkestra, and members of the Blues Project to make the *Batman and Robin* record as a side project, on January 13, 1966, the Clinical Psychiatrists' convention was held in New York with Warhol as a guest lecturer. He used the opportunity to put on a show, "Andy Warhol's Up-Tight," a multimedia Happening with immersive film and light show projections, freeform dancers, and music by the Velvet Underground and Nico. The performance including confrontational intrusions into the audience by the filmmaker Barbara Rubin (who asked attendees about their sexual practices), an immersive onslaught meant to *épater les bourgeoisie* by turning the tables on the uptight therapists. This was a prototype of the Exploding Plastic Inevitable, once Rubin was removed from the equation and the show was adapted to allow for a participating audience in the form of dancers. Different audiences became the target of the EPI's sensory barrage as it moved among venues in the early part of the year, including Jonas Mekas' Film-Makers' Cinematheque on 41st St., for which Gerard Malanga recruited Bibbe Hansen (later the mother of the Alternative musician, Beck) as part of the show—as a go-go dancer. Malanga later complained to Warhol that *he* of course was himself an interpretive artist, not a mere go-go dancer.[27] In a 1966 TV interview, Warhol announced that he was "sponsoring" a band called the Velvet Underground. He explained that since he no longer believed in painting, he wanted to combine music and art and films "all together" to make "the biggest discotheque in the world," but with twenty-one screens and "I don't know, three or four bands."[28] In other words, the EPI was always intended to be a kind of portable avant-garde nightclub, and it inspired other nightclubs for years thereafter.

In April 1966, the EPI began a residence at an actual nightclub, the Dom, in the old Polish social club building on St. Marks Place. ("Dom" means "home" in Polish, but the word undoubtedly also had BDSM connotations for some in the Factory crowd, and, of course, it's also "MOD" spelled backwards). There, Malanga and Woronov continued to perform their leather-and-whip dance while films were projected on the walls and the dancers and an immersive light show was projected over the entire room, with blobs and polka dots and color washes. Washing over it all was the immersive sound of the Velvet Underground playing loud.

The idea of "the biggest discotheque" may have been a joke by Warhol, but the discotheque part was true. The Dom remained essentially what it had originally been, a dance hall, with an open floor and tables and chairs around the perimeter. The Velvet Underground served as "the house band of that scene," Danny Fields later said, "and everybody danced to them."[29] This was at the height of the go-go discotheque craze. In New York, it included clubs like the Cheetah, opened in 1966, and Arthur, opened in 1965, the name of which came from a joke in the Beatles' *A Hard Day's Night*: George is asked by a reporter, "what do you call your haircut?," and he replies, deadpan, "Arthur." Such clubs attracted a mix of celebrities and hip young people, all dancing the frug, the jerk, the Watusi, the monkey, etc. Turntable DJs, live bands, and of course go-go dancers, often on platforms or in glass boxes or in cages, modeling the new dances, inspiring moves, and titillating the crowd. (A few clubs featured male go-go dancers.) The later disco era of the 1970s was in some ways just a continuation of this earlier discotheque craze, reinvigorated by the music and culture of gay and Black clubs. In the 1960s, some rock venues reacted to the first-wave discotheque trend with a pointed oppositional self-definition. They declared themselves the antithesis of the trend. The Cafe Au Go Go in the Village, for example, with its dark, low-ceilinged room used mostly for folk and rock performances or dark ("sick") stand-up comedy, was named satirically, as a downtown put-down mocking the go-go trend. At the Acid Tests and multimedia ballroom shows at the Avalon, the Fillmore(s) West and East, or one-off events in large convention centers or warehouses, psychedelic dance concerts offered deliberate alternatives to dancing in more traditional nightclubs. They were *not-discotheques*, as it were, places where free-form, trippy dancing, and participatory performance, or just sitting in a corner bathed in the light show, replaced the recognizable dance steps, drinking rituals, and structured social interactions of the clubs.

THIS AIN'T NO DISCO

The Dom and the EPI were similarly defined in opposition to the go-go trend, but they took everything further, took it too far on purpose, the sounds, the light, the dancing, the drugs. Despite the Velvets Underground's consistent hostility toward the West Coast, there was clearly some cross-fertilization between the Acid Tests and ballroom scene in California (remember, the Blues Project was playing the Avalon that very same summer) and what the EPI was trying to do.[30] It was the anti-discotheque ethos that formed the context out of which the Velvet Underground emerged. Their first album was a snapshot of that alternative scene, like one of Warhol's Polaroids. The band's later catalog includes various bootlegs and live tracks that give listeners an attenuated taste of what went on in the live performances, beyond the shorter studio songs on the first-release official albums—for example, "Melody Laughter" or "Nothing Song."

Even among the songs on the first album, the noise of "European Son" hints at the overdriven drone that made up the sonic texture for much of the live EPI shows. These long freeform jams were often based on using single-chord drones to create a hypnotic wall of noise. Besides referencing Phil Spector and La Monte Young, interestingly, John Cale also said that the band's droning sound, using viola, guitar, and echo, "was itself a psychedelic experience," that "there was already a very strong psychedelic element in sustained sound."[31] Lou Reed's guitar on "All Tomorrow's Parties" sometimes sounds like the pseudo-raga of "Eight Miles High," which is no coincidence. Yardbirds and Led Zeppelin guitarist Jimmy Page saw the Velvets in 1966 and said he asked Reed what his favorite guitar solo was. Reportedly, Reed answered, "without a doubt, it's

'Eight Miles High.'"[32] Mary Woronov's classification of West Coast and East Coast music scenes was based on drugs of choice, but the distinction was never that precise (Cale openly associated their scene with heroin rather than amphetamine, to set against the LSD of California). But part of the psychedelic scene was always dark, always about exploring the scary side of inner experience. *Bad* trips also came with the territory. In that way, among West Coast bands, the Velvet Underground had something in common with Arthur Lee's band, Love, for example, or with Jim Morrison and the Doors—as opposed to the Bay Area's Jefferson Airplane or the Grateful Dead.

SOLO NICO

After she left the Velvet Underground, Nico was herself part of that dark California scene for a while, staying at the famous goth hangout the Castle (which housed the band Love among others), while she was in a relationship with Jim Morrison (whose style, in turn, may have owed something to the Velvets in general and Gerard Malanga in particular), and attending the Monterey Pop festival with Brian Jones. Dropped by the Velvet Underground, she quickly made her first solo album, *Chelsea Girl*, produced by Tom Wilson. It may have been Warhol who brought her to the band, but Wilson seems to have been her champion. In 1966, Wilson told Paul Morrisey, "The only thing I don't like about the record is, there's not enough Nico."[33]

For the banana album, Wilson wanted to record a proper single that could be played on the radio, one sung by Nico. In response, Reed wrote "Sunday Morning," with Nico slated to do the vocal. The song's chiming bells and lilting melody—not to mention the vague associations of the title and first two words of the lyric—were a deceptive trap. The song is actually about regret and paranoia: "Watch out, the world's behind you / There's always someone around you who will call . . ." In Nico's husky voice it would have made perfect sense as another cabaret song, like "I'll Be Your Mirror" or "Femme Fatale." But Reed decided he wanted to sing it, though he did so in a softer-than-usual, more femme voice. (Wilson mixed in Nico singing la-la-la's at the end.) This is just one example of the tensions in the band around the presence of Nico, who had some obvious troubles with pitch, for example, and liked to burn ritual candles before shows and was often late to the shows or to the stage. She had undeniable physical beauty, was a former model and Warhol superstar, and there were some of the usual sexist assumptions at work about women vocalists—"girl singers," as they were then known. But it's also possible she posed something of a threat to Cale and Reed when it came to the never-ending search for underground credibility. She was undeniably cool.

Indeed, Nico would soon come to present herself as an example of an alternative way to engage the cosmopolitan avant-garde. She was big in modera fashion and was known in some music circles before she ever met Reed and Cale. She was directly linked to the bohemian demimonde of Europe, a world later invoked by David Bowie's Berlin period, for example, the extension of the Weimar culture seen and heard in *Cabaret*, and earlier in Bertolt Brecht and Kurt Weil songs, and—to name an actor and chanteuse with whom Nico was often compared—Marlene Dietrich. (Dietrich herself released pop albums and singles in the mid-1960s, such as *Die neue Marlene* [1965], which included a German-language cover of Dylan's "Blowin' in the Wind," with accordion—and flute.) Nico was comfortable in the worlds of cinema and fashion/art photography, as well as music. Everyone knew she had been cast in Fellini's *La Dolce Vita*. In London, she had posed for David Bailey, the fashion photographer who inspired the mod-photographer character in Antonioni's film *Blow-Up* (released in late 1966). And she had an affair with the actor Alain Delon, with whom she had a child, Ari. Delon had appeared at around that time in another Antonioni film, *L'Eclisse*. Nico had been with Bob Dylan and Brian Jones, brief relationships that, at least as far as she was concerned, were based as much on mutual artistic interests as on sex. Jones facilitated her recording a single Gordon Lightfoot song ("I'm Not Sayin'," which also featured Jimmy Page on guitar), which is how Warhol had proof she could sing in the first place. As her career after the Velvet Underground showed, she understood the fashionably underground appeal of her own dark-goth style. When she showed up in New York, she was already a kind of transmedia artist, in effect playing herself at the Factory as she would continue to do in the new band.

Cale and Reed never really liked her fronting the band they had founded. She was always Warhol's blond protégée, the model and "girl singer" brought in for her glamour and sex appeal. There was also a transatlantic culture barrier. When she tried to get Cale and Reed to pronounce "femme fatale" the proper French way, they mocked her and refused. You can hear it in the punky vocals, defiantly American English in their street-level pronunciation, that short first "e" in "femme" and the final syllable of "fa-taaaal" drawled out to make the point. It's possible to agree that the "boys" in this case were right about how to sing that particular lyric and still recognize the typical sexism behind their response. This reaction extended beyond the band. During a performance in L.A. in 1967, local underground hero Zappa cruelly parodied Nico's singing style from the stage. When she later transformed herself into the prototype of the dark-goth poet, dyeing her hair jet black and dressing in black gowns, accompanying herself on harmonium, it was arguably a way of rejecting the mod pop-art style that had given her fame. It was as if she wanted to dismiss any grounds for judging her outside the underground credibility as an artist. No longer mistakable for window dressing, she didn't want to be a tambourine-playing girl singer.[34] She sought her own voice in a sometime viciously competitive underground scene.

CHELSEA GIRLS

One final story captures the strangeness of the downtown scene just a few years later, at the end of the 1960s. In it, the competition for credibility and cool play themselves out in a lurid conflict. Probably late in 1970,[35] Nico was back in New York, at the El Quixote restaurant, connected off the bohemian Chelsea Hotel on West 23rd Street. At a nearby table sat another group that included the young Black singer and actor Emmaretta Marks. You'll recall her from chapter 2 as the background singer for the Blues Project, 1966–1967. In 1967, she moved on, eventually appearing on Broadway in the original cast of *Hair*. Accounts differ on the details of what happened at the Chelsea, but all agree that Nico physically assaulted Marks. The Black singer was apparently talking about racism in America. Nico objected to something she said and shouted something to the effect that Marks (a Black woman in America) didn't know anything about true suffering. According to some accounts, Nico went on to make a racist remark. Manager Danny Fields recalled her saying "I hate Black people."[36] Then, Nico attacked Marks with a broken wine or beer glass. Among the accounts, it's disputed whether she threw the glass in the other singer's face or, as some people (Fields among them) say, broke it and used it to stab her in the eye socket. At any rate, Marks was rushed to the hospital.

The story may sound at first like yet another parable about bad vibes at the end of the sixties, in keeping with the Manson Family murders and the concert at Altamont: this is where all the peace and love ended up. It's almost always recounted when the question of Nico's racism and antisemitism comes up. It was clearly traumatic for Nico—she spoke about it for years thereafter. We hear less often about its effect on Marks, the victim of assault who ended up in the hospital. Nico said that *she* went into exile afterwards in fear of her life, claiming that a contract had been put out on her by the Black Panthers, who were supposedly friends of Marks's. Sometimes she even said that Marks herself was a member of the Black Panther Party (which had been founded in 1966).[37] Someone in Marks's circle—it might have been a friend or family member—may well have telephoned Nico to tell her she was no longer welcome in New York. That sounds plausible, understandable even, given the nature of the assault. The part about the Black Panthers, especially the supposed murder contract, might also have been a more general threat, or even a bluff, by the caller, whoever they were. Or it may have been a paranoid fantasy of Nico's. She was known for such paranoia and for making racist remarks. She once said in an interview—later self-reported—that she did not like Black facial features and compared them to those of apes and cannibals. The remarks led her record label at the time to drop her.[38]

The Chelsea El Quixote story is often told as revealing Nico's personal character. Sometimes Marks isn't even identified, referred to only as the "young Black woman" who was attacked. What if we were to treat Marks as a significant figure in the story, her own story, rather than just Nico's victim (or, worse, a stereotypically militant and threatening Black woman). We could start by acknowledging that this is a story about *two professional musicians*. Only a few years earlier, they had both been part of New York's downtown underground, just in slightly different, if partly overlapping, scenes. And back in 1966, they had Wilson in common. The producer may even conceivably have played a role in both of the women being hired into or remaining in their respective bands for as long as they did. Warhol actually brought Nico to Cale and Reed. But when the artist was asked about Wilson years later, Warhol, interestingly enough, recalled him as "a friend of Nico's."[39] As for Marks, as we've seen, in 1965 she was with Eric Burdon of the Animals and was thus part of Wilson's circle. In 1966, she was asked to join the Blues Project as a background singer. Kooper and the other members of the Blues Project were, like Reed and Cale, less than enthusiastic about having a "girl singer" in *their* band. For whatever reasons (it was said she missed rehearsals and held up performances, among other things), Marks left the Blues Project in 1967 and went on to other gigs, among them the role in the zeitgeist-reflecting *Hair*. In that production, among other numbers, she performed the song "White Boys" as part of a Supremes-like trio.[40]

The fight at El Quixote makes these women seem worlds apart, but there they both were, hanging out at the Chelsea. Back in 1966, for a few weeks that summer, the Blues Project and the Velvet Underground had performed only about a mile apart. History has calcified the differences between the genres and genealogies of the two bands, and the Velvet Underground has by now far eclipsed the Blues Project in terms of cultural and artistic influence and significance. But both bands mattered a good deal at the time, coming from different but overlapping New York scenes. Their genre divisions and hybrid combinations were part of strategic self-fashioning by both bands, taking advantage of a burgeoning musical eclecticism in 1966.

The Blues Project was what it was because it was *not* a folk group or jug band. Their electric blues-rock allied them, in their own minds, with the sound of Chicago's South Side (though not, they insisted, as mere preservationists). Increasingly, they tried to identify their own music as something new, still mostly blues-based but in spirit psychedelic. The Velvet Underground was pointedly *not* a folk-rock band, but the early demo tape shows how much Reed's songs were based in folk. And it was *not* a blues band. The band members made a point of staking out their own territory in the New York scene as an underground avant-garde art-rock band. It's interesting in this context that Steve Katz later referred to the Blues Project as "New York's hip underground rock band," and the Project may well have been more widely known at the time than the Velvets were.[41] The boundaries between their opposed genres, genre hybrids, and different scenes were actually crossed and recrossed all the time, as the bands toured and records were made and songs were covered or inspired new songs. But the boundaries were there, nonetheless, and they were sometimes hotly contested. Each band worked to set itself apart, and each had a moment when it was what was happening downtown. In each case, but especially in the case of the Velvet Underground, fans saw them as underground-authentic—which means they loved them at least in part for what they were not.

CHAPTER FIVE

A HIT BY VARÈSE

Frank Zappa and the Mothers of Invention, *Freak Out!* (1966); *Absolutely Free* (1967)

A MUSICAL GENIUS

Pauline Butcher, who worked as a secretary in London, writes about bumping into Tom Wilson in the fall of 1967 on her way to meet Frank Zappa for the first time. The musician was in England on tour and had hired her to transcribe and type up his lyrics so they could be printed in an underground newspaper. Wilson was doing his usual A&R work with the Mothers of Invention. At the hotel, she got in the elevator with a "tall, handsome black man with features like Sidney Poitier and a small beard on his chin."

> He wore a dark suit and tie and a beige cashmere coat slung casually over his shoulders. We stepped into the lift together: I pressed the fourth-floor button; he pressed the fifth. My hair was cut by Vidal Sassoon in a Faye-Dunaway-*Bonny-and-Clyde* style, and when the stranger appraised me up and down—admiring my flat, white calf-length boots and green dress with its little white collar and remarked, "Wow, even in California girls don't wear skirts *that* short," I was ready to flirt.[1]

She tells him, "this is London," and "in fashion, we lead the world." He replies that he's from Hollywood, which leads the world in "entertainment." Does he work in film, she asks? He says no, "Music. Rock 'n' Roll." Then she goes to meet the scary-looking but surprisingly polite Zappa. A little later, Wilson reappears in Zappa's suite—he was headed there too but had taken the elevator to the wrong floor—and she's introduced. "Par-leen, you're working for Frank, godammit? Frank, how come you get the best-looking secretaries?" Then Wilson takes her aside and says: "That guy is a musical genius. Stick by him and you'll go far."[2]

Besides transcribing a bit of his Texas accent as heard by a swinging Londoner, the anecdote reveals that Wilson was in 1967 thinking of himself as "from Hollywood" (at least for the purposes of elevator conversation) and working in "Rock 'n' Roll." We also hear that he was attuned to the latest fashions—and to the genius of Frank Zappa. In the first program of *The Music Factory* radio show, recorded that same year he met Butcher in London, Wilson comments on the Mothers' European tour and says that some people might feel that Zappa and the Mothers of Invention were "pop art"—by which he seems to mean ironically distanced, camp, insincere. But, no, he says, Zappa is an "activist" and the band is socially engaged, "has something to say." He then plays "Trouble Every Day," from *Freak Out!*, a song about the Watts riots of 1965.

TROUBLE BLUES

It was that song, the only one he heard the band perform at the Whisky a Go Go in Los Angeles in 1965, that led Wilson to sign Zappa and the Mothers to a contract in the first place, under the misapprehension that it was typical of their oeuvre, that they were another white blues-rock band. Only when they were all in the studio together a little later, ready to make an album, did Wilson discover how truly weird Zappa's music was on the whole. (Zappa says it was when they began to play the descending chromatic notes of "Who Are the Brain Police?") But even "Trouble Every Day," a blues number built on a repeated guitar riff, contains a bit of self-mockery when it comes to its own "blooze" pretensions. At around the five-minute mark, referring to the lack of social mobility of a character who is "watchin' rats go across the floor / And mak[ing] up songs about being poor," Zappa calls out: "Blow your harmonica, son!"—a catchphrase of the blues musician Lightnin' Slim—and the harmonica solo begins. In an earlier spoken bit, Zappa declares, "Hey, you know something people? I'm not black but there's a whole lotsa times I wish I could say I'm not white."

That kind of deflecting irony characterizes Zappa's approach to race and musical identity throughout his work, including a notorious later album cover (*Joe's Garage*) in which he appears to be in blackface (he denied that was his intent), and as late as "You Are What You Is" from the 1981 album of the same name, which mocks white blues artists (and uses the N-word while falling back on a kind of both-sides, "color blind," essentialism). All of this has to be set alongside Zappa's mixed-race bands and projects throughout his career and his often-professed veneration for Black musicians. The memoirist and former secretary we heard from at the beginning of this chapter, Pauline Butcher, also recalled a later visit to Frank and Gail Zappa in the couple's apartment in Greenwich Village. At one point, Frank played her a 7-inch 45 rpm record by Muddy Waters, who he said was "just about the best blues player on the planet."[3] While the record played, he told her: "This is the music to listen to, not the Beatles or the Rolling Stones." Though she was a little insulted that he presumed to know her taste based on her nationality, she listened politely. "Frank proceeded with a lecture on the blues and various black musicians, including John Lee Hooker and Booker T. He showed me sleeves of their records and I was flattered by his desire to enlighten me."[4] Next, she says, he played her a favorite doo-wop record—a genre juxtaposition we return to below.

The truth is, blues motifs, from twelve-bar song structure to pentatonic guitar riffs, run throughout the Mothers' second album (produced by Wilson, 1966–1967), *Absolutely Free*, and blues and R&B traditions influenced Zappa throughout his career. Wilson's initial assumption about the Mothers was not as far off-base as Zappa's story might suggest. You can hear the blues behind later songs like "Willy the Pimp," on 1969's *Hot Rats*, for example, as well as some of the instrumental tracks released as *Funky Nothingness* (2023). Zappa's 1971 underground film, *200 Motels*, includes a scene in which a band member argues that "white guys can play the blues, you know." When he was a student at Antelope Valley High School in Lancaster, California, Zappa had led and played drums in a racially integrated horn-based R&B band (sometimes referred to as a "blues band"), the Blackouts. For that matter, the early 1960s band that would become the Mothers (for motherfuckers, a musician's term of respect; after anxious pressure from the record label, they became the Mothers of Invention) had begun as an R&B group, the Soul Giants. As a guitar player, Zappa always cited Black musicians Clarence "Gatemouth" Brown and Johnny "Guitar" Watson as his main influences.

As a composer, though, he repeatedly cited modernist and contemporary classical musicians Igor Stravinsky and Edgard Varèse. That hybrid combination—blues and R&B (with the stylings of 1950s doo-wop) on the one hand; often atonal avant-garde twentieth-century orchestral music on the other—defined Zappa's musical identity. Any number of his songs could be cited as incorporating both kinds of music. Take, for example, "Cosmik Debris" (1974). It's basically a slow-talking blues with a sung chorus, complete with showy electric guitar solos, but it also incorporates asymmetrical dissonant flourishes. The lyric is about failed authenticity, that is, phoniness. It tells the story of seeing through a fraudulent guru—and seeing through phoniness in general ("Who you jivin' with that cosmik debris?" . . . "Is that a real poncho or a Sears poncho?"). The blues licks exist alongside the modernist melodic runs in such a way that neither side can be taken too seriously. Just as the speaker/singer refuses to be taken in by the guru, the song refuses to take at face value the supposedly "authentic" coolness of the blues. Still, musically, it's the blues that drives the song, while the lyrics are all about exposing the phoniness of "eastern" religious charlatans.

Zappa was a satirist. In that role, nothing is sacred and everything is seen through, in particular the "plastic people" and bourgeois hypocrisy that characterized midcentury middle-American "straight" culture—but also the flower-power advocates among the hippies. As with most satirists, from Juvenal to Robert Crumb, this caustic satirical weaponry depended on the satirist's having a sense of his own fearless, truth-telling integrity. Underneath all the ridicule is a satirical perspective based on a clear-eyed negative truth. In 1966 terms, we might think of Zappa's self-representation as based on the supposed authenticity of seeing through false claims to sincerity and authenticity in a banal, corrupt, and "plastic" culture. Despite his conflicted satire of blues pretensions, both aural (as in the overblown guitar soloing in "Cosmik Debris" and other songs) and topical (as in "Trouble Every Day"), Zappa clearly thought of Muddy Waters, for example, as operating in a zone of musical authority and artistic authenticity relative to his imitators in the British Invasion.

AVANT GARDE A GO GO

As for the other pole of his musical commitments: Zappa pursued avant-garde modernist composition with serious dedication until he died from prostate cancer in 1993. At fifteen, the boy Zappa actually telephoned, cold, his musical hero, the composer and early electronic-music experimentalist Edgard Varèse.[5] The musician was not at home at the time, but Zappa was able to speak with

Varèse's wife, and he later corresponded with the composer himself, whom he idolized for the rest of his career, even keeping a letter from him above his desk. That career included adapted versions performed by the Mothers of Invention, e.g., "Octandre," memorialized on *Whisky a Go Go, 1968*. And it would eventually include Zappa's conducting his own original works for orchestra. Near the end of his life in 1993, Zappa recorded his own versions of Varèse music, the collection titled *The Rage and The Fury*, which remains unreleased.

Zappa was not alone in his fandom. Jazz icon Charlie Parker also idolized Varèse and reportedly even sought to take music lessons from him in the 1950s when the composer was living in Greenwich Village.[6] The idolization of Varèse as a living symbol of modernism and musical experimentation was widespread in the 1960s among rock and pop musicians. Zappa had a lot to do with that. For example, the title of this chapter cites a song by the horn-based rock band Chicago, "A Hit By Varèse" (1972), which makes Varèse a synecdoche for musical innovation and musical freedom in general, including in pop music you might in some ideal future hear on the radio ("attempt something new / The people need you / A seed that will lead to a hit by Varèse"). It's no surprise that Robert Lamm of Chicago writes in a liner note that *he* first heard about Varèse from Zappa's references to the composer in *his* liner notes to *Freak Out!*

Zappa was also a fan of Igor Stravinsky, from whom he borrowed melodies and motifs for a range of his own compositions, and Béla Bartók, whose piano concertos he recommended in response to a 1967 interviewer's asking him to name records people should listen to. The Bartók concertos, he said, were "all very groovy and good to dance to." Then he specified which recordings by which orchestras he had heard, including, interestingly, a "version of the first" that he heard played "at Andy Kulberg's, of the Blues Project, who has an extensive collection of modern music."[7] (As we've seen, Kulberg was also a trained flute player.) It's a reminder that Zappa wasn't alone among musicians of the 1960s in playing blues records and modern classical records on the same turntable—and having one's own music influenced by both. It also suggests the likely influence on both musicians of the evangelically eclectic Tom Wilson.

ÉPATER LA BOURGEOISIE (ON TV)

Zappa began as a boy with eclectic musical interests, and he never abandoned them. If anything, his ambitions as a composer and conductor came first and were to some degree deferred by his successful career as a rock musician. He always saw himself as a composer. In March 1963, when he was twenty-two, he appeared on TV as a guest on *The Steve Allen Show.* Clean-cut and beardless, he calmly demonstrates how to play a bicycle—much to the amusement of the host and the live audience. Zappa approaches the TV appearance with a combination of earnestness and understated comedic timing. When Allen asks him how long he's been playing the bicycle, he deadpans, "about two weeks." But he also already identifies himself, with evident seriousness, as a composer. He demonstrates the different tones and timbres he can achieve by striking different parts of the bike, one with a bike turned upside-down, using drumsticks, bowing the wheel-spokes with a borrowed bass bow, or blowing through the hollow handlebars like horns. Allen tries his hand for a bit, cracking up when the band makes funny noises for him. Underneath the schtick, and despite Zappa's deadpan irony, the young musician seems genuinely interested in the possibilities for found-object sound production. And Allen, himself a musician, appears to become a little interested himself. Then Allen and Zappa perform together an "improvisation for two bicycles, prerecorded tape, and small musical ensemble." Zappa in effect conducts Allen and the house band in a spontaneous composition. The final result is actually a fairly impressive found-object + *musique concrète* piece—despite all the jokes and TV patter. For a later listener, the sound of Zappa's playing the aluminum spokes with drumsticks might even briefly foreshadow all those xylophone and vibraphone parts that would come to characterize many of his later compositions. Ruth Underwood is the musician we think of as playing these parts, but it's worth remembering that Zappa himself started out as a drummer.

This kind of sketch was already a TV trope, a comic bit, its conventions descended from vaudeville and music hall variety shows: some outrageous artist or performer is featured onstage as a way for the host or emcee to play off them and prompt the audience to laugh at the absurdity of (in this case) experimental modern music on display. But such sound experiments were already by then quite common in avant-garde music. They had been around since the early decades of the twentieth century. Take, for example, certain works by John Cage. Cage had himself appeared in a similar TV bit on *I've Got a Secret* in 1960, performing his *Water Walk* on various household appliances and found objects, as well as a tape recorder and relatively conventional instruments like a prepared piano and cymbals. The audience laughed, as expected, despite a fairly serious and respectful introduction by the host, which included his holding up a legitimizing newspaper review.

CONDUCTING THE FREAK SCENE

During his give and take with Allen, Zappa mentions the score he'd written for a movie by independent director Timothy Carey, *The World's Greatest Sinner*. Carey, Zappa says, was in the film, along with "a cast of about a thousand people he found down on main street someplace." Even Zappa can't help but laugh a little as he tells this story. This artistic strategy for making a film—recruiting a crowd of bystanders as in effect found objects/performers to be directed—seems to have stayed with him. Exactly three years after the TV appearance on Allen's show, in March 1966, now with his familiar beard and long hair, the twenty-five-year-old Zappa was in the recording studio with the Mothers of Invention making the band's first album, *Freak Out!*, produced by Wilson. "Tom Wilson was a great guy. He had vision, you know? And he really stood by us," Zappa later said.[8] Despite signing the band under something of a misunderstanding, Wilson already had so much faith in the genius of Zappa, in fact, that he helped him secure the record label's approval to bring in $500's worth of special percussion instruments and invite a crowd of "all the freaks from Sunset Boulevard into the studio" to participate in a midnight session on Friday, March 12, "to do something special."[9] This group of extras, as it were, participated in a kind of structured collective improvisation, making animal sounds, doing heavy breathing, bursting out with orgasmic exclamations, chanting short phrases, sometimes singing and playing percussion instruments. The result was a series of connected pieces released on sides 3 and 4 of the double album—making an avant-garde climax for the record that had opened boldly on side 1, track 1, with "Hungry Freaks, Daddy" (with its weird mix of sounds, including nonverbal vocals, kazoo fanfares, and blues-rock solos). Zappa said the long-form works at the end of the album, as they were recorded, remained unfinished. They still added up to over twenty minutes: "Help, I'm a Rock (Suite in Three Movements)" and "The Return of the Son of Monster Magnet (Unfinished Ballet in Two Tableaux)." The three movements of the first are: "Okay to Tap Dance," "In Memoriam Edgar[d] Varèse," and "It Can't Happen Here." The two tableaux of the second are: "I. Ritual Dance of the Child-Killers" and "II. Nullis Pretii (No Commercial Potential)"—the last phrase supposedly something Zappa had heard a record executive say about the Mothers themselves.

Remember, this was a recording session for a first album by a mostly unknown band, for what would be a *double* album, perhaps the first double album in rock music. Wilson not only approved the session, he was right there in the sound booth. On acid. Allegedly, anyway. Zappa said that Wilson himself told him so, and Zappa commented: "I've tried to imagine what he must have been thinking, sitting in the control room listening to all that weird shit coming out of the speakers, and being responsible to telling the engineer, Ami Hadani (who was not on acid), what to do."[10] LSD was that year seeing record use, just as it was on the way to being made illegal in the United States. Either way, the experimental session on March 12, 1966, was a trip. It didn't involve just any street people; some of the Freaks were key players in the local scene. They were straight off the streets of Hollywood, but Zappa knew them well. He brought them into the studio, handed them percussion instruments, and conducted them in a series of structured improvisations. That night, Zappa was in effect conducting the Freak scene. He was the controlling composer of the whole. And Wilson was directing the whole production from the booth.

I'm suspicious of Zappa's retrospective joking characterization of Wilson as being yet again shocked or taken aback by the Mothers' shenanigans. Surely by then Wilson knew what to expect from the band, or at least knew to expect some surprises. He was already heavily invested (literally, using MGM/Verve's funds) in Zappa's genius. He was, as even Zappa's amused version of the story admits, still telling the engineer what to do, despite everything going on and the added lysergic filter, collaborating with Zappa the composer to make the album into what it was going to be. Wilson was a cosmopolitan professional, experienced with avant-garde music from his days at Harvard and running his own Transition Records in Boston, which had been focused on cutting-edge jazz performers like Sun Ra and Cecil Taylor. By 1966, he was interested in a wide spectrum of diverse forms of cultural expression. He was unlikely actually to play straight man to the Mothers of Invention or the Freak ensemble (especially if he were on acid).

MAPPING THE FREAK SCENE

The Los Angeles Freak scene in 1965–1966 centered on a group of artists, filmmakers, and dancers associated with the sculptor Vito Paulekas. These included Carl Franzoni and the groupie and performer Pamela Des Barres, among others. (Des Barres would later be a member of the Zappa-sponsored all-female band the GTOs.) They were locally famous for living communally, promoting free love, and indulging in various forms of self-expression, and for literally making the scene—turning a club, concert, street corner, or diner into a scene just by showing up and performing, "freaking out" through display of their hairstyles and clothes, engaging in free-form dancing, chanting, vocalizing. Their unofficial affiliation with the Mothers of Invention was reciprocal and mutually beneficial. They made concerts into happenings just through their participation/performances, and the Mothers in turn contributed their outrageous music to the overall soundtrack for the Freak scene. The album, *Freak Out!*, was a kind of musical representation of and tribute to that scene, from the title to the jacket copy, to the lyrics, to the extras, the paratextual materials and paraphernalia for promoting and shaping the experience of the album.

The liner note by Zappa himself on the lefthand side of the album's gatefold gives the listener a basic definition—"WHAT IS FREAKING OUT[?]"—that's only half-mocking: "On a personal level, Freaking Out is a process whereby an individual casts off outmoded and restricting standards of thinking, dress, and social etiquette in order to express CREATIVELY his relationship to his immediate environment and the social structure as a whole." Collectively, he adds, when groups of Freaks get together for free expression, "through music or dance," the result "is generally referred to as a FREAK OUT." But the context of the album is less universal than this might suggest, more local, more about the limited scene in L.A. at that particular historical moment. Lyrics reference the Watts riots, for example, and the police presence at Ben Frank's restaurant in West Hollywood. The idea of the Freaks—which is what makes this, in some ways, one of the first concept albums—is an L.A. thing. "It Can't Happen Here," one track goes, but it was definitely happening already in 1966 on and around Hollywood Boulevard and Sunset Boulevard.

The *Freak Out!* inside jacket, in early printings, included an address you could write to for a paper map of "FREAK OUT Hot Spots!" in Los Angeles—"Only $1.00 in magnificent color (mostly black)." The map is copyrighted 1966, signed as "designed by" Frank Zappa and M.O.I. (Mothers of Invention). It's actually printed in black and reddish ink, with cartoony symbols to mark recent police busts and little car icons or silhouettes of people to show traffic. It's the kind of simplified map—with a key, text and image insets, and little symbolic icons—used by tourists to locate celebrities' homes in the Hollywood Hills, for example. By the Summer of Love in 1967, there were maps of this sort to hippie hotspots in the Haight-Ashbury district of San Francisco, carried by slightly more intrepid visitors than those on the guided-bus tours. In fact, one such map had printed right on it an admonition: "Note: Please dig this scene <u>on foot</u>. We love you but not your car!" The Freak Out Hot Spots! map was a kind of parody before-the-fact of those hippie tour maps.

The Freak Out map depicts a segment of L.A. as if it were Middle-earth or the Hundred Acre Wood, in the kind of image you might find printed on the flyleaf of a children's book. Hollywood and West Hollywood are labeled in big red letters, and the upper-left quadrant is dominated by a foliage-textured Laurel Canyon, labeled "Freak Sanctuary" but also "Caution!"—and, along the border of the red-inked "woods," "Mysterious Hallucinogenic Wasteland." The lower-right corner of the map, on the other hand, is labeled "cultural desert," and is filled with icons of cookie-cutter suburban houses, farms, trucks, factories, and oversized child icons.

On the map, Sunset Boulevard is an obvious vector for what's hot. It has tiny human and car icons in black, and red mushroom clouds signifying police busts or violence, and it's dense with labeled spots identified and described in the key, including the Cinematheque (featuring "rare and interesting films from the Great Underground"), music venues like the Trip ("used to be the center of the Freak Scene See it now") and, of course, the Whisky a Go Go ("still happens every night with Top Pop Music Acts [and, occasionally, lesser known fill-in groups like us]. Yay gang! Lotsa fun!") and Ben Frank's restaurant ("used to be the place to go after the dancing stopped"). All the past-tense verbs suggest the essential nature of any hip scene: that it's always changing, always passing into what *used* to be cool. In this case, there's a suggestion that police crackdowns are a major force in defining where people hang out and don't hang out any more. Buffalo Springfield would record "For What It's Worth" in December 1966, about the Sunset Strip riots in November over curfews and police harassment ("There's something happenin' here . . ."). The Freak Out Hot Spots! map foreshadows those troubles soon to come. In "Help, I'm a Rock!," Zappa voices a character who speculates about getting his driver's license so he might be able to "get a gig driving that bus that picks the freaks up in front of Ben Frank's," before switching the chant to "Help, I'm a cop!" And the map includes an inset photograph of a police bust, a still image from "A highly recommended film: Blue Fascism." An arrow points to the photo from a reproduction of an ID card labeled "A COP-OUT CARD carried by FINKS for protection during a ROUTINE INVESTIGATION."

MAPPING THE MUSIC

If we read the map's key just for the music venues that it identifies, we get a sense of how the subscenes were being defined at the time according to shifting genres—often hyphenated, hybrid genres—a situation that Zappa mocks but also documents as the way things were in 1966:

> #6 The Troubadour gives you not only folk music, but folk-rock music, rock music itself, and other hybrids, all IN CONCERT.
>
> #11 The Sea Witch is one of the teeny-bopper (no offense, gang) IN SPOTS, featuring the new local bands in performances of psychedelic music b/w Cokes and Coffee.
>
> #20 The Ash Grove features ETHNIC ETHNICAL ETHNOCENTRIC Folque Musique.

When *The Monkees* TV show had placed an ad for a casting call the previous fall, it not only referenced Ben Frank's diner but name-checked one of the same hybrid genres, in a similarly half-mocking tone:

> Madness!! Auditions. Folk & Roll Musicians-Singers for acting roles in new TV series. Running Parts for 4 insane boys, age 17–21. Want spirited Ben Frank's–types. Have courage to work. Must come down for interview.

Chapter 8 has a lot more to say about the TV band that ad created. On the Freak Out Hot Spots! map, #26 to the east on Sunset, is "TTG RECORDING STUDIOS where we cut our album"—that is, *Freak Out!*, the very album where you got the address for ordering the map, and which might be playing on your turntable as you peruse it.

The map is a kind of paratext, which, you'll recall from chapter 1, is a textual object associated with the main text, in this case the album, that shapes the way the main text is received. Especially in the theory of Gérard Genette, the paratext is a "threshold," a way into the text and, by logical extension, also a way out of the text into the radiating contexts that inevitably surround it in the material world. Another example is the promotional jigsaw puzzle Zappa had made from the album cover image, pieces of which were sent to local DJs at radio stations, one piece at a time, a game-like teaser for the album's release. In both cases, the map and the puzzle, the album is connected to the world at large, the geography and the airwaves of L.A. In some ways, these are parodic versions of the box-top coupons and souvenirs, paratextual objects as advertising tie-ins, like decoder rings, for example, that had been around since the radio serials of the 1930s. In the same line, in 1967 the Beatles included a sheet of cardboard cutouts, including a droopy mustache, faux military stripes, and a band button, with copies of the *Sgt. Pepper's* album.

On the Freak Out Hot Spots! map, sardonic descriptions in the key qualify some of the lyrics on the album, as in "Help, I'm a Rock!" and the references in "Trouble Every Day" to the 1965 Watts riots. In fact, in 1967, the first song on the next album—what would be the Mothers' second, *Absolutely Free*—"Plastic People," was still name-checking L.A.'s hot spots, in that case, Pandora's Box ("Down Sunset Boulevard to Crescent Heights") and the "vast quantity of plastic people" to be found there. The Hot Spots! map had called Pandora's Box "another teenie-bop underground stronghold" with "cops and ingenue freakos and lots of atmosphere, but tiny." In 1967, "Plastic People" just picked up where the map had left off.

The map makes it clear how much *Freak Out!* is the product of a scene, including actual places, venues, and the detailed urban topography of that part of L.A. That scene, in turn, is associated with specific, shifting musical genres, including hybrid, hyphenated, and hyper-differentiated genres. The album and map tie the Freak scene to the Mothers' brand of avant-garde rock, infused with elements of modern experimental classical music, which, despite Zappa's intentions, thanks in part to the Freaks themselves, was recognizably psychedelic music. Zappa repeatedly protested that "psychedelic rock" was only a marketing term. But *Freak Out!* was *received* as a psychedelic album, anyway, a stubborn reminder that the scene defined the music as much as the music defined the scene.

In one 1967 interview, Zappa tried to separate the meaning of *Freak Out!* as he intended it from the psychedelic music with which it had become associated. When the album came out, he insists, "there was no such thing as psychedelic music" (which is definitely not true), no such thing as "Freak Out."[11] It "wasn't the happening thing." The term "Freak Out" he calls a "colloquial localism" of the scene in L.A. So, the term as he used it in the album's title, he says, was not meant to refer to "a bad LSD trip" but that local Freak scene. He was worried people would associate the album with LSD, which they did. "What can you do?," he says rhetorically. One thing you can try to do (or your heirs can try to do) is to include this very interview excerpt in the 4-CD deluxe edition of *Freak Out!* that appeared in 2006. But the widespread association, in terms of genre, of *Freak Out!* as psychedelic music (if of a particular, idiosyncratic kind) was already long established by then.

One of the hot spots on the map is Vito's Studio ("& store & cult HQ & sanctuary & genetic laboratory which is REALLY THE PLACE TO SEE") on Laurel Avenue. This was the home of Vito Paulekas, who with his wife Szou ran an art studio there, where they taught sculpture and dance classes. This was headquarters for the original Freaks, as led by Vito and Szou and Carl Franzoni, in particular. As "Vito and the Hands," a group of them even released a single of their own in 1966, "Where It's At," and Vito's home studio was also used as a rehearsal space for various other L.A. bands.

FREAKING OUT IN THE STUDIO

These were among the very Freaks Zappa invited into TTG studios on March 12, 1966, where he gave them some basic instructions, handed out all the special percussion instruments, and conducted their improvisations. Among the instruments they used was a Lion's Roar drum, a bass drum or tom-tom rigged with a horsehair cord that you pull through a hole in the drumhead to make a deep and disturbing sound created through the friction. This kind of instrument has roots in Africa; its sound—as the name suggests—is low-pitched and animal-like. It had already been used in some experimental modern orchestral music, including, most significantly for Zappa, *Ionization* by Edgard Varèse, which was among the pieces Zappa recorded near the end of his life.

The semi-structured improvisation that resulted from Zappa's conducting the Freaks made for the strangest and most characteristic sounds on the album, symphonic or operatic music with the feel of anarchic doo-wop combined with overdriven acid rock. It's a particularly Zappaesque hybrid: a psychedelic-Varèsean experiment. Zappa himself clearly thought of these sorts of improvised vocals as forming the artistic core of *Freak Out!* He later tossed off a competitive remark about the Beatles' *Sgt. Pepper's Lonely Hearts Club Band* (which Paul McCartney would later admit was indeed inspired by the Mothers' first album): "I'd like to thank them [the Beatles] very much for doing a wonderful take-off on *Freak Out!* during the song about Rita the meter maid. I thought that it was very clever to have people wheezing, huffing and panting in the background with the music still going on."[12] Of course this was one of the devices Zappa used on *Freak Out!*, as he's implying, but it's also hard not to compare it to his own start in the "recording" business, when he was entrapped by law enforcement into making a "pornographic" audiotape in his own small studio, then arrested for having done so.[13]

If the Beatles imitated the sound of a noisy crowd on some tracks of their record, Zappa recorded an actual crowd. Like Sun Ra's playing the downtown scene on *Strange Strings*, Zappa was in effect playing the L.A. Freak scene, using the recording studio as a venue in which to compose and conduct actual Freaks. It's like that underground film Zappa mentioned on *The Steve Allen Show*: he made use of people on the street as a found cast. But it's also like a whole range of modern and contemporary musical experiments in *musique concrète*, found-instrument, untutored players, and ambient music. It's just that in this case the players were hairy, barefoot Freaks making animal noises, prancing around and chanting, playing the lion's-roar drum and other weird musical instruments.

The later-released *Freak Out!* CD (*MOFO Project/Object*) includes a track with Zappa's instructions to the Freaks after their part of the recording session had ended: "Ladies & gentlemen, attention, please. I'd really like to thank you for coming up here to this, uh, musical thing and, uh, when the record comes out you can all buy it, and listen to yourselves freaking out . . . but we have to clear the room right now. . . . No. I would also like to request that everybody kindly leave all the instruments in the studio. They don't belong to us. Bless your hearts."

ABSOLUTELY FREE IN NEW YORK

By the end of 1966, *Freak Out!* had sold only about 30,000 copies. Recording for the second album by Frank Zappa and the Mothers of Invention, *Absolutely Free* (also produced by Wilson), began in November 1966, with a much smaller recording budget—in fact about half that of the first album. It opens with "Plastic People," as we've seen, another treatment of the theme of American cultural phoniness. Track 3, "Amnesia Vivace," is an avant-garde piece with abstract melody and improvised vocals. Track 6, "Invocation and Ritual Dance of the Young Pumpkin," begins with a modernist instrumental, then moves into a blues guitar riff played by Zappa, which in turn opens up to include flute and other instruments in a long jam, all of it adding up to about seven minutes. But the song is only the second movement of a vegetable-themed three-part suite: slotted between track 5, "Call Any Vegetable," and track 7, "Soft-Sell Conclusion"—the latter including a deadpan comic monologue by Zappa spoken over the instrumental. Much of that suite and the album in general involves the kind of improvisation that worked well in live performance.

Right after recording *Absolutely Free*, the band relocated to New York City, where they settled into a residency at the Garrick Theater in the spring of 1967. There they played two shows a night, six nights a week, performing much of the music from the new album, with some other numbers and plenty of extended improvisations. The show was at first called "Pigs & Repugnant," and then "Absolutely Freeee: A Musical." It was a kind of Dada off-off-Broadway review, complete with props (stuffed animals, dolls, whipped cream, vegetables) and audience participation (Zappa called it "enforced recreation"). The result, like a good deal of experimental theater at the time, invoked a tradition running from Alfred Jarry's *Ubu Roi* through surrealism and Dada, to Andy Warhol's Up-Tight, to the Living Theatre.

The Garrick Theater was upstairs in the same building as the Cafe Au Go Go, at 152 Bleecker Street—the venue where the Blues Project had recorded their debut live album and where they were booked for a series of shows at around that same time. An otherwise dismissive *New York Times* review describes the *music* of the Absolutely Freeee show in glowing terms: "As pure sound . . . this approaches genius. From an electrified kitchen of percussion, saxes, guitars, flutes, etc., they produce a thick, black sound shot through with odd treble sunbursts and pinwheels—the exact aural equivalent of the nervous ever-changing abstract projections flashing on the screen behind them. Beneath the Lenin beards and the John-the-Baptist hairdos, these are fine musicians."[14]

The Garrick was a narrow art-house movie theater that seated about two hundred. One photo shows "The Mothers of Invention / Absolutely Freeee" on the Garrick marquee just above the Cafe Au Go Go awning. In the photo we see a rope line set up outside the window of a poster shop next door, and a sandwich board on the sidewalk with large headshots of Zappa and the Mothers. There was a passageway and stairs at the back of the Cafe Au Go Go that connected it to the Garrick upstairs. Musicians and their companions and entourages regularly traveled between the two venues (they had the same owner). Once, for example, Jimi Hendrix came up to sit in with the Mothers. Once the initial rush of ticket buyers for Absolutely Freeee subsided after the Easter vacation in March, the crowds thinned out, Zappa recalled.[15] Sometimes there were only a handful in the audience, fewer people than the band onstage. Zappa tells a story about one such sparsely attended night: "There was a passageway in back of the Garrick that led downstairs to the Cafe au-Go-Go's kitchen. Everybody in the band went down and got hot cider and bunches of little snacks. We put towels over our arms, like waiters, went back, served our audience their refreshments and talked with them for an hour and a half."[16]

Only about a year separated these New York shows at the Garrick from the earlier recording of *Freak Out!* in L.A. The categorizing bins of music history, with the need to separate genres, bands, and, by extension, scenes and eras, creates an artificial distance between the psychedelic blues-rock of the Blues Project and the crypto-psychedelic Dada of the Mothers of Invention, when in fact the two were closely related, just in a mundane professional way. There was a kind of traffic between their different musics that was as easy as using that backstairs passageway between the downstairs club and the upstairs theater. Or Zappa's listening to Bartók at Andy Kulberg's apartment. This sort of traffic was the rule, not the exception. Such intermingling in overlapping spaces was a feature of pop music of various kinds, and not only in 1966–1967. In this case, we have to imagine, yet again, Wilson on the scene, visiting both venues that year (as he likely did), while traveling back and forth between New York and L.A. and dealing with other musicians—himself a key vector for the spread of musical influence.

MEMORIES OF DOO-WOP

Zappa's own eclecticism wasn't limited to the blues and modern classical music. He was also a fan of 1950s doo-wop. (Lou Reed was a fan of the genre as well.) The Mothers recorded a whole album in 1967–1968, part of it during the stint at the Garrick, titled *Cruisin' with Ruben & the Jets*, containing doo-wop songs by a fictitious band of the title. Zappa thought of it as one part of a three-album cluster, along with *We're Only in It for the Money* and *Uncle Meat*, that he called the No Commercial Potential project. Members of the Mothers of Invention seem to have relished performing the tunes on *Ruben & the Jets*. Zappa always extolled doo-wop and rejected the idea that his take on it was parodic. Instead, he said, it was an experiment in stretching the limits of an established, conventional form.[17] He compared it to what Stravinsky did in his own adaptation of the forms of earlier classical music: "It wasn't really a parody. If you are familiar with the development of the music of Igor Stravinsky; at one point he started writing a whole series of compositions that were in a style grossly unpopular at the time."[18]

Zappa said that a doo-wop record was the first rock 'n' roll album he remembers seeing back in 1957: *Teenage Dance Party*. Its cover showed white kids dancing to music performed by Black doo-wop groups.[19] There were some white doo-wop groups, but the form grew out of R&B and was associated with the street-corner harmony singing of Black neighborhoods. Examples of doo-wop run throughout Zappa's catalog. They often featured Roy Estrada's period-perfect falsetto, including as early as "Go Cry on Somebody Else's Shoulder," for example, on *Freak Out!*, the lyrics of which are meant in a mocking, sophomoric way to satirize 1950s and early 1960s clichés: hot-rod cars, going steady, pompadour hairdos. But mockery isn't mutually exclusive with appreciation of doo-wop as a form. In fact, Zappa wrote a song with Ray Collins, who would later be in the Mothers of Invention, called "Memories of El Monte," that was recorded and released in 1963 by Cleve Duncan, a vocalist with the Penguins, a Black doo-wop group Zappa admired. The Mothers performed "Memories of El Monte." It can be heard on *Whisky a Go Go, 1968*, for example, where the song gives way to a partly improvised medley of lines from doo-wop songs by groups such as the Shields, the Heartbeats, the Meadowlarks, and others. Just to name one more example: the first and last tracks of 1970's *Burnt Weeny Sandwich* are covers of doo-wop tunes by Black groups of the 1950s, "WPLJ" (originally by the Four Deuces) and "Valarie" (originally by Jackie & the Starlites). "Valarie" was another song the Mothers covered live. On the version recorded for the *Whisky* album, Zappa inserts a spoken parody in the voice of a lovesick teenager, who recounts how on prom night he got to "make it" with his "teenage queen," only to find that she had given him "the clap." That ironic double-voice—honoring the musical form of doo-wop while mocking its themes from the perspective of the mid- to late 1960s sexual mores—was one way that Zappa framed his use of the form. But he also used the juxtapositions created through the structure of the LP album to suggest the formal ironies of his deep eclecticism. Two other tracks on the mostly instrumental album, *Burnt Weeny Sandwich*, pay tribute to Stravinsky: "Igor's Boogie, Phase One" and "Igor's Boogie, Phase Two"—even the titles indicate that these are genre hybrids in pursuit of avant-garde effects.

In 1969, three years after *Freak Out!* was released, a Columbia University a cappella group mutated into the nostalgia band Sha Na Na. With the encouragement of Jimi Hendrix, of all people, they performed at Woodstock and thus were included on the famous triple album in 1970. The early to mid-1970s nostalgia craze for 1950s music and styles began in the 1960s and owes a good deal to that performance by Sha Na Na—and also to Zappa's interest in doo-wop. Even in the mid-1960s, in the heart of the hippie era, even if it was often tongue-in-cheek, musicians and music fans were pleased to find street-smart falsetto-voiced predecessors from the 1950s in the record bins. When I was a young teenager, my family came to possess a radio/record player in a birds-eye maple cabinet with a dial that glowed in the dark. Inside was the previous owner's impressive collection of 45s, which ran from early rock 'n' roll and doo-wop to singles by Peter, Paul & Mary, Bob Dylan (both pre- and post-going electric), and the Byrds (including covers of Dylan songs: "Chimes of Freedom" stood out for me). I devoured all of it. I now see that cabinet full of records as a vivid illustration of the diversity of genres pop music saw in that decade or so, but also of the continuities between the genres—just as expressed through that one collector's taste—from 1950s rock 'n' roll and doo-wop to 1960s folk and folk-rock and psychedelic music.

TOM & JERRY FREAK OUT!

On November 13–14, 1970, Frank Zappa and the Mothers were on the same bill as Sha Na Na at the Fillmore East. Zappa's ironic affection (or affectionate irony) towards doo-wop, part of his sometimes-defiant genre eclecticism, helps to explain that double bill. It also helps to explain an earlier and even stranger double bill: the Mothers of Invention + Simon & Garfunkel. Zappa said in print that the concert took place in 1967,[20] but it seems to have actually been 1969, at the University at Buffalo. Zappa had met Paul Simon and invited the folk duo to join them in Buffalo, but unofficially, under their previous pseudonyms, Tom & Jerry. Zappa told the story simply: "Tom and Jerry" came out, to the audience's chagrin, and only in the encore was it revealed they were really "the one, and only, the magnificent, SIMON & GARFUNKEL," as they performed the huge hit "The Sound of Silence."[21]

In fact, it was even weirder than that. The billing for the show was clearly a piece of performance art by Zappa, not unlike those shows at the Garrick, a way of testing the audience's assumptions about genre and pop music authenticity. A review in the university newspaper reported with a wink of its own that Tom & Jerry "seemed best suited for the folk idiom," but performed "struggling" versions "of several early Everly Brothers tunes and a sloppy version of 'Earth Angel.'"[22] The student reporter then reveals what was not at first obvious to the crowd that evening, that they were Simon & Garfunkel, "leaders of the folk world," who had come to Buffalo to "visit Dada Frank and Company." After the Mothers' set, the duo returned to the stage for an encore—more Everly Brothers and what the reporter sarcastically describes as "a stirring rendition of 'Sounds [sic] of Silence,' circa 1950, complete with shu-bops and dong-dongs, and 'Oh, baby lets do it once in silence.'" Tom & Jerry, a blatantly inauthentic product of the 1950s, played the meta-roles usually reserved in the Mothers' shows for the falsetto-voiced doo-wop singers, the fictional Ruben & the Jets, with the added advantage of shocking the folkies in the audience. In Zappa's own telling, he clearly relishes an encounter after the show with "a college-educated woman" who was offended that he had "made fun" of Simon & Garfunkel, had made them the butt of "some kind of cruel joke."[23] Zappa responds by making fun of *her*, the sincere folk-music fan, for thinking he could have "forced" such "superstars" to sing "OOO-boppa-loochy-bah, she's mine" (what they actually sang was "who-bop-a-loo-chi-bop, you're mine," from their first record, "Hey, Schoolgirl"). The aggrieved audience member didn't know about the earlier life of her folk heroes, so Zappa is also mocking her ignorance. But the larger target of the evening's performance and its retelling is the very idea of authentic and sincere, sacrosanct and pure, genres of music.

The teenage duo, Tom & Jerry (a.k.a. Simon & Garfunkel), were actual high school students when their song, "Hey, Schoolgirl," became a hit way back in 1957. Coincidentally, you'll recall that this was the same year Zappa discovered that first rock 'n' roll doo-wop record with the picture of white kids at a teenage dance party on its cover. Zappa may or may not have differentiated between the doo-wop he admired and the ersatz Everly Brothers in the duo's music. Either way, the experimental billing was clearly about testing the limits of genre, taste, race (implicitly, since doo-wop was for Zappa primarily a Black form), and authenticity of various kinds. The student reviewer in the University of Buffalo newspaper had it right when it came to the central importance of genre for that weird show: the Mothers, he wrote, played "some of the most progressive and engrossing 'modern' music which fell somewhere between the John Cage and Bill Haley and the Comets idiom." His review also observed, apropos of Zappa's closing remarks to the audience, "I have never been told to go screw myself more subtly in my life."

PLAYING (WITH) POP

That satirical disdain Zappa showed his audience and the reporter's sarcasm aside, the review makes a serious point. Zappa did indeed work at the crossroads of rock 'n' roll and modern avant-garde orchestral music, where "Earth

Angel" met Varèse, Ruben & the Jets met Stravinsky. This was no mere personal quirk of the eccentric genius. It grew out of a radical eclecticism that embraced found musical genres, found performers, indeed, found anything. Zappa articulated a philosophy of composition and creativity he aspired to follow in his own work in the acronymic motto, AAAFNRAA: "Anything Anytime Anyplace For No Reason At All."[24] It's a kind of absurdist relative of John Cage's embrace of chance, ambience, and aleatory sounds, and it formally comports with the atonalities and free tempos of Stravinsky and Varèse. Conceptually, as a theory of music making and music appreciation, we can see how it would have dovetailed with Wilson's views. On his radio show, *The Music Factory* (program 5), Wilson told the story of being on tour with the Mothers in Europe. At the Amsterdam concert, Wilson says, Zappa directed them in a passage from Stravinsky's ballet, *Petrushka*. This eclectic performance, Wilson says, "underlines what we say on the [radio] show: that everything is everything."

Wilson shared with Zappa a commitment to a radical eclecticism, which he claimed was the spirit of the age in 1960s pop, as we've seen. When he says that Zappa is not *actually* "pop art," he means that he is engaged in social issues, not cynically ironic (and, maybe with unintended irony, or to defend his initial impression of the band, he cites "Trouble Every Day" as evidence). At the same time, he acknowledges that there is a widespread perception to the contrary. At this distance, it's apparent that both things are true: Zappa was both a relentless satirist who made fun of everything *and* a musician who was serious about music, even when it meant playing found genres. He was also serious about certain fundamental social attachments. He later made tentative forays into electoral politics, served in a kind of ad hoc ambassadorial relationship with Václav Havel and the government of the Czech Republic, and battled Tipper Gore and her organization over labeling and censorship of albums for their offensive lyrics. A similar duality characterized his attitude to musical genres. He both mocked doo-wop and was seriously fond of it. He mocked the L.A. Freak scene but clearly considered himself a part of it. He mocked Simon & Garfunkel's earnest folkie fans and set the duo up in Buffalo as part of an experiment in authenticity, a performance that provoked the audience and revealed the distance between their sentimental folk-music ideals and the raucous rock 'n' roll of Tom & Jerry. In the process, Zappa may have evinced some real affection for the latter's early rock, at least its formal qualities. After all, Tom & Jerry's "Hey, Schoolgirl" was closely adjacent to his own beloved doo-wop.

PLAYING WITH *THE MONKEES*

The same kind of duality applies to Zappa's admiration for the Monkees. He had a similar, partly tongue-in-cheek, appreciation for the prefab made-for-TV band. With whatever degree of sincerity, he seems to have been a fan. He no doubt relished the idea of bucking conventional taste, preferring the Prefab Four over the Fab Four, for example. And he appreciated the musicianship of the actual Monkees, even if it was relatively limited, but also appreciated the early studio-musician-made records released in their name. After all, Zappa and Wilson had hired some of the same "Wrecking Crew" studio musicians for the Animals session that Wilson put him in charge of. Most of all, though, I suspect he enjoyed defying the Authenticity Police, all those who railed against the Monkees as nothing but bubblegum, a commercial pop concoction tantamount to a fraud on the public. For Zappa, they may have seemed like the perfect accidental Dada project: a band found via casting call, turned into a popular recording act, who were becoming something of an interesting creative group in their own right.

Zappa actually appeared on *The Monkees* in a segment for an episode that aired March 11, 1968, near the end of the show's run later that same month. The show added segments to some episodes, brief scenes that broke the frame of the fictional TV world, with the stars sitting in folding chairs revealing that they're on set, not acting but candidly responding as themselves to a question from off-camera. In the final season, each of the Monkees was allowed to invite a guest musician to talk and perform during one of these tag-scene segments. Peter Tork apparently declined. For his segment, Micky Dolenz brought in Tim Buckley, whom he just introduced straight and let sing. Davy Jones sat at the piano with his invited guest, Charlie Smalls, the Black composer, session musician, and performer who would go on to write the music and lyrics for *The Wiz* for Broadway. An awkward exchange ensued about "Black soul" and "white soul," reducing the difference between them to which beats in a measure the music emphasizes, either the downbeat or the upbeat, the 1 and the 3, or the 2 and the 4. Smalls plays an example from Latin music that combines the two. The result, as Jones is just a little too quick (and relieved) to say, proves that "*everyone's* got soul!"

When it was his turn, Michael Nesmith invited Frank Zappa, who was made up to look like Mike on the show, complete with the signature green stocking cap and double-breasted button-up blue shirt. Nesmith, in turn, wears a wig, a fake beard, and a prosthetic nose in order to play Zappa. The two improvise a stilted conversation in each other's characters (sometimes confusingly slipping out of character), about the differences between the Monkees and the Mothers, among other topics. For example, Zappa to Nesmith (playing Zappa), asks, "When you first got into the psychedelic music business, was it very difficult?" Then, with a quick cut, they move together to a piano, and Zappa (playing Nesmith) asks: "You know that, after I quit the show, I'm gonna join the Byrds, don't'cha?" And Nesmith (playing Zappa) refers to the Monkees' music as "sometimes thought of as banal and insipid" and asks about the "soul" of Monkees music. The skit thus becomes a satiric retort to Jones's segment with Smalls, which had aired just the previous week, mocking the whole idea that musical beats could reflect essential racial or (sub)cultural differences.

Rather than play the piano, they move on to a loading dock on set where they proceed to "play" an antique car. Nesmith conducts Zappa, who smashes the car with a chain and a sledgehammer. He ends up spraying a fire extinguisher on the exploding engine, then turning the extinguisher on the camera. The whole thing may have been inspired by Zappa's earlier TV appearance on Steve Allen's show, but with a car instead of a bike and demonstrating a more extreme and violent form of "playing." The bit is sped up like a Keystone Cops movie (or a Monkees "romp"). Zappa/Nesmith smashes the car while we hear a bit of the Mothers of Invention's "Mother People" (from *We're Only in It for the Money*). Avant-garde absurdity serves as a refuge from the whole slippery notion, often racially inflected, of musical authenticity.

Later that same year, in November 1968, the Monkees' semi-underground movie, *Head*, was released, and Zappa had a brief surreal cameo in the film. Zappa shows up absurdly leading a cow, and laconically engages Jones in a bit of dialogue about music, race, and the popular audience ("That song was pretty white"). Zappa is theoretically playing a character, "the Critic," but the scene likely reflects his actual attitude about the music business. It takes swipes at the uncomprehending youth audience (he tells Jones, mock-sincerely, that the youth of America are counting on him), and thus, obliquely, at the exaggerated self-importance of pop musicians. But he reads the lines as himself a "pretty white" and self-important musician, who was always looking for found instruments, sounds, and performers, as the means to realize his own compositions. The paradox is the point, the place where Zappa always situated himself as he sought to exploit the productive tensions of the space *between* pop and serious composition, the blues and Stravinsky, doo-wop and Varèse.

CHAPTER SIX

YOUNG MAN WITH A HORN

Hugh Masekela, *The Americanization of Ooga Booga* (1966);
Hugh Masekela's Next Album (1966);
Grrr (recorded 1965; released 1966)

OUT OF THE (VILLAGE) GATE

November 1965, Greenwich Village: Tom Wilson was busy that month collecting live recordings of the Blues Project at the Cafe Au Go Go at 152 Bleecker Street. The recordings were captured on tape out of the parade of blues and blues-rock bands that played "The Blues Bag" show he had booked there. Together with other tracks recorded a couple of months later, these performances by the Blues Project would become the band's first album. At around that same time, Wilson regularly dropped into the venue across the street, the Village Gate. Earlier, in March 1965, for example, he could theoretically have seen there his friends from the Transition Records days, Sun Ra and Cecil Taylor, along with Albert Ayler, John Coltrane, and others, who were all on the same bill at the Village Gate for a benefit concert in support of Amiri Baraka's Black Arts Repertory Theatre School in Harlem. Performances by most participants—but not Sun Ra and the Arkestra—were released in November as an album on Impulse! Records, *The New Wave in Jazz*. On multiple nights that year Wilson heard electrifying sets at the same club by a jazz quartet fronted by a gifted twenty-five-year-old trumpet player from South Africa, Hugh Masekela. Masekela later declared that Wilson "never missed any of [his] performances at the Village Gate."[1]

Wilson moved to sign and begin producing the young trumpeter, whose global aspirations were so in sync with his own attitude about the eclectic diversity of world music. As Masekela later said, the songs he wrote and performed "were a hybrid of traditional and ethnic chants, township dance, and Caribbean calypso-like grooves mixed with jazz and Brazilian sambas. It was a potpourri of the music of the African diaspora."[2] Masekela's albums (and not only those produced by Wilson) were crossover projects linking South African township music, pan-African, and global diasporic sounds to American jazz, but also to contemporary R&B and global pop music. This ambitious crossing, this cosmopolitan openness so in tune with Wilson's professed catholicity of taste, was no doubt reinforced by his exile from apartheid South Africa. But it was also the kind of diverse mix out of which his music had emerged in the first place: such eclecticism was for Masekela the heart of modern African music.

GRAZING IN THE GENRES

Even if you don't know it by title, you have probably heard the 1968 pop instrumental by Masekela, "Grazing in the Grass." The global hit song remains instantly recognizable, with its infectious up-and-down guitar riff (played on the record by Bruce Langhorne), piano-chord rhythm, and rapid sixteenth-note cowbell (played by Masekela with drumsticks and held up by Langhorne) to establish its highly danceable groove. But the true hook is its melody, composed by Philemon Hou and played by Masekela on the trumpet, notes that soar above the beat. The song was created casually, on the spot, just to fill out an album, but once it was released the single shot up the charts. The single was inducted into the Grammy Hall of Fame in 2018, the year Masekela died. He once called it "the biggest record that I ever had," and in a cool understatement, said it was just "a typical South African dance tune," recorded in "half an hour," in one take.[3] It is in fact a perfect pop record, combining features of R&B, jazz, *and* South African township music with a dance beat and a highly memorable tune.

So, it's interesting that the B side of that monster hit single was a more obviously and self-consciously African song, "Bajabula Bonke (Healing Song)," which the trumpeter first released in 1966 as the opening track on his live album, *The Americanization of Ooga Booga*. *That* song, by contrast, is built on a slow-walking two-chord piano part, backed with bass and percussion, supporting a syncopated, partly improvised, wide-ranging vocal in the Zulu language, sung by Masekela, with backing by pianist Larry Willis and other members of the group. Introducing it on the live album, Masekela tells the audience that the song is from Swaziland (now Eswatini), and that he learned it from his then-wife, the celebrated singer Miriam Makeba (she's in fact credited as the songwriter), who in turn had learned it from her mother, a traditional healer. In other words, it's a kind of African folk song. Its essential story is kin to the familiar blues tradition ("nobody loves you when you're down and out"), a lament that everyone is rejoicing in the singer's illness. Masekela's arrangement and style of playing, however, sets the folk song in the frame of meditative jazz. He would go on to record other versions and perform it live many times, arranging it differently with different combos, sometimes including trombone and saxophone, for example.

The most famous version of "Bajabula Bonke (Healing Song)," is probably his performance of it at the Monterey Pop festival in 1967.[4] Wearing oval horn-rimmed glasses and a striped sweater with a beaded necklace, Masekela shouts out the tune, backed by the band, including a turbaned Big Black (Danny Rey) on congas. Masekela improvises the vocal as if he were playing a loud and powerful horn. About halfway in, he follows a trombone solo by joining in with his trumpet in a rhythmic horn section—trumpet, saxophone, and trombone. It's an exciting performance by the group, a remarkable demonstration of Zulu-language folk music folded into a swinging jazz mix. Because this was the summer of 1967, animated op-art psychedelic projections run on big screens behind the band.

On the B side of the 7-inch single, African folk music with a jazz twist; on the A side, a jazzy pop tune based on township dance music. Each song was genre-crossing in its own way. Or, more like genre crisscrossing: the pair of songs taken together also represent the hybridity Masekela said he was after. This chapter is about that genre (criss)crossing, first fully realized in a pair of albums that appeared in 1966: *The Americanization of Ooga Booga* and *Hugh Masekela's Next Album*. Both were produced by Tom Wilson. (There was only a brief window when the two collaborated. I refer below to a third album from that same year—one not produced by Wilson. It was the first record Masekela made after he left Wilson and MGM—*The Emancipation of Hugh Masekela*.) One of the two albums, *The Americanization of Ooga Booga*, prominently featured Masekela's "ethnic"-music/jazz hybrid; the other, *Hugh Masekela's Next Album*, was mostly a collection of covers of contemporary pop songs, including by the Mamas & the Papas, the Beatles, and Paul Simon, along with a few original tunes.

Taken together, the two albums of 1966–1967 tell us everything about Masekela's ambitions in 1966. He wanted to create his own version of a South African jazz hybrid, and he wanted to make a dent in the American pop charts. His eclecticism was grounded in ambition. The two albums also suggest that his eclecticism was very likely influenced and enhanced by Wilson. He had attempted to make Sun Ra's experimental jazz accessible to a wider audience with *The Futuristic Sounds of Sun Ra*, in the belief that Sun Ra's own hybrid music might speak to the eclecticism of the times. Though it originated on another continent, in Masekela's case the music was not otherworldly, like Sun Ra's, but deliberately down to earth, representing local township style, remixed and hybridized for a global audience. International, intercultural, inescapably political, the music was the result of a series of complex crossings made by the young aspiring musician. In this way, Masekela's music of 1966 helps us to understand the ambiguities of identity and the shifts in genre that characterized American pop as a whole that year.

POTPOURRI OF THE DIASPORA

In 1964, Masekela was living in New York, newly exiled. He had left South Africa after the 1960 Sharpeville Massacre and subsequent violent clampdown by the apartheid government. In 1963 he decided, on the advice of Harry Belafonte and others, that it would not be safe for him to return home. As he was finishing his studies at the Manhattan School of Music, he played some gigs in New York clubs and began developing his own sound, not just American jazz or South African pop but a hybrid of the two (with additional influences in the mix). Even back in South Africa, Masekela remembered, when he had played in shebeens (township bars) with the Jazz Epistles big band, they were writing original music that was "a cross between mbaqanga [a Zulu musical style that was itself influenced by American swing and pop music] and bebop."[5] Masekela labeled this hybrid "township bop." In fact, South African big bands in the 1950s had already been composing "township versions of American swing music," coming up with "styles that came to be known as *marabi*, *mbhaqanga*, *jit*, and *kwela*, hybrids that have stood the test of time."[6] When Masekela was young he heard all of these styles: "township Kwela bands, penny whistle combos, male and female trios and quartets, famous singers from home and abroad, gospel choirs and American swing bands."[7]

Masekela's pursuit of hybrids was variously motivated: it was a protest against the apartheid system's rigid segregation and a countercultural demonstration of the power of racial intermixtures, as well as being a synthetic act of musical creativity. Kathleen Boyle's liner notes for 1968's *The Lasting Impression of Hugh Masekela* explicitly connect the trumpeter's world music, his sudden fame, and the timing of the "Black is Beautiful" cultural movement. His appeal crossed both genre and racial boundaries. To illustrate the point, Boyle describes the audience at another of his concerts from that time: "An equal mix of dashikis and mini-skirts, of Afros and 'hippy' hair." Masekela always told his story as an assertion of independence and a search for his own authentic musical identity. But his story unfolded on an international stage. It reflected the musician's pragmatic idea of the value of shared traditions and cultural exchange, and it took place against the backdrop of apartheid back home in South Africa, where racial and ethnic identity were highly contested matters of life and death.

As we've seen, *The Americanization of Ooga Booga* was recorded live at the Village Gate in November 1965 and released in June 1966. Along with its introductions, crowd responses, vocals by the band, and varied mix of songs, it's a document of a kind of workshop/performance, a demonstration of Masekela's way of combining musical styles. Some of the recorded tapes were set aside. Six additional tracks not included on the album were later released in December 1968 as a separate album (mentioned above), *The Lasting Impression of Hugh Masekela*.[8] In 1966, Masekela was himself a young man with a horn, coming into some renown. He played mostly instrumental jazz on trumpet (sometimes cornet or flugelhorn) and foregrounded his experiments in genre. Despite his use of the term "potpourri," Masekela's music was less a blended mixture than a multiply-grafted tree, a series of performative displays of his often-flamboyant acts of genre-splicing.

WITH A HORN

A word, here, about trumpet music in 1966. The electric guitar was already at that point a symbol and synecdoche for rock 'n' roll. All the same, there were horns everywhere at the time, including in rock and pop. Saxophone had remained prominent in rock, as it would continue to do. Trumpets were rarer. But sometimes a solo trumpet was even featured on a track by a guitar-playing band, where it stood out from the mix, adding something different to the usual stringed-instrument combo. For example, the Byrds' "So You Want to Be a Rock 'n' Roll Star" (1967) featured a signature trumpet solo by Masekela himself.

In pop as a whole, by far the most prominent trumpet on the airwaves in 1966 belonged to Herb Alpert. His catchy instrumentals, many mariachi-inspired (Alpert, who was Jewish, named the band the Tijuana Brass and promoted the image), topped the charts in 1965–1966: *Whipped Cream & Other Delights* (1965), *Going Places* (1966), *What Now My Love* (1966), and *S.R.O.* (1966). Like Masekela, Alpert mixed a derivative "ethnic" music (in his case, heard while traveling in Mexico) with contemporary pop and jazz. Years later, the two collaborated on an album in 1978 that included tracks written or cowritten by Masekela's friend and colleague, South African composer Caiphus Semenya. That same year, 1978, Masekela and Alpert released a joint live album, *Main Event Live*, which employed a funky rhythm section. Its track list included several songs by South African composer and jazz trombonist Jonas Gwangwa (who also played on the album).

There are many examples in 1966–1967, from the iconic trumpet solo on "These Boots Are Made for Walkin'" (1966), to the baroque piccolo trumpet solo in the Beatles's "Penny Lane" (released as a single in February 1967), and the soul-review horn section in "Got to Get You into My Life," from *Revolver* (1966). When Al Kooper left the Blues Project in 1967 and, with Steve Katz, formed Blood, Sweat & Tears, it was at least partly over the conflict of whether to add horns to the band (Kooper pushed for it). His landmark *Super Session* album of 1968, with Mike Bloomfield and Stephen Stills, included a horn section arranged in an R&B style. Many R&B and funk records of the mid- to late 1960s included horns—especially solo alto or tenor saxophone, but also sometimes brass ensembles or solo trumpets. James Brown's music is one powerful example, as are Cynthia Robinson's trumpet parts for Sly & the Family Stone. See also Otis Redding and countless Motown and Stax/Volt R&B and soul records. Masekela later recalled that Motown and Stax "had the greatest impact" on him at that time.[9] Besides going to a lot of jazz clubs after he arrived in New York, Masekela recalls once going uptown to hear Brown at the Apollo.[10] Even psychedelic pop sometimes featured horns, for example as part of the larger orchestral arrangements for Brian Wilson and the Beach Boys' *Pet Sounds*. A less well-known example is Arthur Lee and Love's "Alone Again Or," released as the opening track of Love's album, *Forever Changes* (1967). Its Latin rhythm, acoustic guitar, string section, and brass—including a key trumpet solo at the bridge—give the song a mariachi-on-acid feel.[11]

The trumpet remained central in 1960s jazz. Prominent examples included Dizzy Gillespie, Miles Davis, and, still having an outsized influence, Louis Armstrong. Masekela knew them all. Armstrong had sent him a trumpet when he was still a student, but he was especially close to Dizzy, who was among the handful of influential Black musicians in America who took him under their wing when he first came to New York to study. Masekela also knew Davis, the most important innovator on the trumpet of the era. The young South African wrote a song, "Mixolydia," the title a play on both the musical mode and a fictional woman's name. When introducing it on *Ooga Booga*, Masekela dedicates the song to Miles Davis and John Coltrane, "two very great musicians who have had a very heavy impact on the cause of modern music." Miles, then recording with his second quintet, was on the cusp of fusion and funk experiments, including his own version of "going electric," using microphones and special distortion effects, eventually the wah-wah pedal, for example, to augment his use of mutes and a range of techniques to achieve a variety of tones linked to different genres.[12]

THE MOTION PICTURE

Masekela was always a fan of American jazz, traditional and modern, across a wide spectrum of styles. His own self-created origin story as a musician begins with seeing the movie *Young Man with a Horn* in 1953.[13] In the film, Kirk Douglas plays Rick Martin, a white trumpet player, based in part on Bix Beiderbecke; the big-band musician Harry James overdubbed the trumpet parts. Martin is inspired by listening to Black jazz musicians, starting with his friend and mentor, a Black bandleader named Art Hazzard. Martin is a loner who becomes a doomed addict, but he has a transcendent talent. He carries his trumpet with him like a fetish object everywhere he goes, even when he's down and out. His is also a story about the conflict between racially inflected subgenres: swing, played by mostly white bands, and blues-based New Orleans–style jazz, played by a mostly Black band. At one point, Martin admits that he leads a musical double life, that he had "started playing two ways"—one way for money, with the mostly white dance bands, and one way for himself, which he calls "the way of feeling"—with an all-Black small combo engaging in freewheeling improvisation. Hired by one big band, he is immediately warned in thinly veiled racist terms: "no blues and no low-down jive." Naturally he starts a hot jam session and gets fired. Before that happens, though, he plays a lot of fancy evening gigs with the refined swing band, then escapes after-hours to a dive bar where he can let loose with the Black musicians whose music he really loves, jamming with a group led by Hazzard, his old mentor. The white swing-band director refers to the Hazzard group dismissively as only a "spasm band," a derogatory term derived from New Orleans street music, implying a rag-tag, unprofessional style and sometimes relying on found objects as instruments (bucket drums, washtub bass). Martin shuffles back and forth between these two musical worlds, always feeling torn, self-divided. When he finally suffers an alcoholic breakdown, he finds himself wandering in the Black part of town. There he collapses, desperately clutching a pawn-shop trumpet. He is discovered and taken to a sanatorium.

It seems like a strange story to inspire a young musician. But in his autobiography, Masekela emphasizes in his own story echoes of the early part of the movie's plot—how he finally got a horn, first a second-hand pawn-shop trumpet, then, eventually, one he received from America as a gift from Louis Armstrong. He carried that gift horn with him to music schools in London and New York. In the film, the main character always has the horn with him and clings to it as he falls prey to alcoholism. In his memoir, Masekela tells of his own experiences with drugs after he became successful. For Masekela, the Armstrong trumpet was invested with symbolic significance, providing a link "not just to Armstrong, but to a long, powerful tradition that had crisscrossed the Atlantic from Africa to America and back."[14] That crisscrossing journey, of course, mirrored his own.

The movie represents two divided worlds and Martin's ultimately failed attempt to cross and recross the boundary between them. Masekela's mother had a white father, but she refused on principle the relative privileges afforded a "colored person" in apartheid South Africa, Masekela says; he and his sisters "were never considered black enough to be seen as African, nor were we light enough to be totally accepted by our colored relatives."[15] Seeing Kirk Douglas in the film while he was living in South Africa, hearing the real-life white musician Harry James play the trumpet parts, inspired the young Masekela to play the trumpet himself: that movie, with that soundtrack, viewed in that particular situation. His inspiration was always linked to the problem of divided musical styles and genres, the divisions mapped onto different racial identities and cultures. The tragedy of the movie's lead character is that he can't help but try to cross the lines, even though he never really finds a home on either side. Masekela's own career would be spent in similar, though more successful, border crossings, of musical genres as well as racial and (in his case) national identities. He chafed against any assumed division as a barrier to personal expression. He had played the raucous township scene with the Black bebop band, the Jazz Epistles; he studied music theory and trumpet technique in London and New York; he made a mark on the downtown jazz scene; he moved to California, where he recorded with rock and pop musicians and performed at famous venues and landmark festivals. He was consistently outspoken against apartheid in his own country and spoke against racism and discrimination globally. That outspokenness is one reason he was advised not to return immediately to South Africa. Early on, his mentors were Harry Belafonte and Miriam Makeba (he had known Makeba in South Africa, and the two were married from 1964–1966).[16] He would eventually work with Fela Kuti and many other African musicians, and would return to Africa in the 1980s, by then a revered artist and activist. In 1987, he performed with Paul Simon—whom he had first met in Wilson's office in Manhattan—and an ensemble of other African musicians on the *Graceland* tour.

OOGA BOOGA

In *Young Man with a Horn*, Martin carries around a large record collection as he moves from place to place—his most important possession after his trumpet. "We ought to make our own records," he says, at one point, but the market for popular music is crowding out jazz. Once again, the convenient scapegoats, "high-school girls," are blamed. They buy only new pop records, we're told, to learn the words—they don't truly care about the music. In one recording studio scene, the band cuts a record straight to vinyl, using a recording machine in the booth with its needle set on a blank disc. Making records, as well as collecting them, is mythologized in the movie as much as playing live jazz is.

Masekela was planning to make records of his own from the time he arrived in New York and watched Makeba's recording career on the rise. Belafonte and others encouraged him, and so he made his first album, *Trumpet Africaine*, in 1962—a record he quickly came to regret as "a disaster, an unlistenable mixture of elevator and shopping mall music."[17] Its arrangements and song choice were to blame, he thought—in effect its overall production. Belafonte himself dismissed the results as "antiseptic, jive, white music."[18] Thereafter, Masekela consciously tried to lose his "fascination with all things American"—or perhaps he means *white* American—and look more to his experience with South African music as inspiration. In the years that immediately followed, after listening to the advice of fellow musicians, Masekela decided to pursue a more interesting and, for him, authentic mixture of South African township music and American jazz (with a contemporary international pop flavor).

It was this canny hybrid music that Wilson heard him play with his ensemble downtown at the Village Gate. It's no wonder that Wilson—with his own ideal of global eclecticism, his background in jazz, and his interest in musical hybrids of all kinds—immediately signed Masekela to a record deal at MGM. The result was technically Masekela's third album (more on that in a minute), *The Americanization of Ooga Booga* (1966). It's a live album, an audio snapshot of the scene at the Village Gate in late 1965. You can hear the back-and-forth between the audience and the band between songs (there seem to have been a number of fellow South African musicians in the audience). The mocking title actually makes a serious point about the energetic fusion of worlds that Masekela sought to bring to that scene. But it is mocking since this fusion of worlds was nothing as simple as "Americanization." On the contrary, Masekela's performances, as documented in the album, represented a kind of Africanization of the downtown New York jazz scene. Soon he would do the same on the record charts.

What is "ooga booga?" The offensiveness of the term is the whole point. Exiled South African musicians in Masekela's circle used it as a sort of jive satire, reclaiming the term and turning it around on their white audiences. The liner notes by Wilson explain it with a bit of a fractured fairy tale, in which "GOLDILOCKS" exclaims, "My, my, an African! How cultural! What language do you speak?" and "MASEKELA" replies, "OOGA BOOGA, Lady."

A bystander asks about the exchange and "MASEKELA" explains that when he was a boy, he saw Tarzan in the movies, which included "parodies of Africa and Africans." Even the young Masekela was bothered by those fake movie Africans spouting phrases like "Ooga Booga Bwana!" Many still entertain such B-movie clichés, he says, and "when one of those gushing types at a cocktail party twists my arm to say something in African, I just say, 'Ooga Booga'—which I learned from Tarzan. And, they dig it." Wilson continues in his own voice: "With a sort of black-humor twist, Ooga Booga has become the password of expatriate South African musicians in the States." He suggests, half seriously, that Masekela is the leader of a musical movement, "brilliant, earthy, hard-swinging, rebellious Ooga-Boogists." In his autobiography, Masekela is blunt about his own actual experience when it came to exchanges about "authentic" African identity, about being "shocked" at how many Americans still "believed the outrageous, stereotypical bullshit about Africans still living in the Stone Age gathered from Tarzan films, Nyoka the Jungle Girl, Jungle Jim cinema serials, comic books, and other ignorant portrayals."[19] Interestingly, the example he cites is a Thanksgiving visit to a Black American family. Even the kids in this Black family ask him to speak African languages and marvel at the exotic sounds. Later, he says, when he met other African Americans who were free of such primitivist stereotypes ("bullshit"), he assumes that they've had to overcome a conservative disinformation campaign that has limited what most Black Americans know about their African ancestry.[20]

The cover of the album reinforces the "black-humor twist" as Wilson calls it (pun surely intended). It's a caricature of the fetish of "authentic" African identity. The title is set in a red, white, and blue border around a photo of Masekela, wearing a suit, carrying a briefcase, newspaper and hat in hand—and barefoot. He stands on some rocks, amid tropical foliage. He looks up at the camera with a serious expression on his face. Among other things, it's a parody of the flood of exotica records on the market at the time that advertised African, Afro-Caribbean, Polynesian, or Latin music of South America, or the idea of such music, using "primitive" jungle or tribal imagery. In fact, it may well be a direct parody of the cover of Les Baxter's *Jungle Jazz* (1959), which shows what appears to be an Amazonian man in a loincloth, holding a machete and standing amid tropical-jungle foliage, in a pose similar to the one on the Masekela cover. Many of the Baxter album's tracks have place-name titles—"Brazilia," "Rain Forest," and "Amazon Falls," but also "Isle of Cuba" and "Voodoo Dreams"—that reveal just how generalized (and race-based) its idea of "jungle" music is. Baxter put out another album that same year (1959) called *African Jazz*. Its cover shows a grinning woman in bizarre "tribal" makeup and headgear. On his album, on the other hand, Masekela's defiant stare and business suit defy the kind of exoticism seen on Baxter's album cover, and defy the record-buying public's expectations, as well, their desire for the Tarzan-style primitivism he routinely responded to with the mocking "ooga booga."

Masekela was raised to resist any such reductive primitivism. He recalls that his father, a self-educated but learned man, a sculptor who was friends with a well-known painter Gerard Sekoto, was adamant in this regard. Masekela's father and Sekoto would not accept the titles of "woodcarvers and sketchers, the terms used for African artists. They demanded to be called sculptors and artists just like their white counterparts, who often copied their styles and made huge profits by doing so."[21] Masekela was fully aware of the economic exploitation that underlay promotions of the supposedly "authentic" African art and culture as "exotic" and "primitive."

The satirical album cover for *The Americanization of Ooga Booga* strikes a kind of preemptive blow against reductive exploitation. That satire existed in tension with the fact that the record companies—and even, to a degree, Wilson—leveraged the public's ideas about African music and culture at the time, the very ideas Masekela's cover image was mocking. Indeed, Wilson himself had earlier (1959) produced an album for United Artists by the jazz flautist Herbie Mann called *Herbie Mann's African Suite*. The Afro-jazz sound on the album is supported by the vibraphone of Johnny Rae (the album was originally attributed to Rae instead of Mann to skirt a contractual obligation Mann still had to Verve at the time), and the swinging flute of Mann himself. The cover for the album is typical exotica: a red- and green-lit multiple-exposure photomontage of entangled male and female dancers, semi-topless in sarongs, bodies posed ecstatically, erotically, behind a rough-carved African drum.

By 1966, the satire of the *Ooga Booga* cover image fit with Wilson's own acerbic sense of humor as well as Masekela's, although it's hard to know precisely how much influence the producer had over the photo session and cover design. At Verve, Art Director Acy R. Lehman is credited with design. Lehman was also the art director responsible for the peelable banana cover based on a print by Andy Warhol used for *The Velvet Underground & Nico*. For the later release of the additional Masekela tracks from that 1965 show at the Village Gate on another album, *The Lasting Impression of Hugh Masekela* (1968), the cover design showed a closeup of barefoot footprints in dark mud, with a trumpet standing upright on its bell.

IMAGES OF CONTESTED IDENTITY

To better understand these satirical cover images, we can set them against a more famous shot of Masekela, taken by the later-famous South African photographer Alf Kumalo in 1956. Masekela was only sixteen at the time, but he was already playing in the Huddleston Jazz Band at his boarding school in Johannesburg. And he was recently the recipient of that iconic gift-trumpet sent by

Armstrong. So Kumalo arranged a portrait of the young man with *that* horn, as Masekela would later recall:

> He took me to Sophiatown, Joburg's glamorous township, where he made me take off my expensive shoes, roll up my pants' cuffs and jump into the air holding the trumpet high above my head. I hated the picture because it was so square and unhip; an image that would lose me buddies like myself who were into beautiful threads, not to mention my girlfriends.[22]

Kumalo reassures him, predicting the photo would become famous. It did. It was later used for various publicity purposes, and Masekela agreed to use it for the cover image of his autobiography, *Still Grazing*.

In the photo, the young Masekela is caught midair, spread-eagled, the horn in his right hand and his tongue hanging out. (It's oddly like a premonition of Michael Jordan's famous image being used as the "Jumpman" logo for Nike.) What you notice secondarily, behind the jumping body, is a crowd of urban township residents in the background, standing and watching, most with serious expressions. One man in particular wears a suit and hat, standing off to the right of the frame, a little sideways, with his hands in his pockets, and appears unimpressed by the staged-for-the-camera celebration. Masekela's own reaction to the photo—he said that later in life Kumalo constantly tried to get him to reenact it, but he refused—was brutally simple in his own adolescent mind: the staged "spontaneous" joy was embarrassing, fake African authenticity. His image was too "country," he complained, with his rolled-up pants. It was phony in its performed simplicity.

The images for the 1966–1968 albums serve as one answer from the adult Masekela to that 1956 photo—however much he knew and loved the photographer, his friend, and however excited he truly was to have the horn from Armstrong. In addition, the album covers, centered around Masekela's serious gaze, aimed at the camera, preemptively say that the musician sees through it all, including the faux-African exotica and the stereotype of African jazz held by many in the record-buying audience. It's all ooga booga (which is bullshit). He's too cool to take it seriously, too busy playing the sophisticated music actually recorded on the albums to care about the "Americanization" of his identity. The voice of the bandleader as he quietly introduces tracks and addresses the "ladies and gentlemen" of the audience in the club is that of a serious professional artist—and also of a confident, cosmopolitan ambassador of sorts for the real South Africa he had left behind.

One more example of Masekela's using this kind of mocking, preemptive satire—and of how closely tied up it was with his professional ambitions. When he formed his own production company with saxophonist Stewart Levine, he named it Oo-Bwana, pronounced "double-o Bwana," after the 007 of the international spy, James Bond—combined with the East-African word for "boss." Another deliberate cultural hybrid. The partnership with Levine was inspired by the partnership of Stan Getz and João Gilberto, whose "Girl from Ipanema" had conquered the pop charts in 1964 and won a Grammy in 1965 (the album had, incidentally, come out on Verve Records). "We figured that if Stewart assumed a similar kind of persona on his saxophone and fused South African township music with American jazz, we could come up with a popular hybrid."[23] Note that the project involved assuming a somewhat artificial musical persona, and that the hybrid forms that Masekela and Stewart were after were meant from the start to be broadly popular.

MAKING HYBRIDITY HAPPEN

Each of the tracks on *The Americanization of Ooga Booga* demonstrates this search for a popular hybrid of township music and jazz, as Masekela's later comments make clear. Once Masekela had formed the quartet, the first song he composed for them was "U-Dwi (Song to My Mother)" (track 5), the title being his mother's nickname. He calls it, tellingly, "an uptempo mbhaqanga shuffle, which had a heavy bebop and merengue groove."[24] Note the genre mixture: a township dance tune grafted onto modern jazz and Latin rhythms. Then, traditional African folk tunes, "Dzinorabiro (The Good Old Days)" and "Abangoma (Song of Praise)" (tracks 2 and 7) are included, with call-and-response vocals by Masekela and pianist Larry Willis—"before jazzing up our solos," as he says. You can hear the "seam" of the combination, where the hybrid is formed, a little over halfway through "Dzinorabiro," when Willis takes off from the folk song melody in a swinging solo. African vocal styles clearly influence the improvisational structures of the instrumentals. Masekela's solos often include horn-specific sound effects, such as valve flutters, tonguing, half-valve squawks, creating a whole palette of tones and timbres that echo the sonic variety of his and Willis's vocals, which contain traditional folk song growls and Xhosa-language clicks and broken-up or scaled melodies.[25] Vocal sound effects—growls, syllabic bass rhythm parts, shouting—are part of township singing and chanting.

All of these African elements in the sound would surely have read as "ethnic" folk music for many audience members at the time. The folk craze had not entirely dissipated, even in Greenwich Village. Framing the music as folk would have followed a familiar set of conventions. Indeed, the album often sounds as if Masekela were teaching a seminar or leading a workshop at a folk festival, where the provenance of a song and its cultural contexts are given to educate and enhance the listener's full appreciation. Those contexts can be contemporary as well as traditional. Songs like "Bajabula Bonke (Healing Song)" (track 1) are juxtaposed with new songs like "U'nhlanhla (Lucky Boy)" (track 3), written by Masekela's daughter about her cousin in South Africa, which Masekela later characterized simply as "a mid-tempo shuffle." The audience is led to compare the modern jazz tunes by the African trumpeter with reimagined African folk songs played in a similar jazz mode.

American jazz, including contemporary bebop and post-bop music, runs throughout the Masekela quartet's sound. Referring to those passages when the band breaks into "a furious double tempo, with Henry and Hal playing feverishly against Larry's vamping and my solo," Masekela calls the sound "reminiscent of Coltrane's quintet." And then there's the album's closing track (number 8), "Mixolydia," that callout to modal jazz that on the album he introduces as a tribute to Miles Davis and John Coltrane in particular. Later he called the tune "a cross between . . . 'All Blues,' and 'Trane's 'Favorite Things.'" Track 4 is a cover of Herbie Hancock's "Cantaloupe Island," which had been included on Hancock's 1964 Blue Note album, *Empyrean Isles*. Hancock was at that moment in the mid-1960s on the cusp of engaging hybrid fusions in his own music, like his jazz-pop soundtrack for the 1966 film *Blow-Up*, released as an album in 1967. A Latin influence is also present on the *Ooga Booga* album, as on track 6, "Masquenada," by the Brazilian guitarist, Jorge Ben. Among other tracks from the live recordings that evening, one that was not included on *Ooga Booga* but appeared on the *Lasting Impression* album in 1968 is "Con Mucho Carino," which Masekela describes as "a fast-paced Juajuanco-jazz kind of salsa"—referring to the genre of Afro-Cuban Guaguancó rumba music.[26]

The introductions, with brief descriptions and stories by the bandleader, contextualize the music, letting us know in particular how the songs and modes of playing emerged from township culture. We are told about the musicians and the menial day jobs they are forced to take in the townships (selling cigarettes, for example, or serving as "messenger boys"), but also about their playing together at night in the shebeens and dancehalls, and how "they burn those places up till daybreak." Introducing track 2, "Dzinoraboro," Masekela says it's the kind of song rural workers sing as they ride trains to labor in the coal mines of Johannesburg. The lyrics, he says, are about "reminiscing" about "times of old," celebrating not a primitive but a precolonial Africa, "when the sky was the roof and the ground was the floor and things were much less complicated." He introduces track 7, "Abangoma," as being about the people of the same name who are among the few to still "live the old life of our forefathers." But he reframes the nostalgia, which verges on romantic primitivism, in the wider context of actual Africans' awareness of African heritage, saying that people "all over the countryside are always singing [the] praises" of these contemporary people, who are actively preserving a traditional way of life in the present. Masekela characterizes the song as just another example of "singing the praises" of the Abangoma, placing it in the context of a broader contemporary African culture that deliberately holds up traditional ways of life as an act of resistance to colonialism and apartheid.

The album as a whole is structured so that it opens with the traditional Zulu-language "Healing Song" ("Bajabula Bonke") and ends with "Myxolydia," the cheeky tribute to contemporary bebop and modal jazz. The point is clear: Masekela is a cosmopolitan musician engaged in a deliberate program of crossing, of artistic hybridization. He's on a musical mission. The result is nothing like the vague primitivism or exoticism the record-buying public might expect.

NEXT

Soon after *The Americanization of Ooga Booga* was released in June 1966, a second Masekela album came out, also produced by Tom Wilson, *Hugh Masekela's Next Album*. The two, so close in release time, have to be seen as deliberate bookends. In a key scene in *Young Man with a Horn*, Kirk Douglas's Rick Martin has moved to New York City. The camera follows him, excited, as he walks diagonally across Times Square—right in front of the giant Bond clothing store sign and the marquee of the Criterion Theatre. The cover photo for *Hugh Masekela's Next Album* was shot at that same spot one quiet Sunday morning, from almost the same camera angle. In this tableau Masekela poses in the middle of the street, a different young man with a horn, staking his own territorial claim to the usually very busy intersection. The urban intersection invites the metaphor: Masekela's music-making takes place at the intersection of radically different styles and cultures, through a cosmopolitan hybridity on which he was now prepared to base his career.

In the image, once again Masekela stands barefoot in a suit, mocking the viewer's likely expectations about Africans, exposing the general ignorance of actual South African culture and the musician's origins in complex urban townships. Once again there's a briefcase and hat, this time dropped to the pavement beside him. Instead of striding through the jungle, he's on the street, casually leaning with one elbow on a near life-sized stuffed giraffe. It's absurd, silly looking. But he stares down the camera lens, daring the viewer to indulge in the reductive stereotypes. Masekela holds a tall spear in one hand and a trumpet in the other, fingers on the valves, ready to play—the horn, rather than the spear, a weapon in an artistic battle. Even the font used for the title on the album cover contributes to the dissonance. It's a wiggly typeface that signified the "exotic" at the time.[27] But it's read against the New York streets. In case you miss the point, Tom Wilson's liner note for the *Ooga Booga* album paints a vivid picture:

> Johannesburg at that time was a colorful jumble of tribal and urban traditions. It was a brilliant whirl of rainbow robes, double-breasted suits, rubber boots, feathers, spears, dice, bibles, black, yellow, brown, the wail of Xosa chants overlaid with the bittersweet sound of bebop blaring from gramophones. Hugh remembers Friday nights when Zulus, Xosas, Pedis, Lozis, and Sothos piled together into town from the countryside bringing laughter, music, and dancing to the streets. The ultimate contrast: a proud Abangoma warrior, in full tribal regalia, calmly cooking his supper on the concrete steps of a soaring skyscraper.

This may now sound like a romanticized celebration of multiculturalism. But Wilson says it was based on Masekela's own descriptions of the multiethnic African diversity of city and township culture. The point Wilson is trying to make is that Masekela's cultural roots in South Africa were *already* complex, urbane, hybrid, many-layered. He didn't need Americanization. What he needed in 1966 was to build on the foundation of his African background and experience to produce in America new albums for a global audience.

Musically, *Hugh Masekela's Next Album* gives us the contemporary pop side of Masekela's experiments. But this time, he's not watering down anything, as he had been led to do with *Trumpet Africaine*. He's just opportunistically sampling a list of hit songs from the radio airwaves (mostly), but playing them his way, alongside a handful of original tunes. The track list is printed on the front cover as a kind of advertisement for the contemporary tunes found on the disc. After the intimate live jazz from the Village Gate on the first album, this one is aimed at commercial airplay on the radio. It's made up mostly of pop hits of the moment, including "California Dreamin,'" "Norwegian Wood," "Sounds [sic] of Silence," "It's Not Unusual," "From Me to You," and "If I Needed Someone." But besides those contemporary covers, there are three original tracks cowritten by Masekela, and one cowritten by his friend Caiphus Semenya with other South African musicians. Probably at Wilson's suggestion, the final track on the album is a cover of Bob Lind's international folk-rock hit "Elusive Butterfly." Lind is the same singer-songwriter who wrote "Cheryl's Goin' Home," a tune covered by the Blues Project that same year. Wilson, the connecting thread and the self-described "Folk-Rock Tzar," likely saw to it that the opening and closing tracks of *Hugh Masekela's Next Album* were both folk-rock songs: "California Dreamin'" and "Elusive Butterfly." Naturally, Masekela's arrangements jazz them up. His singing on "Elusive Butterfly," for example, echoes bossa nova. The rhythm and the trumpet solos make the song over into a Latin swing tune.

To appreciate the push for commercial and artistic success represented by those two rapidly released albums, we can compare them with a *third* Masekela album that appeared in 1966, titled *Grrr.* It was actually recorded in the previous year, before the trumpeter came to MGM/Verve to work with Wilson. To repeat the order of appearance: *The Americanization of Ooga Booga* was recorded in the fall of 1965 and released the following summer of 1966; *Hugh Masekela's Next Album* was recorded and released late in 1966. *Grrr* had been recorded for Mercury Records before the other two, back in spring 1965. It was released a year later, just as the other two records entered the market—which makes the "Next" in the title of *Next Album* look like it's making an argumentative point. It's the true second album, despite the potentially confusing belated appearance of *Grrr.* The record titled *Grrr* was originally intended by Masekela to foreground his African cultural roots. It featured Eric Gale on guitar, along with Larry Willis and other South African musicians in Masekela's circle. But it was dismissed by the record company as a failure before it really had a chance to succeed. It remained unreleased until after Masekela had found success with Wilson at MGM. Then, Mercury rushed it out to try to cash in on that success. Its cover image features an overly cute baby tiger growling at an upright trumpet. Masekela seems to have been offended by the album's title and by the fact that the cover showed a *baby* tiger, and also by the failure to release the album on time, when it was first finished.

EMANCIPATION

As it turns out, a similar conflict with record-company executives would repeat itself at MGM. After his new company appeared not to promote him sufficiently, Masekela was referred by Wilson to the head of MGM. He was told the company thought that his records were "too African" for the American market. MGM/Verve failed to renew his contract, so he left and moved to his own new Chisa record label to release a *fourth* album for 1966: *The Emancipation of Hugh Masekela*. It made for a remarkable cluster of albums released during a single year. It was indeed a pivotal year for Masekela's career. *The Emancipation* was recorded in Los Angeles and featured the pianist Charlie Smalls, among others. It was influenced by West Coast musical genres, folk-rock, and then-emergent psychedelic pop. See, for example, "Why Are You Blowing My Mind?," "She Doesn't Write," and especially (both the tune and the lyrics) "What Is Wrong with Groovin'?" The album cover this time is a photo of Masekela, shirtless and smiling, wearing an Abraham Lincoln beard and top hat. The lyric is simple: "What is wrong with groovin'? / Can't a fellow have a little happy without any hide-n-seek? / . . . Why do they follow me around just like their name was 0-0-7?" It's worth remembering that Masekela was actually under surveillance by the FBI during this period and for some time afterwards.[28]

Masekela moved with Stewart Levine and their production company, Oo-Bwana, to California in 1966, living first in Sausalito and then in L.A., just off the Sunset Strip. There he became part of the local scene. In 1967, his band played the Whisky a Go Go, where he says they were only the second Black act to headline, after Otis Redding.[29] They recorded a live album at the club the following year. They also played a number of public gigs in California, including antiwar concerts that included bands like Jefferson Airplane and the Grateful Dead, as well as Eric Burdon & the Animals and the Byrds. As Masekela says, his band was "part of the sound and the fury of the Flower Power era."[30] The context for Masekela's music had shifted from Broadway in New York to the Canyon in California, and the emphasis also shifted, to some degree, from jazz to pop.

MONTEREY

In June 1967, Masekela and his band played at the three-day Monterey Pop Festival, another sign of their bid for broad popularity and crossover success. Besides the list of stellar rock performers, Jimi Hendrix, Janis Joplin, and the Who among them, Masekela remembers the event as "the largest group high" he had ever seen: "Almost everybody in the audience was tripping on LSD."[31] He played a set on the second night, going on just after the psychedelic band Moby Grape and just before the quintessential folk-rock band the Byrds. The performance, Masekela said, looking back, brought his music to the attention of what was at the time a "massive psychedelic community."[32] Eric Burdon & the Animals were there as well and later commemorated the festival with the blissed-out song "Monterey," which, as a kind of audio documentary of a festival, predates Joni Mitchell's "Woodstock" by two years, recounting performances by the Byrds, Jefferson Airplane, Ravi Shankar, the Who, the Grateful Dead, and Jimi Hendrix, as well as Masekela, whose music Burdon calls "black as night." With the diversity of performers, it's notable that Burdon's summary epithet for Masekela's music celebrates its Blackness, its identity as a product of Africa, though now mixed into the global pop potpourri.

Also playing at Monterey that year, as we've seen, was the Blues Project. They were introduced by Paul Simon and performed their psychedelic jazz-rock number "Flute Thing." Al Kooper, who had recently left the Project, performed a set of his own that included blues and gospel-inflected songs he had recorded with the band, "I Can't Keep from Cryin'" and "Wake Me, Shake Me." Simon & Garfunkel played their folk-rock hit "The Sound of Silence." Monkee Peter Tork came to the mic to introduce the folk-rock group the Buffalo Springfield, which included his old friend and roommate Stephen Stills. Masekela, with the formidable Big Black on percussion, performed "Bajabula Bonke (Healing Song)" and the Beatles' "Here, There, and Everywhere," as well as teen singer/songwriter Janis Ian's pop hit "Society's Child" about a doomed youthful mixed-race relationship. The mixed genres of the set—from township folk music to British Invasion to contemporary folk-rock, all filtered through Masekela's jazz trumpet sound—made a statement of their own.

SO YOU WANT TO BE

At Monterey, the Byrds followed Masekela on the bill. They were indeed flying high that year, as Burdon's song said, their album *Younger Than Yesterday* having just been released in February. The opening track of that album was the fast-paced folk-rock number "So You Want to Be a Rock 'n' Roll Star." Its chiming riff, played on the twelve-string Rickenbacker by Roger McGuinn, helped to make it a hit. "Just get an electric guitar / Then take some time and learn how to play," the lyric advises, with sardonic understatement—and a soundtrack of screaming fans fades in as if to support the argument ("The girls'll tear you apart"). As you listen to the recorded version, you can imagine the mixing-board slider bringing up, then back down, the scream-track, which was recorded at an actual Byrds concert. In 1967, the electric guitar was more than another musical instrument—it had become a symbolic object, a metonym that stood for rock 'n' roll as a genre and a style. But when the repetitive twelve-string riff reaches its climax, guest instrumentalist Masekela's jazzy trumpet soars over the top of the mix, heavy with echo, a sustained note that ends with a flourish. Live at Monterey, Masekela and Big Black came back out onstage with the Byrds to play the parts they had recorded for the song. The whole song was a cross-genre, international collaboration. To close the circle, the memorable bass riff was developed in the first place by Chris Hillman while doing session work with Masekela, Caiphus Semenya, and David Crosby for an album by the South African singer Letta Mbulu (*Letta Mbulu Sings*, 1967).[33]

"So You Want to Be a Rock 'n' Roll Star," it was pretty obvious to everybody, was written about the manufactured TV-show band the Monkees. The ersatz Beatles, the madcap group was invented, from the series treatment on, to get ratings and to sell records. Then the lyric says, "it's time to . . . / Sell your soul to the company / Who are waiting there to sell plasticware." Masekela was first and last a jazz musician, if one with eclectic tastes and a mixed-culture background. But he also wanted to be a pop star, to reach a wide audience and have his records on the charts. He had to deal with the same music-business issues the Byrds' song is about. He more than once refused to sell his soul, changing record companies instead, but he still had to deal with the commercial imperative to sell records, which are always in danger of being reduced to a literally plastic commodity. The company and its executives were gatekeepers standing between him and the audience he hoped to reach. During his year with Wilson, however, he was encouraged to sell records, but also encouraged to experiment with his own hybrid form of South African township music and jazz (+ pop and R&B). The eclecticism and genre-crossing can be seen within the tracks on his albums and also between the albums that came out in 1966, two produced by Wilson. The trumpeter was perfectly willing to record music that crossed over to contemporary pop, as *Hugh Masekela's Next Album* made clear. When the record company got in the way, he moved on, but his desires for hybrid forms and successful crossings continued for the rest of his life. By 1967, he was well on his way to being a rock star in the general sense, as the term was then starting to be used. But as the Byrds' song reminds us, the star-making machinery was a "strange game," pulling you in the opposite direction of the elusive ideal of authenticity that rock music was increasingly claiming as its own.

That contradiction, the claim of artistic authenticity coming from obviously manufactured rock 'n' roll stars, was the starting point of the Monkees, as we see in chapter 8. But first, in the next chapter, chapter 7, we look at another band with an animal name—in fact *the* Animals, from England. In 1966, they were another Wilson production. The journey taken that year by their frontman, Eric Burdon, whose "Monterey" praised Masekela's music, sums up the key issues of 1966. Burdon's search for what he understood as an authentic musical identity took him from covering blues and R&B songs, to making the quintessential folk-rock single ("House of the Rising Sun"), to a brief pop-crooner experiment, and finally into full-blown psychedelia, an inward-trending journey aided by ballroom light shows, Owsley acid, and the formidable Frank Zappa. In the span of about a year, he went from "See See Rider" to "anything is everything." The next chapter traces that trajectory.

CHAPTER SEVEN

BLUES OF MY MIND

The Animals, *Animalism* (1966);
Eric Burdon & the Animals, *Eric Is Here* (1967);
Eric Burdon & the [New] Animals, *Winds of Change* (1967)

OUT OF THIS PLACE

Sometime in late 1967 or early 1968, the English singer Eric Burdon's image was clipped from a photo and included in the weird collage for the gatefold of Frank Zappa and the Mothers of Invention's *We're Only in It for the Money* (released March 1968). The scruffy rocker from Newcastle upon Tyne stands there in a wildly eclectic group that includes cutouts of Edgard Varèse and R&B singer Big Mama (Willie Mae) Thornton, for example, and Jimi Hendrix (live in the studio) and Frank Zappa's English secretary, Pauline Butcher, whom we met in chapter 5. And Tom Wilson—producer of both Burdon and Zappa—standing stately out at the lefthand edge of the frame.

As it turned out, that image marked the culmination of a momentous year-plus for Burdon. His career path rose quickly in the mid-1960s through a series of radical changes, culminating in the 1970s with being lead singer for the Black pop-funk band War. In this chapter, I focus on the turning point in 1966–1967 when Burdon went from being frontman for the Animals (and making their first album in America), to making a weird solo album (crooning pop tunes with orchestral settings), to fronting a new psychedelic blues band, Eric Burdon & the *New* Animals. In that year-plus, the rough British bluesman was transformed into a psychedelic bard. He went from Newcastle to Monterey, from Tyneside to Laurel Canyon (with visits to the Bay Area). By 1967 we find him riding a motorcycle along the coast, wearing love beads and hanging out with Jim Morrison, Frank Zappa, Janis Joplin, and the Grateful Dead. Burdon's changes were not that unusual. In fact, his was just a more extreme example of the journey followed by much of pop music in 1966–1967. In his typically blunt style, Burdon tellingly explained the journey as a turning inward, from playing the blues to playing the blues of his *mind.*

Even before the Animals came to America, their recordings had come over as part of the British Invasion. In the summer of 1965, they had a big pop hit with "We Gotta Get Outta This Place," about the desire of a couple of young lovers to escape the "dirty old part of the city"—invoking gritty Newcastle. In the fall of 1965, they had another hit with "It's My Life" ("It's a hard world to get a break in"). Just before the band's in-person arrival in America, they were brought together with Wilson as their producer. Soon, as we've seen, the Blues Project was complaining that Wilson treated them as second fiddle to Eric Burdon & the Animals. The Animals were working-class "Geordie" musicians. They had started out in local clubs like the Downbeat and the Club A' Go Go in Newcastle, and, in many ways, they actually *were* the white R&B band Wilson *thought* he was getting when he signed the Mothers of Invention. Previously they had been the Alan Price Rhythm & Blues Combo (Price was the keyboard player). The Animals always traded on their working-class credibility, which, it was implied, gave them a connection to American Black culture, the blues, and R&B. Their name turned a pearl-clutching insult by polite society (they're just *animals*) into a defiant badge of honor, and their early repertoire included songs by John Lee Hooker, Muddy Waters, B. B. King, Ma Rainey, Chuck Berry, Joe Tex, and Screamin' Jay Hawkins. Burdon's vocals—sung looking out from beneath shaggy bangs and perpetually arched eyebrows, the high notes shouted with his eyes closed—channeled those artists and others, his musical idols. The official essay on the band for their induction into the Rock 'n' Roll Hall of Fame was still saying that "Burdon's deep, raspy vocals . . . sounded more authentically black than many of his English R&B contemporaries" (not just more Black, but more *authentically* so).[1] Listening to Burdon now, it's easy to hear those moments of overreach when he goes for what he deems "Black" vocal stylings and comes up short. But he usually sounds relatively more natural or more comfortable in his appropriations than many of his peers (including the young Mick Jagger, for example). It wasn't just the vocals or choice of songs. The playing on the early albums was audibly committed to the raw instrumental sounds of the early R&B records the Animals admired.

Eric Burdon was open about his fascination with what he called "the American black experience."[2] When he was young, "America's black music had become the new secret underground teen language"—not just a genre but a shared language.[3] The young Burdon believed that his affinity with American R&B provided him with a kind of "underground" authenticity. He persisted in this belief well into the 1970s. The Animals' 1964 debut album included "The Story of Bo Diddley," a talking song with a sung chorus over the famous Bo Diddley beat. In telling the story, Burdon awkwardly does different voices, including voices of the Black musicians and their entourage. It culminates in what turns out to be an invented meeting between the Black singer and guitarist ("the man himself") and the Animals, whom he supposedly came to hear in Newcastle. In a self-deprecating joke, Burdon has Diddley dismiss the young Brits: "He said, Man, that sure is the biggest load of rubbish I ever heard in my life."

Except, it never happened. Diddley did play Newcastle and the band may have met some of his musicians, but the rest is made up. The story expresses a would-be self-deprecating fantasy: the Animals imagine engaging with one of their heroes, but he gives them the thumbs down. On the other hand, just the fact of the song—with this self-owning punchline—worked as self-promotion and staked a claim to a supposed (if unearned) familiarity with American Black music. The song reveals the band's insecurity and self-consciousness about their musical identity, about what they idealized as artistic authenticity via American blues and R&B music.

Burdon didn't encounter Bo Diddley that night. But in the years that followed he met his heroes and shared the stage with a number of prominent Black musicians. Just after his arrival in America, he visited John Lee Hooker at the blues singer's home in Detroit; he regularly hung out at the Apollo Theater in Harlem; and he went out of his way to travel to Stax/Volt Records studio in Memphis, where he says he was present when Sam & Dave were recording "Hold On, I'm Comin'";[4] he was a close friend and collaborator of Jimi Hendrix. All of these experiences became part of his own story and were crucial to his personal identity. For Burdon, working with the African American producer Wilson seems to have been of a piece with all of that. In one of the liner-note acknowledgments for *Winds of Change* in 1967, he described Wilson as "tall" and "brown," and said that he "taught me to leave my negro hangups behind, and to use what I'd learnt from black people to my own avail." We'll come back to that teaching and Burdon's response to it, but it's hard not to hear in it an echo of Wilson's oft-repeated advice to white singers not to try to sing like Black blues musicians. "Robert Johnson had his thing and I exhort everybody to develop their own," he said.[5] Burdon says he took Wilson's advice as a spur to develop *his* own thing—and it was a psychedelic thing.

THE CIRCLE OF INSPIRATION ("HOUSE OF THE RISING SUN")

Before they met Wilson, the Animals were a hard-driving R&B band. But even before "It's My Life" and "We Gotta Get Out of This Place," there was "House of the Rising Sun" (1964). Trying to differentiate their sound from Chuck Berry, with whom they were on tour in Britain at the time, the band decided to try out an arrangement of the traditional folk song—"House of the Rising Sun"—also known as "Rising Sun Blues." It worked. Audiences loved it.[6] The A-minor chord progression (Am-C-D-F) had already begun to circulate among folk singers and guitar players everywhere. Bob Dylan's own 1962 version was taken from Dave Van Ronk's. But there had been numerous versions before that.[7] With a lyric in the voice of a female prostitute trapped in a New Orleans brothel, Dylan's recording made a highly significant contribution to the history of the song. The Animals knew that version, and their guitarist Hilton Valentine said outright that it was their main source.[8] Burdon, however, equivocated, saying they had *first* heard the song in Newcastle clubs performed by British folk singers, though he too admitted the importance of Dylan's version (if only for the additional lyrics it provided). But for most of his career, Burdon claimed that the origins of the song were in Black American culture (he sometimes identified Josh White's version as a key influence). In fact, "House of the Rising Sun" had been recorded first by a white singer in 1933, and a version was captured by Alan Lomax in 1937 in a performance by a young white woman, Georgia Turner.[9] It's really pointless to try to fix on one source for a song of this kind, which was always "in a constant state of production, refinement, and reproduction."[10] But it's nonetheless significant that the supposed Black roots of the song mattered so much to Burdon, precisely because it was part of his own search for musical authenticity.[11]

The Animals' version featured electric guitar playing 6/8-time arpeggios, set against a diabolical-sounding Vox organ played by Alan Price, pumping out chords, calliope style. Which is to say, it was a folk-rock tune.[12] Burdon sang the lyric gender-swapped, the sin also swapped from whoring to gambling (those alternatives were already present in the song's long and varied history). With the electric arrangement, the Animals had a different *kind* of song, a folk-rock version. The record was made in one take on May 18, 1964. Once released in June, the single quickly become what was arguably the first international folk-rock hit. Dylan's version probably inspired the Animals' version, at least in part. But the circle of inspiration didn't stop there. Reportedly, Dylan was in turn inspired by hearing the Animals' electric folk-rock arrangement. The story goes that he was driving when the Animals' "House" came on the radio. He stopped, got out of the car, and smacked the hood to punctuate the eureka moment: *this* was how he could "go electric"—a folk song he had already covered, in a new version by the Animals, showed him how he could also play folk-rock. The rest is history. Or myth. Both, no doubt.[13] At any rate, the Animals were in a musical crucible in 1964, a shared space out of which folk-rock emerged.

The truth is, everything was happening all at once in a transatlantic swirl of live performances, radio play, record-swapping, and word of mouth. Six months after the Animals recorded "House of the Rising Sun," Dylan was in the studio with Wilson to make one of the prototypical folk-rock albums (at least for half of its tracks), *Bringing It All Back Home.* In December 1964, Wilson recorded a remix of Dylan's 1962 acoustic "House" overdubbed with tremolo electric guitar, bass, and drums, creating another hybrid folk-rock version. Perhaps the overdub was just an experiment. But, given the timing, it may well have been inspired by the Animals' record—which, again, was partly inspired by Dylan's original in the first place.[14] Wilson's electric overdub was not released at the time.[15] Alan Price's prominent organ part isn't replicated on the overdub. But it's interesting that a year later Al Kooper's organ would turn out to be the key ingredient added to "Like a Rolling Stone."[16] Whatever circles of influence we trace, the folk-rock hit by the Animals was a major presence at the time, part of the spread of a hybrid sound that included the Byrds, just to name another example, and that led to the sound Wilson and Dylan captured in 1965. To bring the circle around once more: Wilson's electric overdub of Simon & Garfunkel's "The Sound of Silence" was released in September 1965 via the same process of adding electric instruments and drums to a folk record. By the beginning of 1966, the self-described folk-rock tzar would find himself producing Eric Burdon & the Animals.

ANIMALISM/S/IZATION

Billboard magazine contained a notice on September 25, 1965, about the Animals having "been lured" away from British producer Mickie Most by their deal with MGM. Most's contract with the band did not actually run out until February 1966. At that point, the Animals' new producer officially became Wilson. The result of this transatlantic transition was that a confusingly titled cluster of albums (and singles) appeared in 1966–1967 produced by Wilson:

May 1966: *Animalisms* (U.K.)

August 1966: *Animalization* (its track list overlaps with that of *Animalisms*)

November 1966: *Animalism*

March 1967: *Eric Is Here*

October 1967: *Winds of Change*

Animalisms and *Animalization* were transitional albums that accompanied the band's breakout in America. All the albums are marked by a flurry of major changes, including the departure of Price, who was replaced by Dave Rowberry on keyboards, and then the breakup of the original Animals, who were replaced by a new slate of musicians later in 1966.

In April 1966, the band took a working vacation in the Bahamas, part of it spent on a yacht. Wilson showed up with portable equipment to start recording in a local hotel ballroom.[17] Technical conditions were primitive, but at least one single came out of those recording sessions ("Don't Bring Me Down"), as well as one track for what was then the forthcoming album *Animalism* (a cover of Donovan's "Hey Gyp"). The first song on *Animalization* when it appeared in August was Joe Tex's R&B number "One Monkey Don't Stop the Show," which, in Tex's version, had reached number 20 on Billboard's R&B chart in 1965. (Joe Tex was later well known for the funky/goofy 1972 hit, "I Gotcha.") Multiple versions were recorded by various artists, but "One Monkey Don't Stop the Show," is—ironically—a showstopper, with a rousing chorus and bump-and-grind rhythm, a juke-joint number with a corrupted gospel feel. It left plenty of space for Burdon to do what he did best, improvise a spirited vocal, speaking, growling, and singing. The Animals' version of the lyric cheekily overwrites the geography, replacing the American South and New York with the U.K.'s London ("the Smoke") and Newcastle. The title phrase just barely makes it into the song right at the end, repeated during the closing chorus as the final payoff. *Animalization* also includes several songs that sound like pop music for the radio, especially in America, given Burdon's British Invasion accent: for example, the original tunes, "You're on My Mind" and "She'll Return It." And there's a pretty faithful cover of Chuck Berry's "Sweet Little Sixteen," with Rowberry's piano at the front of the mix. The Gerry Goffin and Carole King lead-off track, "Don't Bring Me Down," with chords and glissandos on the organ by Rowberry, and fuzz-tone and tremolo guitar by Hilton Valentine, made for a hit single.

November's *Animalism* opens with a sign of things to come, a track called "All Night Long." The song is a genre-splice—a psychedelic pop tune grafted onto a traditional blues stomp, forced together into one song by the writer and arranger, Frank Zappa, who also plays guitar on it. Different time signatures mark the different genres. A change of meter signals the transition back and forth—between a raga-like (or Byrds-like) guitar solo by Zappa, shifting to a pounding electric blues riff. The result is effectively schizoid, as if the psychedelic pop tune were repeatedly bursting out of the skin of the blues number, only to be resubmerged until the next chorus. A key change near the end enhances the graft effect. Zappa also arranged and played bass on the other obvious pop song on the album, songwriter Fred Neil's "The Other Side of This Life" (track 3).

Track 2 is an R&B dance number the Animals played live as a frenzied rave-up, Sam Cooke's "Shake." It foregrounds Rowberry's organ and Valentine's fuzz-tone guitar but is dominated by Burdon's howl. Other blues or blues-rock songs on *Animalism* include a stripped-down "Rock Me Baby" by B. B. King (track 4), an upbeat "Lucille" by Albert Collins (track 5), a walking-pace "Smokestack Lightning" by Howlin' Wolf (track 6; the arrangement begins with just a heavy-reverb guitar riff and Burdon's shouting vocal), a version of "Louisiana Blues" by Muddy Waters (side 2, track 4), and the blues standard "Going Down Slow" (side 2, track 6), which closes the album. Side 2 opens with the Donovan cover, "Hey Gyp," one of the songs recorded in the Bahamas. Donovan's song is actually a variation on a traditional blues dialogue song by Memphis Minnie and Kansas Joe, "Can I Do It for You." Side 2 of *Animalism* also includes a bluesy version of "Hit the Road Jack" (track 2) with heavy drums and organ, a song by Percy Mayfield that had been made famous by Ray Charles in 1961. The track list is rounded out with soul and R&B songs, "Outcast" and "That's All I Am to You" (side 2, tracks 3 and 5). The cover photo shows the band in performance, shot from close in, in front of the organ, all of them standing clustered together (as bands often did on a small stage in those days). Burdon faces in the general direction of the organ and the camera, his mouth wide open, mid-howl.

The liner notes (in this case not written by Wilson) include two telling observations about genre and the band's supposed self-expression: "To put a name to Eric's soul music we'll call it rhythm & blues, but it's more than that . . . it's an 'Animalization' of rhythm & blues." The term "Animalization" calls back to the earlier Animals album title, but it also declares the intention of the band to add "something else" to the R&B and blues music they were playing—to somehow make it their own and, in that sense, to *Animalize* it. The second telling statement in the note is about why they were so intent on doing this. It could be that this was the only way they could claim what had become in 1966 the sine qua non for rock bands, authenticity. Burdon, we are assured, "pours all the sincerity he contains into a song, and feels every word he utters." In 1966, this amounted to a kind of manufacturer's guarantee. On this album you would get the real thing, authentic, sincere self-expression. Not just R&B, but "Animalized," made the band's own thing. Never mind that it was mostly Black music played by a white band from the North of England—it was sincerely felt and authentically stamped as . . . something else.

ERIC IS HERE

The first incarnation of the Animals was abruptly dissolved on September 5, 1966. *Animalism* was already recorded, and it was released in late November. In the same month, Burdon's first solo album was recorded. *Eric Is Here* is an obvious anomaly in his catalog. On the album cover is a drawing by Nancy Reiner, an artist who would a little later provide a spacey drawing of Jimi Hendrix set against a cloud-fleeced sky for the cover of *The Cry of Love* (1971). Here, she sketches Burdon as a kind of bearded British gnome, whose body in repose is also a landscape sprouting grass and flowers, with some kind of tiny piper or flute player standing on him (or the horizon), under a small sun. Seeing the image, it's hard not to think just a few years ahead to the fantasy song Burdon would record with the band War, "Spill the Wine," in which we're regaled by "an overfed longhaired leaping gnome" about a dream he had about lying in "a big field of tall grass" as a flute plays a bluesy riff.

The title of the 1967 solo album probably cites, tongue-in-cheek, a TV commercial slogan for Erik cigars.[18] In the commercial, a Scandinavian-looking man on a Viking ship smokes a cigar as he arrives in New York Harbor (the voiceover says: "Erik Is Here"). Then, as in so many 1960s TV commercials, a blond shows up to embrace him. The reference seems like a joking admission that the album was intended to market Burdon as a new, addictive product, just arrived on American shores from Europe. The album *Eric Is Here* (1967) is credited to Eric Burdon & the Animals, but for the most part drummer Barry Jenkins is the only other member of his band playing on it—it was made in the brief gap between the original Animals and the New Animals. Wilson recruited saxophone player Benny Golson and pianist Horace Ott as co-arrangers. Their combined orchestras provided most of the session players. Golson, a serious jazz musician, is nonetheless an appropriate choice for this album named for a TV commercial and aimed at a popular audience. As we've seen, in April 1967, he also worked with Wilson as the arranger of *Tune In, Turn On*, the album of TV-commercial jingles.

On *Eric Is Here*, Burdon effectively croons or shouts the pop tunes over orchestral arrangements that include a prominent brass section and a rock-band rhythm section. With a few exceptions, he avoids the "Black"-sounding voice we hear on so many Animals blues tracks, even sometimes singing in his native English accent. Still, Burdon's voice stands out in contrast to the dense strings and horns. Sometimes he seems to struggle to find exactly the right mix of talk-singing, improvising, and melody, and the effect of that can sound a little strange. But it's not the "disaster" Burdon later labeled it.[19] As Sean Egan says, "There's not one track that's truly bad and its high production values, good musicianship and—naturally—fine singing make it an enjoyable album to have on in the background even if its lack of layering militates against undistracted scrutiny."[20] I agree. Except, I find most of it fairly enjoyable to listen to in the foreground too.

Burdon's vocal stylings on top of such orchestrations sometimes call to mind certain Jim Morrison songs with the Doors or David Clayton Thomas's singing with Blood, Sweat & Tears—both of which can at times cross into lounge-singer territory—but it's ultimately less pretentious than either of those examples. Thanks to the influence of the Beatles and George Martin, orchestral arrangements were finding their way into all sorts of rock and pop records at the time. Soul music and R&B stars like Ray Charles had often sung over big arrangements. As for orchestral pop records in general, they were decidedly not cool by the late 1960s, but there were a lot of them being released anyway. Elvis Presley and other rock 'n' roll singers had made even more lushly produced albums, as had soul groups like the Temptations (though theirs were consistently funky), divas like Diana Ross, or the Welsh baritone Tom Jones. In fact, two songs on *Eric Is Here* had recently been released by Jones himself: "True Love Comes Only Once in a Lifetime," which had a strangely childlike female backup vocal that Burdon's version seems to be imitating (though pitched a little higher and with a slightly different cadence), and "It's Been a Long Time Comin'." Orchestral instrumentation with a rock rhythm section was conventional at the time on records showcasing pop vocalists. *Eric Is Here* is more soulful than many such records, thanks in part to Burdon's distinctive voice. (Although at times there are moments of vocal strain, like the high part on "It's Not Easy.") Finally, Wilson's mix, created with the sound engineers, brings forward the rock-band instruments—drum kit; echo-saturated piano, organ, or electric clavichord; tremolo guitar; bass; tambourine—to a greater extent than in many other orchestrated pop records at the time. In fact, Wilson produced other orchestral pop records: in 1966, for example, he is credited with three separate albums by the singer Connie Francis, who had been a smash hit in the 1950s and was still making records like *Movie Greats of the 60s*, for example (1966).

Many of the songs on *Eric Is Here* are interesting, even well crafted. Among these, there are three tracks by then-emerging American composer Randy Newman: "Mamma Told Me Not to Come," "I Think It's Gonna Rain Today," and "Wait Until Next Year." That last—both its lyrics and its lounge-piano tune—is typical of Newman's dark humor. It's sung in the voice of a loser and blowhard (whose "manners need refinin'") making empty promises that even he doesn't seem to believe. Burdon half-talks/half-sings the verses in his Geordie accent—until the very end, when he puts on a posh London accent to promise that we'll see "a marked improvement in [his] mannerisms" next year. The English accents are notable in part because they diverge from Burdon's usual R&B and blues accents. There's a Gerry Goffin and Carole King number, "This Side of Goodbye"; and the album opens with a song by Tommy Boyce and Bobby Hart—the duo who wrote, and in the beginning performed, the early hits for the Monkees—"In the Night." In his biographical notes for the back cover of what would be the next album, *Winds of Change*, Burdon describes the guitarist Vic Briggs with reference to that hit TV show about a rock band: "Had he been born in the U.S.," he says of Briggs, "he might have been one of the Monkees." It's not clear whether there's a backhanded insult contained in the joke.

The single from *Eric Is Here*, "Help Me Girl," was written by Scott English and Larry Weiss. The song made the charts at the end of 1966, just before the album was released. The final track on the album, "It's Been a Long Time

Comin'," is a gospel-influenced soul song by Jimmy Radcliffe and Joey Brooks, which had been recorded by Tom Jones on his album *A-Tom-ic Jones*, released January 14, 1966.[21] It's likely, in fact, that Wilson had Jones in mind as a model for the kind of pop singer's showcase the *Eric Is Here* album could be.

The instrumental arrangements on the album are not undifferentiated easy listening. Some distinctive sounds add color to the tracks. For example, "Losin' Control," by Carl D'Ericco and Roger Atkins (a team who had written the Animals' hit single, "It's My Life" [1965]) opens with a tightly woven flute duet, a part that recurs throughout the song. Another sonically catchy tag opens "The Biggest Bundle of Them All," the penultimate track on *Eric Is Here*: an echoey piano + electric keyboard (?) + plucked guitar melody, each layer added to create the song's hook. This is an album of songwriters' songs, interpreted by Burdon and the two arrangers with Wilson's input. It diverges from the new paradigm then just beginning to dominate the recording process: a rock band working things out together in the studio, recording successive takes and overdubs.

What if, to understand the album, we took seriously for a moment the idea that Wilson thought of Burdon not just as a frontman for a rock band but as a powerful, talented singer? In that case, *Eric Is Here* might have seemed to him like an opportunity for another experiment in crossing genres (or sounds), an attempt to combine radio-friendly pop tunes in orchestral arrangements with Burdon's distinctive gritty vocals. At the same time, commercially, it might have seemed like a chance to capture a different demographic from the usual fans of the Animals. Once we give up the idea that this album was a wrong turn away from the Animals' signature blues rock sound, and consider it on its own terms, *Eric Is Here* is actually an enjoyable pop album. It shows that Burdon, under Wilson's direction, was trying to stretch his sound in new directions, though new combinations, demonstrating that he "wasn't constrained by the blues' limited horizons and was ready to open out his music."[22] It's possible that the prominent use of electric violin on the next album, *Winds of Change*—which, like John Cale's electric viola in the Velvet Underground, sometimes signaled artistic pretensions—might not have happened at all without Burdon's experience with the orchestra in making *Eric Is Here*, whatever he felt about the album in later years.

FRANK ZAPPA ZAPPED

One of Burdon's signature song forms was a kind of name-dropping catalog of musicians, which he thought of as "musical journalism" aimed at "documenting the times."[23] The prime example is "Monterey" (1967; on the album *The Twain Shall Meet*, 1968), about the June 1967 festival—the same event at which the Blues Project performed "Flute Thing," Hugh Masekela performed "Bajabula Bonke (Healing Song)" and sat in with the Byrds on "So You Want to Be a Rock 'n' Roll Star." The Animals' "Monterey" starts with Burdon whispering a parody of Genesis, "in the beginning . . ." etc. Then he proceeds to tell the story of the festival as a catalog of vignettes, a roster of participating musicians, with epithets or brief identifying actions (e.g., "The Byrds and the Airplane did fly," and "Hugh Masekela's music was black as night"). The point is to sketch not just that significant festival, or even "the times" per se, but that scene, comprised of different scenes brought together, to register impressionistically a slice of contemporary musical and cultural history. Indeed, a song like this, by a prominent insider like Burdon, helps to create the scene and immediately becomes part of its lore.

Other times, Burdon's catalog songs take the form of the recitation of a lineage, therein creating a history for contemporary music and making a myth through the song. This is how the title track on the album *Winds of Change* works. Over John Weider's electric violin and the sound effect of blowing wind (dynamically channel-shifted in the stereo mix for an even trippier effect), Burdon chants a list of the names of jazz, blues, and R&B greats (e.g., Duke Ellington, Jelly Roll Morton, Bessie Smith, Robert Johnson, and the "Father of R&B," Louis Jordan) until he gets to rock 'n' roll and then, ca. 1964, the reverb suddenly kicks in on his vocal, as he calls out the Beatles and the Rolling Stones, then declares, "Frank Zappa zapped." Whatever "zapped" might mean in this context, Zappa is clearly meant to have a special place in the litany. He connects other British Invasion bands with Burdon's own newly adopted California scene.

Burdon met Zappa through Wilson. The producer asked Zappa to provide arrangements and musical direction for an Animals recording session for the album *Animalism* on July 4, 1966. Zappa was at home in the recording studio, comfortably in charge, as the making of *Freak Out!* had shown. He could arrange, conduct (often literally waving his arm to set tempos and direct musicians), and produce. The Animals met Zappa when they were in the studio next to the Mothers of Invention sessions for *Freak Out!* So it makes perfect sense that Wilson should delegate some of the work of producing to him that day. Burdon later put it this way: "The record company lent Frank Zappa to our new production, and we cut two tracks together: 'All Night Long' and 'The Other Side of This Life.'"[24] For his part, Zappa said, "I was told: just go in there, tell the musicians what you want and they'll play it."[25] So he hired top session musicians, including the great Wrecking Crew bassist Carol Kaye (who had played twelve-string guitar on *Freak Out!*). They recorded some initial tracks before the Animals even showed up later that day. But a kind of musical and cultural transfer took place that day.

And that night. After the session ended, Burdon went to Zappa's house in Laurel Canyon, where they played R&B records and watched some of Zappa's 16mm experimental films. For Burdon, the encounter was life-changing. That summer of 1966, he had recently discovered LSD and was in the midst of discovering American culture—L.A.'s Laurel Canyon in particular. He and his music were going through changes. Zappa recognized this and attributed it to experiences at his own house in the Canyon, and an enthusiastic immersion on Burdon's part in his own music with the Mothers of Invention. Zappa says he's not sure what happened, but after attending a party at his house ("I believe he was a little bit psychedelically jacked-up that evening or the two nights that he spent over at my place"), suddenly "there's this album that they recorded about a month or two ago with [Tom] Wilson in Los Angeles; their new group is psychedelic." He cites a new seven-minute track about the Black Plague and a song about a policeman in San Francisco. And this psychedelic turn goes along with an obsession with the music of the Mothers of Invention: "they went into the studio and played 'Suzy Creamcheese' note for note . . . played 'Return of the Son of Monster Magnet' note for note."[26] At one point on the day of the *Animalism* session, Zappa says that Wilson showed up to the studio around 11:00 a.m. and asked, "Where are the Animals?" Zappa replied drily, "Gee, I dunno, Tom." They showed up later, after the tracks had already been cut with the session musicians.

It was a ripe moment in the history of pop: Wilson delegated to Zappa some production and arranging of Eric Burdon & the Animals. That night, Burdon, possibly on acid, socialized with Zappa and others in L.A. as part of his initiation into California culture. This involved exposure to Zappa's underground films. Soon Burdon and his music had mutated into something else. Something psychedelic.

WINDS OF CHANGE

Zappa's retrospective account of the *Animalism* session refers to songs on the 1967 album, *Winds of Change*: "The Black Plague" and "San Franciscan Nights." These he suggests were products of his influence on Burdon. The first was, as Zappa said, essentially a spoken-word narrative over solemn musical soundtrack of heavy bass, ringing bell, and monkish chants ("bring out your dead"). It's a kind of harbinger of prog-rock or metal pseudo-medievalism to come, but it, along with other spoken-word pieces on the album ("Man-Woman," for example), may have been partly the result of Burdon's acting ambitions.[27] Here Burdon essentially narrates a medieval story about class difference, inequality, and death as Grim Reaper and universal leveler. It's a story about the division between the peasant rabble locked outside the castle walls and the aristocracy locked inside, thinking they are protected from the plague but finding that they are not, of course, protected in the end. Meanwhile, one heroic rebel crosses the line to care for the dying. There's a whiff of Spinal Tap in the sometimes pompous-sounding dramatic recitation (Sean Egan says the song is "from the substantial flaky end of hippiedom"[28]). But, if you put the lyrics aside, you can hear a resemblance to the art-rock experiments of John Cale and Lou Reed. It's a droning soundtrack under a solemnly narrated story or poem, like the Velvet Underground's "The Black Angel's Death Song" or "The Gift." Interestingly, Burdon linked "The Black Plague" to the Animals' own earlier favorite genre, calling it "a blues about the Bubonic Plague of the 14th Century."[29] He may simply mean that, like the blues, the song exposes the suffering caused by class distinctions. But if we put aside the lyrics, it's possible he means to suggest a *musical* resemblance between "The Black Plague" and the dark feel of one-chord, drone-like blues tunes by Howlin' Wolf, for example, or Robert Johnson.

The second song Zappa mentions, "San Franciscan Nights," is a hippie ballad crossed with one of Burdon's journalistic scene-sketches. It starts with a parody of the opening voiceover for the TV show *Dragnet*, the familiar four-note theme followed by a spoken-word bit recited over a marching beat (but with Los Angeles changed to San Francisco): "This following program is dedicated to the city and people of San Francisco, who may not know it but they are beautiful, and so is their city." Burdon invites fellow Europeans, who may not get it, to fly "Trans-Love Airways" to come over and see for themselves. Then the singing begins, as if a troubadour were describing a film clip of the Fillmore or the

Avalon: "Strobe lights beam, creates dreams / Walls move, minds do too / On a warm San Franciscan night." The beat-poetry lyric then lists area musicians, Hells Angels, Harleys, and blue jeans, "cool" children *and* cops, with a rapid mandolin- or bouzouki-sound from a twelve-string guitar plays, baroquely, as the chorus ends: "There's no place left to go: San Francisco."

Even though Burdon eventually had a house in L.A.'s Laurel Canyon, he also liked to hang out with fellow musicians in Northern California. Everyone laughed at the idea of warm nights in the chilly City by the Bay, teasing him about what they assumed was a rookie error on the part of the Englishman, but Burdon said he wrote "San Franciscan Nights" about one particular visit he made during an unusual warm spell. That night, he met Janis Joplin at the Fillmore, who handed him a tab of Owsley acid, and he witnessed a Hells Angels beat-down right there on the dance floor—but was also immersed in a psychedelic communal experience. Except maybe for that violence in the club, it was a long way from the Tyneside Club A' Go Go. As the line "no place left to go" suggests, the final frontier, once you've reached the edge of the North American continent, has to be inward. Burdon would later compare visiting San Francisco in 1964, before "the psychedelic explosion," to his visit in 1967, when he said he experienced a new "feeling, an underlying belief that encouraged a new outlook, psychedelic humor, habits, and dress style."[30]

The first album with the new band, *Winds of Change* (1967), contains several examples of quintessential psychedelia. By then, they were in good company. A number of albums had been released in 1966 with competing claims to being the first to use the word in their title: *The Psychedelic Sounds of the 13th Floor Elevators* by the 13th Floor Elevators; *Psychedelic Lollipop* by the Blues Magoos; and *Psychedelic Moods* by the Deep. A list of other albums that were part of the trend that year would include the Beatles' *Revolver*; the Byrds' *Fifth Dimension*; the Blues Project's *Projections*; Cream's *Fresh Cream*; Donovan's *Sunshine Superman*; Love's *Da Capo*; and the Yardbirds' *Yardbirds*, just to name some of the more prominent. The (New) Animals joined the crowd. Their version of psychedelia was a product of the West Coast scene and the Summer of Love, as Burdon's lyrics made clear. It emerged out of the same milieu as the Grateful Dead (though album releases were never the most important form for that band), and Jefferson Airplane. *The Jefferson Airplane Takes Off* was released in 1966; by the time *Surrealistic Pillow* came out in 1967, they were fully identified with the new movement.

A number of psychedelic records released in 1966–1967 were essentially garage rock with trippy lyrics and layers of weird sound effects. Eric Burdon & the New Animals, on the other hand, tended (with a few exceptions) toward a chamber pop sound, open and porous in arrangement, spare but orchestrated in a way that calls to mind the softer tracks by the Velvet Underground or solo Nico, for example, or some of Donovan's songs. By their second album, *The Twain Shall Meet*, recorded December 1967 and released in May 1968, the orchestration would expand to include strings and horns on some tracks. The sound was indeed influenced by Burdon's encounter with Zappa and the Mothers. But it was also likely influenced by the experience of making *Eric Is Here* with Wilson. The arrangements on *Winds of Change* use twelve-string guitar; percussion instruments including bongos, bells, and cymbals; echoey piano; electric violin; and electric sitar. Although it's possible to tune a guitar in ways that allow a player to approximate something of the sounds of Indian classical music, the electric sitar was basically an electric guitar designed to have the tone of a sitar. Danelectro came out with a popular model, the Coral, in 1967, with a bridge that was designed to move and buzz and a second set of short, sympathetically vibrating drone strings built into the body of the instrument (tuned with a special key), intended to work somewhat like the multiple strings of an actual sitar. A promotional film for the Danelectro Coral said that it made it possible to play "the new, exotic, Eastern sound first introduced by the Beatles." (The Beatles went to India in July 1966, where they bought a range of Indian instruments including the sitar; George Harrison returned to study with Ravi Shankar in September of that year.) The Coral electric sitar is what Vic Briggs uses to play the singsong nursery rhyme–sounding riff and other parts, including playing along with John Weider's electric violin, on the title track, "Winds of Change." (He also plays it on other tracks.) Briggs became seriously interested in Indian classical music at around this time. He would later study Sikh music and learn to play sarod as well as sitar.

Some tracks on the album are almost program music, sounds telling a story or matching the theme of the lyrics, for example, "Hotel Hell," with an echo-saturated mariachi trumpet invoking the setting. All the tracks feature Burdon's storytelling. Some are spoken-word pieces, more like poetry over soundtracks (see "The Black Plague"). The vocals are often treated with heavy echo. Some sound like meditative chants, in stark contrast to the early Animals' blues shouting. A cover of "Paint It Black" goes further than the Rolling Stones' own version into the raga-influenced melody, wordless chants, and droning instrumentation, providing a setting for the lyric's bad-trip breakup imagery.

The song would show up again a few years later in an improvisational medley Burdon created with the percussion-heavy funk band War.

There are several songs with lyrics about music. "It's All Meat" is a hard electric blues number about the blues. Like a number of traditional blues songs, it's reflexive: it audibly demonstrates the blues it refers to in its lyric. A Hendrix-soundalike track, "Yes I Am Experienced," is a direct answer to "Are You Experienced?" When Burdon's song was written, Hendrix's had been performed live but had not yet been released (it would come out in May). It's an insider's call-and-response, a conversation between those in the know. "Some," he says, just don't get it: "And for those who never heard or seen the truth / They're blind." The lyric goes on to promise that those who do get it will be able to "fly with it," thus extending the response line in Hendrix's original: "Well, I have" ("been experienced"). The former bassist for the original Animals, Chas Chandler, was to become Hendrix's manager. Having heard him play in the Village, he helped him go to London, where they put together the band the Experience. Burdon had met Hendrix earlier, but during 1967 the two became close friends, touring partners, and fellow trippers for the few remaining years of Hendrix's life.

SANDOZ WHO TAUGHT ME LOVE

The most explicitly psychedelic song the Animals released in 1967 was a single not included on the album *Winds of Change*, but which helps to explain Burdon's profound transformation at the time, "A Girl Named Sandoz." It's the B side of a single, the A side of which is the nostalgic ballad "When I Was Young." The B-side song is a transparent reference to LSD. Sandoz was the Swiss pharmaceutical company where Dr. Albert Hofmann had first synthesized LSD-25 in 1938 and the company continued to test the hallucinogen until 1965.[31] For context: this song about a metaphorical "girl" was released in the same year as "Lucy in the Sky with Diamonds," which, despite the Beatles' later denials, was taken by most listeners at the time as a coded trip report. (Even if it began with an innocent coincidence in a child's drawing, that doesn't mean the songwriters' intentions for the song stopped there, that they didn't also intend the drug reference.) Burdon's tribute to LSD bluntly invites us to see through the transparent personification. The fact that the two songs—about the girl with kaleidoscope eyes and the old/young girl with many things to teach—were recorded at around the same time testifies to the metastasis of the psychedelic idea at that moment.

Burdon's track is in the form of a simple personification, a love song: "Well I met a girl called Sandoz / And she taught me many, many things." It's an already conventional hallucinogenic landscape, including an oxymoron of a sunny morning with snow on the ground mirroring the ambiguity of the "girl's" age: she's "very old" though she may appear to be young. The idea (it's too abstract to be called an image) of a winged mind is shared by the other Hendrix-sounding song on the album, "Yes I Am Experienced." Both echo the lyrics of Hendrix's own "Little Wing" and "Sweet Angel" ("My mind has wings").

The key word is "mind" ("They could all learn something from your mind"). Transcendent intersubjectivity is how the speaker imagines the drug's effect on him, his own mind communing with the personified universal "mind" opened up by the "girl." The short song's keywords—love, time, mind, strange, and things—are repeated. The end of the verse is just, "Good times, for all time, Sandoz." The phrase "good times" is ironic. These "good times" are like the "good things" the girl has taught the singer; and "times" are part of an eternity whose "time has come"—invoking the psychedelic-soul hit, "Time Has Come Today," by the Chambers Brothers (also released in 1967). "Good times, for all time": the last clause, "for all time," is the point. This is the polar opposite of the sad, sodden "good times" as recounted in the folkish pub song also on the album titled "Good Times": "When I think of all the good times that I've wasted having good times . . . All of that boozin' / I was really losin'." That (anti-) drinking song includes a brief interlude when the rhythm shifts into syncopation and we hear pub noises—clinking glasses, loud voices, raucous laughter, a honky-tonk piano—a British version ("having a jolly good time") of the cocktail-lounge sound effects on Zappa and the Mothers' "America Drinks and Goes Home." Over the years, most of the original Animals have told the story of how a division developed that year between the faction who drank and the faction who dropped acid, a cultural divide that they say led to the breakup of the Animals in 1966.[32] "Good Times" may be a salvo fired in that battle, a justification by Burdon written from the other side of the split.

The ascending and accelerating opening riff of "Good Times" calls to mind the opening piano cadence of the Rolling Stones' "She's a Rainbow," which was recorded in May 1967, yet another psychedelic song in the form of a love song (or vice versa). Musically, "A Girl Named Sandoz" also sounds like another Hendrix imitation, with a syncopated shuffle beat that recalls "Crosstown Traffic," with its growling fuzz bass line and heavy drums, and a counterpoint of chiming high notes on a xylophone—and of course an overdriven lead guitar. Weider shares the writing credit with Burdon, and his electric violin adds a key layer of complexity to the simple song. In a later moment almost thirty years afterwards, during 1990s *neo*-psychedelia, the song was covered by the alternative-rock band the Smashing Pumpkins.

THE PSYCHEDELIC MOMENT

It was called psychedelic music for a (literal) reason. Despite all the public disclaimers at the time, the music was always associated with, if not entirely caused by, the use of LSD, psilocybin, and other hallucinogens. The drug—even more, its collective ideation, the way people thought of it and mythologized it—had a huge effect on music but also on art, fashion, and culture for a brief historical moment. There were plenty of derivative bandwagon gimmicks and cash-in exploitations recorded at the time, but there was also a general shift in the texture and feel of a good deal of pop music between 1966 and 1968 that can be credited to musicians' (and listeners') actual experiences with psychedelics.

LSD had a big year in 1966. Through the 1950s, Sandoz Laboratories had made it widely available for clinical research, but in August 1965, due to a public panic and pressure from law enforcement, the lab halted production. The cat was already out of the bag. At the end of 1963, Harvard psychologist Timothy Leary, with Richard Alpert (later, Ram Dass), had started a communal center for experimentation with psychedelics at the Millbrook estate in upstate New York. In 1964, author Ken Kesey took his band of Merry Pranksters on a cross-country road trip in a painted bus to attend the World's Fair in New York—and to visit Millbrook. By 1966 Leary was an underground celebrity and his slogan, "turn on, tune in, drop out," the title of a book by him, became famous—and notorious. On October 6, 1966, LSD was made illegal in California (the federal law would come later). In San Francisco, Augustus Owsley Stanley III, along with a handful of others around the country, were by then taking up the slack (and then some) synthesizing the drug on their own. The ballroom scene in San Francisco was fueled not by Sandoz but by Owsley acid, at first distributed to and through the Grateful Dead and their inner circle (Owsley was a sound technician for the band).[33] This is the milieu into which Burdon dropped on that famous warm San Franciscan night. He says he was given blotter-paper acid made by Owsley when he arrived at the Fillmore. This was the same scene that the New York–based Blues Project participated in that year, when they played the Avalon Ballroom's opening shows before a swirling audience of "lysergic people," as Danny Kalb hailed them from the stage.

So, as Burdon and Weider were writing and recording "A Girl Named Sandoz," the drug had just been declared illegal in California. Like "Yes I Am Experienced," it's an insider's song, a way of hinting at a psychedelic underground the band was part of but many or most in their listening audience were not. It was a declaration of Burdon's new psychedelic authenticity. As annoying (and often self-serving) as any profession of faith by the newly converted, this sort of declaration was everywhere in the 1960s and early 1970s, a way of staking out one's identity as someone who *knew*, who had been there. It's the core of what Hendrix meant by "experienced" in the first place. Psychedelic experiences can indeed be life changing. See Aldous Huxley's 1954 *The Doors of Perception*, for example, or Dr. Hofmann's own accounts of the brain-altering glimpse of an alternative reality that changes one's whole perspective. But the experience is often difficult to share with those who haven't experienced it for themselves. That sense of having discovered an alternative identity beyond the ego (sometimes paradoxically expressed with an egotistical sense of superiority) is the backstory behind most of the obscure pseudo-symbolist lyrics and forbiddingly dense sounds of much psychedelic rock. Sometimes the music tried to embody an authentic sonic expression of what it was like to be on LSD; sometimes it was a matter of exploiting the power of the blues, for example, to induce an analogous state of trance/transcendence. Sometimes, of course, psychedelic music just repeated LSD tropes and images for commercial purposes, or just to get in on what was happening, to sound hip.

ULTIMATE MUSIC

The insider's vision of an alternative form of mental and spiritual authenticity clearly appealed to Burdon, and it made his music of 1966–1967 sound starkly different from his earlier rowdy R&B. It's also what makes those psychedelic songs sound so dated now, because in them he wears his psychedelic authenticity on his (caftan) sleeve. Burdon enthusiastically embraced the new identity, just as he dissolved the Animals and then reconstituted a new band, the New Animals. Sharing the language of the initiated, he spoke of his new music in strikingly universal terms. In an interview in *Melody Maker*, October 7, 1967, on the occasion of the release of *Winds of Change*, Burdon said that "every track is dedicated to love and humanity."[34] The journalist, Bob Dawbarn, drily comments: "Eric, as you may have gathered, becomes more and more immersed in the new Love philosophy." Burdon explains the dissolution of the original Animals in sweeping terms about what happened in 1966, saying that he and the Animals had been part of a general trend of groups breaking up, because "certain people had changes in thought and they no longer mixed." Then he goes on to explain the significance of the album, *Winds of Change*: "It sounds big-headed," he admitted, "but it is on the verge of creating ultimate music. From the cover to every track and every sound—it's all for everybody." The grand statements continue: "musicians have the answers to the world's problems. They don't know it, but they have. It's up to them to walk the path that I have done." Asked if this meant he was rejecting the blues, he replies, "No . . . I accept everything I have learned from. Now I am singing blues of my mind, 1967 blues, my own blues."[35]

It quickly escalates, as "changes of thought" lead to new musical relationships, in pursuit of a universal ideal, "ultimate music . . . all for everybody." The casually messianic language ("walk the path that I have done") leads to "everything I have learned from" being internalized, including the blues. Burdon revealingly refers to the "blues of my mind." Which is the blues of the times, he says. In other words, 1967 blues is psychedelic blues. Rather than "expression of suffering in song," blues in this case must mean something like "self-expression of the soul," which is more or less the message of "It's All Meat." The song asserts an odd equivalence among Muddy Waters, Ray Charles, Miles Davis, Ravi Shankar, Erkel Darbies (?), Eric Clapton, Muhammed Ali, and an anonymous drunken Irishman—the point being to universalize the blues until it's something more like the marrow of authentic human feeling and its sincere expression: "from the whole wide world / Deep within the souls of men."

TOM WILSON TAUGHT

Burdon later confirmed the rumor that, when he was seventeen, he wrote the word "blues" in his own blood on the cover of a notebook in which he was writing song lyrics.[36] He says he gave the journal to one of his heroes, Nina Simone, who kept it for a few years and then returned it. Afterwards, it was stolen from backstage during a show. This is probably not the same raggedy notebook photographed for the cover of *Winds of Change* or the book Burdon is pictured writing in on the back cover, but the point is that Burdon's romantic image as a *writer* was closely bound up with his dedication to the blues. Burdon never really relinquished his obsession with the blues and American Black culture. Evidence includes his consistent devotion to Black musicians, from Bo Diddley and Chuck Berry to the jazz experimentalist Rahsaan Roland Kirk. And then there's his joining as frontman of the L.A.-based Black soul band Nightshift—which was renamed War.[37] With War, Burdon made hit records (especially "Spill the Wine") and toured successfully, including sharing the stage at Ronnie Scott's Jazz Club in London with Hendrix, in what would turn out to be the guitarist's final show. Burdon later said of the initial idea for his collaboration with War: "Eric Burdon with a black band—now there's a concept."[38] During early rehearsals, he admits, significantly, that it was at first "a bit awkward as I wanted to lean toward the blues. The band didn't. They didn't listen to the blues and didn't want to play it. American blues meant one thing to a group of black guys from Long Beach and quite another to people like me, Eric Clapton, Jimmy Page, and Keith Richards."[39] He left War over conflicting contracts, he later said. They went on to rack up a series of hits in the 1970s, including "The World Is a Ghetto," "Cisco Kid," and "Why Can't We Be Friends?"

But back in the intense moment of 1966–1967, Burdon was looking for a new kind of authenticity, and the effort of that search showed in the albums of that period, sometimes as successful experiments and sometimes as failed experiments. Given what we know about Tom Wilson, it's impossible not to credit him with at least encouraging those experiments and influencing the direction they took. This is true even if Burdon's own experiments with LSD and immersion in California culture framed the results in terms of his finding a psychedelic solution to the problem of identity. For the back cover of *Winds of Change*, as mentioned above, Burdon himself wrote of Wilson—after first characterizing him as "Producer" and then, physically, as "tall" and "brown" (by which he meant to emphasize his Blackness)—that he: "Taught me not to be afraid of being myself. Taught me to leave my negro hangups behind, and to use what I'd learnt from black people to my own avail." Wilson was not just a producer in the technical sense—the person in the booth calling takes and asking for more reverb—he was an A&R executive, someone always thinking about ways to help artists develop their repertoires, to help them develop. As we've seen, he tended to think of such development in terms of the exploration of genres.

Zappa echoed Wilson's advice, specifically in relation to the Animals: "I had an experience arranging some stuff for them, and I found that not only were they were not particularly original, but were hung up in that R&B bag, which is deadening when you get little white boys trying to be little black boys, screaming the blues and being funky and all—that's shitty."[40] (Zappa knew that trap from experience.) Zappa also said of Wilson more generally, "He's been responsible, having been producing a long time, for most major weirdnesses in music"[41]—and he means "weirdnesses" in the most positive sense, as nonconforming musical expressions outside the clichés of the music business, the kind of weirdness that Zappa aspired to in his own music. Wilson clearly encouraged Burdon to develop his own thing, to leave behind his fixation on hoary blues tropes (and Black vocal styles) and to use his deeper understanding of blues and R&B as music, as art forms, for his own authentic artistic expression. Burdon interpreted this as a call to turn inward, to sing the psychedelic blues. That's why the story of Burdon embodies the key story of this book. In pursuit of authenticity, the scruffy British blues singer with a powerful voice was transformed into a beads-wearing psychedelic bard. He literally *idealized* the blues, turning it into something of the mind, of his own mind. Nothing could be more 1966. Unless it's the transformation of a whole band of TV pop stars into beads-wearing psychedelic "heads." I'm referring, of course, to the Monkees. Stay tuned.

CHAPTER EIGHT

HERE THEY COME

The Monkees, *The Monkees* (1966); *More of the Monkees* (1967); *Headquarters* (1967)

WALKIN' DOWN THE STREET

"It Can't Happen Here," along with "Hungry Freaks, Daddy," from Frank Zappa's *Freak Out!*, established the theme of an unwashed horde of countercultural underground youth, freaks or hippies, coming for middle America, in every town and city. *That* ominous theme was still ringing in the air—at least in hip circles that knew the album—when the "(Theme from) The Monkees," by Tommy Boyce and Bobby Hart, played on TV the evening of September 12, 1966: "Here We Come . . . ."[1] A sharp drum snap, then the lyric sung in a minor key, backed with a heavily syncopated bass + high hat + finger snaps. By the time the intro was over and the first episode of *The Monkees* began, viewers had been reassured by the rest of the tune (including an abrupt modulation to a major-key chorus) that, although the long-haired Monkees might be coming to town, there was really nothing to fear. They were just cutups, kids "too busy singin' / To put anybody down." But the reassurance only served to remind some of the threat it was meant to assuage: hippie-types *might* be coming to your town to put people down (and who knows what else). (In the full recorded version, the theme song continued, "just look over your shoulder / Guess who'll be standing there?") By 1968, the sarcasm of a spoken-word track "Ditty Diego–War Chant," from *Head*, made clear that the Monkees had changed their tune into something more ominous, openly admitting they were a "manufactured image / With no philosophies." The Monkees were always both innocuous TV characters and in on the joke, pop entertainment and something darker, commenting on pop. In fact, they were always walking and singing double-entendres. They were a nascent rock band in sheep's clothing whose very existence exposed the machinery behind their own "manufactured image."

WHAT THE MONKEES MEANT

The Monkees were always about more than mass entertainment, though they were that, were in fact created for that purpose. What they meant in 1966 depended on where you sat among the demographic segments of their viewing and listening audience(s). It's common to talk about the band chronologically, as having two eras: before and after their declaration of independence from Don Kirshner. The psychedelic avant-garde film *Head*, which premiered in 1968, was, in this scenario, their final pyrrhic victory. But instead of discrete eras, we can think of these as oppositional possibilities—pop stardom and underground credibility—that were always present in the Monkees' conflicted situation, toggling, jostling for dominance, together making up their ambiguous cultural significance.

Of the two oppositional possibilities, underground credibility was at first out of the question, just given the way the music was made and the publicity that surrounded it. Which is not to say that the music on the first two Monkees albums isn't good. On the contrary, much of it is very good pop. The two albums were professional productions, from the songwriting to the session musicians who played the songs. Both were released in that first year: *The Monkees* and *More of the Monkees*, obviously meant to capitalize on the TV show, but also to materialize the fiction of the band, to give fans music as if from the Monkees they saw on their screens. The third album, *Headquarters*, on which the band played and sang nearly everything themselves, appeared in May 1967, the band's answer to its critics and a response to the embarrassment of their situation. For the first two albums, the producers worked with writers and session musicians to make music for target audiences. The third album, which aimed to subvert that model and stand on its own as an "authentic" album by the Monkees as a band, actually targeted a different audience or segment of their audience—the relatively hipper one.

The standard story of the Monkees goes: a hastily assembled TV band decided to cut their puppet strings and become a real band. But the story is actually less Pinocchio and more Frankenstein. Like Mary Shelley's lumbering monster, the Monkees wanted to be loved—which is to say, recognized as real, as authentic. They were part of a stitched-together fake band that was shocked by success, came alive, and began looking for recognition. Then the Frankenband turned on its creators when it saw the horrified look in their eyes (play their own instruments?! play live?). *Headquarters*, the first album on which the band wrote and played everything, was intended to bite the corporate hand that had fed them. About a year later, the movie *Head* (and its soundtrack album) was the logical follow-on, when, like Frankenstein's creature, they discovered they would never really be accepted on their own terms. So, they burned it all down. On the *album Head*, the band extended their experimentation with underground strands of contemporary pop music on their way out. To achieve even this limited hip credibility, they thought they had to destroy their bubblegum identities. That was the stated purpose of the film. Pop success versus underground authenticity: the story of the Monkees supposedly dramatizes that stark dichotomy as it was imagined everywhere in pop music and pop culture in 1966–1967. But this was always an oversimplification, a theory that ignores the complications of pop music, for one thing, and ignores the limitations of the hip underground, for another.

In fact, the Monkees were the product of messy, dynamic *interchanges* between those opposed options, TV and music, chart singles and albums, effervescent bubblegum pop and underground musical experimentation. They were always a weird amalgam, and that weirdness was key, I think, to their appeal. Davy Jones with cartoony animated stars in his eyes; Micky Dolenz chewing up the scenery—but also playing one of the first spooky-sounding Moog synthesizers in pop music (on "Daily Nightly"); Peter Tork earnestly playing his banjo at solo gigs or standing at the keyboard looking bored or embarrassed to be on TV. The whole group a boy band in matching double-breasted red shirts that included the tall, cerebral, and smirking Michael Nesmith in a green stocking cap, cooking up on the side a lyrically sophisticated country-rock. Producers at Raybert were trying to have a primetime hit that still came off as relatively hip. That double aim, including the inherent contradictions, were what actually made the Monkees watchable and listenable for a variety of audiences. The Monkees franchise as a whole—the hit records, the TV show, the paratextual merchandise, the final underground film—embodied the tensions between creative ambition and the demands of commercial success. No act better expressed those tensions, the contradictions and competing energies that characterized pop in general in 1966.

PRODUCED

The Monkees were a product: they were produced, in more than one sense. We can't forget that the show began with a duo of young TV producers, Bob Rafelson and Bert Schneider, even before Don Kirschner began to produce the music. This book has been focused on the record producer, Tom Wilson. He had nothing to do with the Monkees, but his views on music production help us understand the significance of the media franchise about a rock band. Wilson always said he wanted to give as much rein as possible to his artists' identities and creative impulses. Often, this led people to accuse him of being removed or uninterested, but he seems to have thought of it as a form of therapeutic empowerment. And his commitment to allowing artists to experiment was evident as early as the 1950s at Transition Records, where eccentrics like Sun Ra were given the spotlight, even while Wilson at times tried to steer them in what he thought of as more commercial directions. The role of the producer (or A&R executive) was in transition in the mid-1960s. Bands began to follow the Beatles' lead and go into the studio as creative collectives rather than clay to be molded. (Yet even the Beatles had George Martin, at least for a time, to guide their sessions.) Wilson's sometimes contradictory-sounding attitudes, however tongue-in-cheek, reflected real contradictions within the music industry as it was going through significant changes.

Sometime in the mid- to late 1960s, Wilson gave a speech at a convention about the role of the producer. His opening focuses on the changing media environment:

> First let me make it clear, as the best record producer ever developed in Waco Texas, I have not come here to advocate the standard adversary relationship between the so-called creative guys and the functional guys. I believe that everyone involved with the process of producing and purveying records is creative, or should be. This is especially true now that we are entering into an era of complex mixed media where varied information—pictures, sounds, symbols—will become fused into a freely associative entertainment form. In order to adjust to this new age, we will have to forget the old divisions, the ancient antagonisms that divide A&R, sales, promo-

> tion, distribution, and dealership people into separate warring clans. We must establish a cohesive, creative flow that begins in the studio and ends at the point of sale.[2]

His final sentence (at least in this draft) makes a characteristic joke: "In all of these highly cooperative, mutual agreement-circumstances the producer will be given the benefit of the doubt, because I hope you didn't really believe that I don't think the producer really ought to be in charge." The irony is of the kind Wilson often displayed on *The Music Factory* radio show, for example, in the self-deprecating and arch story about getting a tinfoil "gold record" for *Batman and Robin*. In that case he mocked himself for singing the blues about the faux award, but he also exposed the absurdity of the industry in the process. Yes, he consistently saw the producer as being at the center of the process of making records. But he also pursued the ideal of a collaborative "creative flow" in an era of "complex mixed media," and saw pop music as an arena in which varied kinds of work could contribute to meaningful results.

At one point in the speech, Wilson sounds as if he's channeling Marshall McLuhan when he describes the new "era of complex mixed media where varied information—pictures, sounds, symbols . . . fused into a freely associative entertainment form." In fact, McLuhan had based his theories in part on the kind of music and media that Wilson and others helped to create. The Velvet Underground and psychedelic multimedia happenings like the Exploding Plastic Inevitable figure in his work as examples.[3] This too is what Wilson meant by "everything is everything," an embrace of eclecticism of media and form—including forms of creative labor in the music industry—as well as of genre. The producer works as part of a larger endeavor, as a kind of conductor and media coordinator, not an alienated factory worker running the hit-making machinery. But the music industry is also part of the creative process, or can be, making a vital material contribution to the "everything." After all, Wilson would go on a few years later to become a stakeholder in the founding of the Record Plant studios, which was meant to be an artist-friendly recording space with a "living-room" feel. One of the initial ideas of a name for the new studio, which Wilson helped brainstorm, was "the Music Factory" (the same name as his radio show).[4] "Plant" was chosen as a nicely ambiguous synonym of "Factory."

This capacious way of imagining "production" was broadly compatible with a multiplatform, "manufactured," but no less creative, endeavor like the Monkees. Yes, music director for the show, Kirshner, was part of the residual Brill Building scene, and his initial heavy-handed approach to the actors/musicians eventually led to a break with the cast/band. (After the Monkees, Kirshner went on to have a smash success with the Archies, an entirely imaginary, animated band of comic-book characters, made for Saturday morning TV and the commercial tie-ins that came with it: lunchboxes, posters, toys—and vinyl records.) But even he played a key role in the startup of the Monkees, a franchise that was bigger than he was and was one of the most successful transmedia pop culture productions of the 1960s.

The actor-musicians, Dolenz, Jones, Nesmith, and Tork, were hired into sitcom roles. But the show they were in was about music, and music was featured in its storyline and its soundtrack. From Kirshner's point of view, the records were potentially lucrative spinoffs, opportunities to cash in. But because of the show's premise, the songs were *diegetic* features, as drama theorists might say, media experienced within the show's story world—as when the band performs lip-syncs or improvises an undercranked-looking sped-up "romp" (à la *A Hard Day's Night*) while a particular number plays. But the songs were also nondiegetic, were, we might say, *epitextual*—outside of the show proper—when they were released as singles or as tracks on albums. At the same time, fans connected the music with the show: playing the records on your turntable made the fictional band seem real. At first, professional songwriters and studio musicians made most of the music, though the actors, especially Dolenz and Jones, were allowed to record vocal tracks.

It was inevitable that this situation—a group of youthful rock-music types being used as a front for manufactured commercial pop, for a mixed audience with mixed expectations—would lead to conflict. The whole situation was built on contradictions. The conflict was at first mostly behind the scenes, but it showed through in small ways on camera, such as a sardonic remark by one of the stars that broke the fourth wall. In some ways, *The Monkees* was a kind of reality show before reality TV. It's surprising it lasted as long as it did—about a year and a half—at a time when, as producer Bob Rafelson later said, "authenticity, integrity and a certain kind of pop truth [were] the slogans of the day."[5] It's worth pausing to note that "authenticity" and "a certain kind of pop truth" might be a contradiction in terms.

THE MAKEUP OF *THE MONKEES* (THE ALBUM)

If you listen to the first three albums in a row: *The Monkees*, *More of the Monkees*, and *Headquarters*—and you listen in the context of the TV show and film + soundtrack album, *Head*—you can hear the complications of the Monkees' story, right there between the tracks. The producers of *The Monkees* deliberately set out to exploit the contradictions and "the ambiguity of the situation" the Monkees were in.[6] The albums seem to have been planned to reach a layered audience by mixing lightweight bubblegum pop with semi-hip sounds, fan-club fodder with slightly more daring stuff. The strategy was opportunistic, but it also played on (and reflected) a deep ambiguity in pop culture as a whole, the dynamic opposition between mainstream and underground. This was often experienced by listeners as what Wilson referred to as the difference between "the popular and the *recherché*." There was a certain amount of blatant exploitation of prepubescent fan-club members. But the overall appeal of the Monkees leveraged that opposition, played on the inherent ambiguity of the whole thing. Many viewers and listeners experienced the Monkees as *both* a mass-market confection and as providing a taste, at least, of a hipper underground perspective.

The actor-musicians enjoyed a broad international success as TV celebrities. But what they wanted, it was clear (at least after the first season of the show), was to be hip and to be a *real* band. They would never be 100% hip or 100% real. But they had some sophisticated fans who were not *only* indulging in a camp lark. People are still surprised today to learn that Frank Zappa, John Lennon, and other credible musicians actually admired the Monkees and their music. These artist-fans were likely responding to the possibility of revolt built into the whole project. The show might have gone off the rails at any minute. That was part of the attraction, especially for those who were outside the preteen and teen demographic, but also, I argue, for a portion of that demographic, too, who, more than most people gave them credit for, sensed and responded to the exciting tensions surrounding the Monkees. Not unlike viewers of *The Smothers Brothers*, who were also (from February 1967) playing music on TV, testing the limits of conventions and, in their case, testing the censors, *The Monkees* attracted some viewers who watched through tinted shades, as it were, in a meta-pop frame of mind. Of course it attracted besotted preteens—that was its prime directive. But it appealed to both kinds of viewers.

The Beatles were the first widely known rock band to embody something like this ambiguous meta-pop dynamic in their personae. They were known for their double-entendres onstage, in interviews, and in films—a wink at the camera, playing with the absurdity of the form—as displayed in *A Hard Day's Night*. Their meta-theatrical dialogue in that film was usually delivered dead-pan, starting with the earliest scene on the train, juxtaposed with musical numbers in which the band comes across as fairly sincere, about the music at least, even if they're lip-syncing and eyeing the girls who are standing around. Little Richard and Elvis Presley had made use of similar double-voicing in the previous decade, on stage and in movies. Rock 'n' roll had always been about irreverence and a smart-aleck attitude. This was likely inspired in part by the ironic attitude of some jazz performers, which had inspired similar slyly ironic attitudes among some jazz-influenced American pop singers during the swing era of the 1940s and early 1950s. Rock 'n' roll just did the same thing in leather (except for a brief interlude when it was in mod suits), with more adolescent defiance and with the volume turned up.

The Beatles came across as relatively friendly, famously less threatening than many rock 'n' rollers (and the Teddy Boys who had inspired them). Still, they were the first well-known rock band to consistently deploy hip irony as an artistic strategy, a double-voice flickering between pop effervescence and a rock attitude. They played to screaming young girls at the shows or at home with their record players; hip teens and adults listened to the same records in a slightly different way. Eventually, after 1966, they gave up the screaming, stopped performing live, and made studio art for home listeners, concentrating on the album as their primary form. The Monkees were the first TV rock band to take their cue from the Beatles when it came to that kind of double-voicing for a divided audience. The sitcom writers structured the show that way: Jones sees yet another young girl and his eyes sparkle, a TV-magic special-effect joke about TV magic, framing yet another seduction story. The preteen and teen girls in the viewing audience swoon and rush to join the fan club and buy the records. Others (and just maybe some in the fan club) knowingly appreciate the gimmick and the irony behind it.

The Monkees were the first rock band to do this on TV—unless you count the Beatles' own appearance in an animated cartoon. By 1966, *The Beatles* was a Saturday morning cartoon watched by children eating their breakfast cereal. Before the release of their own animated *Yellow Submarine*, there was the commercial-sponsored Saturday show, four caricatures in stovepipe-leg suits and turtlenecks romping around as if *A Hard Day's Night* or *Help!* had been transformed into 2D, conceptually as well as visually. With voice actors. Also, singalongs. You could literally follow the subtitled lyrics as the cartoon band played Beatles recordings. Every episode was named for songs. The first was "A Hard Day's Night / I Want to Hold Your Hand." It premiered in September 1965, just before *Rubber Soul* was released. By 1966 there was a wider awareness among the general audience of the double-entendre attitude and its association with pop, an awareness a show like *The Monkees* could take for granted and exploit, as the bandmembers looked straight into the camera and dropped the register of their voices to read their ridiculous lines.

The double-voicing for a divided audience structured Monkees records too. Some of the songs were obvious teenybopper bait, like "I'll Be True to You," by Gerry Goffin and Russ Titelman, for example, which was first released by the Hollies in 1965 as "Yes I Will." The Monkees' version includes a saccharine spoken-word bridge by heartthrob Jones. It was supposedly inspired by "If I Fell" from *A Hard Day's Night*.[7] On *The Monkees* album, the teenybopper tearjerker sits right alongside more straight-ahead garage-band ravers ("Let's Dance On"). Some of the tracks are relatively mature pop songs. Lyrically, even radio hits like "Last Train to Clarksville" could be taken in more than one way. It hinted at the Vietnam War as the backstory for the two lovers—they were being separated by the draft. But the song could also be heard more generally as yet another romantic breakup song.

The first two Monkees albums contain some sly references to drugs, sexual freedom, and general rebellion (though rarely any actual politics), as well as tunes with bits of Indian ragas, psychedelic blues (e.g., "Mary, Mary," from *More of the Monkees*, which had been recorded by the Paul Butterfield Blues Band before *The Monkees* TV show aired), and some clowning around that, with camera tricks, crosses over into absurdist humor in the tradition of the Marx Brothers. Even the anodyne theme song—with its insistence that the band was "just tryin' to be friendly," and didn't want to "put anybody down," and yet somehow still had "something to say"—reflects this strategic dichotomy. The ominous tone—"Here we come . . . look over your shoulder . . ."—is, as we've seen, followed by disclaimers. The truth is, they *did* want to put *somebody* down, if gently: stereotypical squares, suburbanites, and uptight aunties, but also, in a backhanded way, the imagined stereotype of the naive girl among their fans.

That stereotypic fangirl is objectified and complicated by songs like "Sweet Young Thing," from *The Monkees*. Nesmith cowrote it with Carole King and Gerry Goffin, and it has a fast-driving country-rock beat, with a bluegrass fiddle drone. Its lyric may hint at the common rock 'n' roll subject of the attractions of underage or near-underage girls (see Chuck Berry's "Sweet Little Sixteen," Papa John Phillips's "Twelve Thirty [Young Girls Are Coming to the Canyon]," and so on). But, in something like the reverse of the Animals' "A Girl Named Sandoz," "Sweet Young Thing" describes the male fantasy of the groupie dream girl in the language of a mind-expanding drug trip.

I know that something very strange
Has happened to my brain
I'm either feeling very good
Or else I am insane.

People "try to talk" to the speaker, but he resists their attempts to bring him down and declares: that he "must yield before / The wisdom of a child." The subject in this case is not explicitly sexual ("it's love you bring"); and the song is not necessarily about a groupie, as "Star Collector" is, for example, also written by Goffin and King (but without Nesmith), included on *Pisces, Aquarius, Capricorn & Jones Ltd.* (1967). *That* one says it out loud: "She only aims to please young celebrities" and "How can I love her, / When I just don't respect her?"[8] Its title, even, is only one modifier away from the Rolling Stones' "Star Star" ("Starfucker"). But on *The Monkees*, "Sweet Young Thing" is a suggestive rock song adjacent to the saccharine "I'll Be True to You." Double-voicing, in this case, is in terms of genre and based on the juxtapositions of the album's track list.

After that opening track of *The Monkees*, the "Theme," we get a straight-ahead pop song, "Saturday's Child," about choosing the girl who just wants to have fun. Its bouncy rhythm, sunny melody, and group harmonies owe something to the Lovin' Spoonful's power-pop hit, "You Didn't Have to Be So Nice" (1965). Indeed, *The Monkees'* producers had considered hiring the Lovin' Spoonful, a real band, to play the TV band.[9] That, in turn, is followed by one of the hit singles from the album, "I Wanna Be Free," a dreamy chamber-pop tune sung by Jones and written by Boyce and Hart. Structurally, it's a folk song with an orchestral arrangement. The genre would have been recognizable to anyone in 1966, a wistful ballad not unlike "500 Miles" or "Hang Down Your Head, Tom Dooley." In Jones's plaintive voice and British accent, the lyric is a calculated heartbreaker. It steals the Beatles' already-tested line, "I want to hold your hand," and paints a montage of chaste beach walks and vague "fun," but "without any strings."

Two very different country-inflected rock songs follow, "Tomorrow's Gonna Be Another Day" (by Boyce) and "Papa Gene's Blues" (by Nesmith). The Nesmith song is pure country rock. Session guitarist James Burton's solos provoke Nesmith to call out, in the style of Bob Wills, "Play it, Magic Fingers," and "Pick it, Luther!"—a reference to Luther Perkins, who played lead guitar for Johnny Cash.[10] Interestingly, the final track on side 1 is a Goffin and King number with psychedelic lyrics, "Take a Giant Step."

DOUBLE-VOICING AND META-THEATRICS

The pattern I'm talking about goes beyond the tried-and-true strategy of alternating slow numbers with fast numbers, ballads with rockers. On these albums a zig-zag pattern of bubblegum tunes alternate with relatively more mature songs across several genres. And the latter sometimes dip into folk-rock or underground music of the moment. Now, there's nothing surprising about a commercial album trying to appeal to diverse audiences. What's interesting in this case is how the zigzagging diversity follows certain genre assumptions about what the mainstream versus (relatively) underground, or at least hip, audience might expect to hear. The genre-eclecticism is commercially interested, of course, but it's also a response to perceived cultural divisions, and the album embodies those divisions.

The TV show clearly aimed to play on these divisions as well. Rafelson and Schneider, the show's producers, were young, with "a streak of hip that traded on being avant-garde and adroitly subversive."[11] After the pilot didn't play well with advance test audiences, they edited in clips from the irreverent screen tests by the band members as themselves: instant meta-theatrics. The show was much better received. Watching these clips, it becomes clear they are meant to display a true authenticity, via hip irony on the actors' parts about the phoniness of TV as a medium. These sincere-because-ironic bits by the Monkees gave hipper viewers a knowing vantage from which to laugh at the rest of the show while still enjoying it. This is very much like what *Batman* had already been doing on a different network, starting back in January, and was still doing during that fall 1966 TV season, when *The Monkees* premiered.

The connections between *The Monkees* and *Batman* include details like the red phone in their "pad" and the Monkeemobile, parodies of the Batphone and the Batmobile, as well as the "Monkeemen" capes and tights the band sometimes wear in fantasy sequences. The Penguin from *Batman*, played by Burgess

Meredith, even had a brief cameo in a late episode. But season 1, episode 23 (February 20, 1967), "Captain Crocodile," goes all out in its tribute. The episode as a whole is a spoof of the children's show *Captain Kangaroo.* Addressing their own situation, the Monkees try to play music on the fictional show, to no avail. When musing about "other TV shows" they might be on, they imagine a takeoff on *Batman* called *Frogman and Reuben the Tadpole,* and the skit is acted out, a spoof within a spoof about another spoofy show. The superheroes in the satire are "the Amphibious Duo" (rather than "the Dynamic Duo," as Batman and Robin were known). There are colored lights, a tilted camera, and a fake-looking fight scene with sound-effect word bubbles ("Rumble!," "Plink," "Plank," and "Plunk," and, inexplicably, "Kretch"—as well as "Miss" when one of the punches doesn't connect). Frogman's and Reuben the Tadpole's suits are kinky red leatherette with zippers. Actually, they are the same "frogman" scuba suits the band wore in another episode, stock wardrobe that probably inspired the name of the superhero bit. The "Captain Crocodile" episode is about the absurdity of television, the band's persistent attempts to play their own music on TV, and the tyranny of catering to underage fans' unreasonable demands. More broadly, it's about the impossibility of being authentic in the "vast wasteland" of the media, especially when television is crossed with the record business. Just to make *that* point, Dolenz reads a story to the kids that begins "Once upon a time, in the land of Kirshner . . ."

None of this required a theory of meta-drama on the part of the show's creators or among its audience. But in the mid-1960s, that and similar concepts associated with the avant-garde drama of Luigi Pirandello, for example, and Antonin Artaud, were just in the air. Notions of dissolving the fourth wall separating the performance from the audience had gone mainstream (this culminated in the success of the musical *Hair* in 1967–1968). Among theories of this sort influencing writers, directors, and actors at the time was Bertolt Brecht's "alienation effect" (*Verfremdungseffekt*).[12] For him, this involved the positive "alienation" or distancing of the audience from the play. In that way, a critical perspective could open up. It relied on staging that revealed the artificiality of the production, ignoring the fourth wall and the conceptual frame of the theater itself. Prominent verbal signs or labels placed on the scenery, or direct addresses to the audience, could expose the artifice of the theater while the play was in progress. Theoretically, in Brecht's view, this could give the audience a distanced perspective from which to critique the play, but also maybe allow them to critique society's dominant ideologies and conventions.

It's unlikely that *The Monkees* producers Rafelson and Schneider intentionally set out to make Brechtian television. But the general concepts behind his theory, and related avant-garde theories, were commonly known. Local college and community theaters were staging works by Beckett, Pirandello, Artaud, and Brecht. In rock music, the Dada-influenced revue of Zappa and the Mothers of Invention in New York in 1967 was likely received by an audience with some awareness of similar avant-garde theater going on downtown and elsewhere. The highly influential Living Theatre, for example, had been a primary example in the years just before Zappa and the Mothers arrived in New York. But there were other similar experimental theater groups in 1966–1967, including small agitprop performances on the street or at protests. An absurdist strain also ran through film at the time: Richard Lester had made an early surreal comedy in the spirit of the avant-garde *The Running Jumping & Standing Still Film* (1959). It was this work that brought him to the attention of the Beatles and led to his making *A Hard Day's Night* and *Help!* These films were wrapped in a recognizably (for those in the know) "experimental" or "underground" aura that was starting to become more widespread at the time of their release. It was both things at once: pop and underground.

That both/and appeal was likely another thing Raybert Productions aimed to imitate with their TV show about a Beatlesque band. The culture was ripe with examples of pop/avant-garde crossovers. Soon after *The Monkees* premiered on American TV, John Lennon met the conceptual artist Yoko Ono at a showing of her works at the hip Indica Gallery in London (November 7, 1966). Paul McCartney had by that time become a kind of "patron of the avant-garde," including helping to found and promote the Indica Gallery and Bookstore.[13] Lennon and the other Beatles became Monkees fans. Members of the two bands socialized. The Beatles even threw a party for the Monkees in 1967 at a London club. Whether in L.A. or in London, the Monkees moved freely from mobs of screaming fans to hip artistic and social circles. The TV show itself was built around that kind of mobility. If we listen, we can hear that mobility reflected in the recorded music as well.

BUT WAIT, THERE'S *MORE*

The Monkees as a TV show aimed at a mass market. Further exploiting that market was the primary reason the second album was made and titled, bluntly, *More of the Monkees*. It was released quickly in January 1967 to build on the show's momentum. The band wasn't even aware it was coming out and hadn't heard it until it was released. The cover photo of the four of them had been shot earlier as part of a promotional tie-in deal with J. C. Penney's department store. In the photo they're wearing dorky button-up shirts and belts and slacks from the uncool mainstream retailer—the company had explicitly pushed for the album cover as part of their deal—and the band was not happy when they learned that the cover had been printed.[14] Kirshner's liner note emphasizes his own role and that of the session musicians at the expense of the Monkees themselves. Soon thereafter, at an angry meeting with Kirshner at the Beverly Hills Hotel, Nesmith famously punched his fist through a wall to emphasize the band's displeasure with the whole arrangement. Kirshner was dismissed as music coordinator at the end of February, the proximate cause being that he released a single in Canada behind everyone's backs.[15]

More of the Monkees was an instant hit. Serving pent-up demand, it replaced *The Monkees* at the top of the charts. The pattern of covering the bases by combining bubblegum pop hits with hipper rock songs (including some psychedelia) shifted with this album in the direction of pure pop. Another division came into sharper focus: between tracks produced by Kirshner's mostly New York–based songwriters, who sometimes also served as the actual producers of the tracks they wrote, and everything else, including the couple of original tunes by Nesmith allowed on each of the first two albums. The outside songwriters were skilled professionals, Carole King and Gerry Goffin, Neil Diamond, Neal Sedaka, Carol Bayer Sager, and Boyce and Hart. Diamond had two songs on *More of the Monkees*, "Look Out (Here Comes Tomorrow)" and what would become the monster hit "I'm a Believer." Boyce and Hart, the original "shadow Monkees" whose songs, and sometimes voices, gave the TV show and the early singles and albums their sound, had two songs on the *More* album, both destined to become Monkees classics, "She" and "(I'm Not) Your Steppin' Stone." The latter, especially, was garage rock at its back-to-basics best. It had been intended at first for Paul Revere & the Raiders and went on to be covered by amateur and professional bands for decades.

There was typically one novelty song on each Monkees album. "Your Auntie Grizelda" (track 5) is the designated example on *More of the Monkees*. It was presented to Tork as a "protest song." It is, in the sense that it expresses a petulant adolescent protest against the Establishment. This might have made it attractive to the adolescent segment of the fan base, as well as slightly older mildly political listeners. Tork wasn't fooled. But he sang it, even though his vocal sounds a bit whiny, maybe vaguely annoyed and perfunctory, especially when it comes to the nonsense sound-effects bridge that seals its status as novelty song. On the other hand, that style of nonsense singing is the kind of playful vocalization sometimes used in in lieu of instrumental solo by folk singers, as former busker and banjo player Tork would know.

On the first album, the novelty song was "Gonna Buy Me a Dog." The composers of that one, Boyce and Hart, originally thought of it as a classic rock tune in the R&B tradition that included "Hound Dog." Pre-Monkees Jones had performed it, go-go style, as a guest on the TV show *The Farmer's Daughter* (1965), ironically, while hiding in a closet and singing for someone else to lip-sync to. A year-plus later, the Monkees' version of "Gonna Buy Me a Dog" slowed the tempo, enhanced the syncopation, and layered on improvised banter and jokes by Dolenz and Jones to make its genre identity perfectly clear. One joke, about training an elephant, references Dolenz's childhood role as Corky in *Circus Boy*. As it fades, Jones recites "they're coming to take me away, Haha-hehe-hoho"—from the "sick"-humor novelty song hit released in the summer of 1966.

The session musicians on *More of the Monkees* again included Wrecking Crew players Carol Kaye (bass), Hal Blaine (drums), James Burton, Glen Campbell, and Al Gorgoni (guitars), among others. Neil Diamond plays guitar on the two songs he had written. The tracks had been recorded during the year, with lead vocals by the Monkees, but it was still very much a professional studio-musician project. It's often said, even by the Monkees themselves, that Nesmith and Tork were the real musicians of the group. But the truth is that all four Monkees were musicians of one kind or another before being cast for the show. In addition to his role in musical theater in *Oliver!*, Jones had made a couple of teen-idol records for the Colpix label by 1966. Dolenz was not only a child actor but had performed on stage, singing and playing guitar. In fact, he played and sang "Johnny B. Goode" for his *Monkees* audition.[16] He was cast as the drummer and took some lessons, but he could already read music and was a typical show-business kid, comfortable singing and playing as well as acting. Tork came to the audition as a multi-instrumentalist, a folk and folk-rock performer. He had played in clubs like the Troubadour in L.A. and was fairly well known locally. His friend and roommate Stephen Stills recommended him for *The Monkees* during his own audition for the show. (The two musician friends looked alike.)

Of the four, Nesmith was the most serious musician, a songwriter, arranger, performer. He had done some producing and contributed songs to the first two albums. Before being cast for the show, he sold songs and made folk records under the name Michael Blessing. He had been a regular performer and emcee ("hootmaster") at the weekly hootenanny at the Troubadour. As a folk singer, Nesmith retained his Texas accent and country inflection. He would soon develop one of the earliest examples of the hybrid country-rock. Like almost everyone at the time, he also played blues sometimes, in certain venues. In one interview in August 1965, Nesmith characterized his music at the time as "folk-n-roll"—the same genre label *The Monkees* producers would use in the casting-call ad for the show published just a month later.[17] He credits Los Angeles D.J. Don Steele for coming up with or promoting the term "folk-n-roll," and cites as examples the Byrds and Sonny & Cher. That same year, surf duo Jan & Dean released an album actually titled *Folk 'n Roll* (1965). Separately, a review article in 1965 used the term for the music trend heard at that year's Newport Folk Festival.[18] More than a witty portmanteau, the term was a precursor to the one that stuck, folk-rock. It reminds us that there was a moment when the hybrid of the two genres seemed something fluid and new.

All of this to say that the story of four naive actors being stood up as cutouts for session musicians was always a reductive oversimplification. The Monkees helped spread the story by outing themselves, doing press in which they revealed that they did not play on the albums. In part, this was to get ahead of the story, as publicists say, and in part it was surely to provoke the crisis of authenticity that led them to make *Headquarters*, an album on which they played and sang almost every part.

CALLING *HEADQUARTERS*

It was their third album. It was the first album to appear *after* the first season of the TV show, and it was the first to be released after their early 1967 rebellion, when they threatened to quit and Kirshner was dismissed. Recorded mostly in March and April 1967, *Headquarters* was released May 22, 1967. It featured the four Monkees as a real live band. They did much of the writing and almost all of the playing and singing. The title is a joke about who was in charge of their corporate operation, of course, but it also contained a bit of typical 1967 humor: the band members got high. They were "heads" and therefore hip. There was a boutique/head shop in Westwood Village in L.A. at the time called Headquarters[19]—no doubt one of many around the country with that punning name. The heads were now running the shop, with something close to creative control.

The album emerged amid the chaotic atmosphere around the TV show and the Monkees' changing roles. Andrew Sandoval's meticulous book, *The Monkees: The Day-by-Day Story of the '60s TV Pop Sensation*, vividly illustrates how everything was happening all at once in early 1967. Taping episodes for the show continued; the Monkees started to perform live; Jones was still recording vocals with Kirshner's session musicians, and he seems to have remained somewhat on the fence at first during the band's dispute with him; the Kirshner sessions continued for a time as if no rebellion were taking place. The band had begun recording some tracks on their own as a band, partly as proof of concept. To actually make the album without Kirshner and his stable of session musicians, they found a new record producer, the musician Chip Douglas. He had been in the Modern Folk Quartet (M.F.Q.) and played bass for the Turtles, whom the Monkees had seen at the Whisky a Go Go. Douglas served as a fifth Monkee on *Headquarters*, contributing one of the key songs ("Forget That Girl"), playing bass and providing backing vocals on some tracks. Jerry Yester of the Lovin' Spoonful also played bass on two tracks, as did Nesmith's friend, John London, who would later join him in forming the First National Band. There were still several tracks on the album written by Boyce and Hart, and several tracks were by other writers. But seven of the fourteen tracks were written by Monkees, alone or as cowriters. The underlying theme of the album is: look Ma, (almost) no session musicians. A kind of demo after the fact of their fame, it was intended as a sincere, and thus authentic, musical expression.

A staggered group count-in, parodying the beginning of the Beatles' *Revolver*, opens the album with Nesmith's "You Told Me." Fourteen tracks later, it closes with Dolenz's "Randy Scouse Git," a hallucinatory flashback to his recent surreal trip to Swinging London: the title is slang that means, roughly, "horny Liverpudlian idiot." In the middle, as you turn the disc over and drop the needle, side 2 begins with "For Pete's Sake," a folk-rock ballad cowritten by Tork on the cusp of the Summer of Love ("In this generation"). This became the closing-credits tune for the TV show during season 2. Thus, the album is anchored by a trio of original tunes: a country/folk-rock guitar and banjo song; a druggy piano-and-timpani production with a rousing noisy chorus; and a flowery transcendental manifesto with psychedelic lyrics. Side 1 does conclude with a tack-hammer piano music-hall tune, sung by Jones song-and-dance style (you can almost hear the tap shoes), that could have been on either of the first two albums: "I Can't Get Her Off My Mind" by Boyce and Hart. Otherwise, the songs, even those written by outsiders, better represent the expanding creative interests of the band in terms of genre: Nesmith's country-flavored folk-rock, Dolenz's rock 'n' roll shouting, and Tork's folkie psyche-pop. There is one sad short-story song à la "Eleanor Rigby"—but with a less sympathetic main character and a country feel (and Nesmith on steel guitar)—about a nebbishy banker who absconds with funds before his forced-retirement party ("Mr. Webster"). It's a bit of black humor by Boyce and Hart with a vaguely anti-establishment message. Structurally, as well, it's mildly adventurous: it comes to a halt and restarts in the middle, then ends abruptly.

As if to prove they were now free to experiment, in place of the usual goofy-but-commercial novelty song, we get a brief spoken-word chant-in-the-round, "Zilch," that plays with found phrases and includes a line that shows up again, sung, in "No Time": "Never mind the furthermore, the plea is self-defense." And there's a throwaway instrumental snippet of the band trying to play, fast, the opening bars of the Warner Brothers *Merrie Melodies* cartoon theme ("Band 6"). They seem to be saying, "You want kids' TV? *We'll* give you kids' TV." It later became common for the Monkees themselves, looking back on it—and for fans and critics, even those who admire it—to call *Headquarters* a garage-rock album. Usually, this is meant as an admission of the limits of their musicianship or of the relatively stripped-down production, as in: "not bad for a garage-rock album." But, except for the twelve-bar jam "No Time," the term doesn't really fit the album as a whole. That is, it doesn't cover the genre diversity or the range of experimental and pop ambitions it shows off.

Perhaps the most performatively sincere track is "Shades of Gray" (track 6). Written by Barry Mann and Cynthia Weil, it's sung mostly by Dolenz and Jones, with a signature bit of piano introduction by Tork (who also arranged the French horn part). The lyric is about borderline states and ambiguous truths, including when it comes to the question of authenticity: "It was easy then to tell truth from lies / Selling out from compromise." But "today," as the refrain says, it's "only shades of gray." They didn't write the song, but they could well have done so. The Monkees surely identified with its nostalgic melancholy, especially when it came to the question of selling out. The song is more than just self-justification, but it is that as well. If everything is ambiguous, who's to say what's authentic, what's real and what's not? The Monkees' place in pop culture at the end of 1966 was ambiguous by design and circumstance, when it came to what was truth and what was lies, what was manufactured and what was organic, what was derivative and what was original, what was sincere and what was satirical. And, in the end, what counted as a real band, an authentic group making authentic music.

The gray area was inherent in the TV show's multilayered paratexts, including commercial marketing campaigns and tie-ins. But it was also inherent in the sometimes jostling artistic ambitions of its producers and the band itself. Rafelson described *The Monkees* in an interview for *TV Week*, December 1966: "the keynote of the show," he said, "was something rare in television—creativity, freedom and *non-phoniness*" (my emphasis).[20] The show everyone thought of as the epitome of phoniness—plastic, manufactured—he claims was actually making a statement against phoniness. Maybe he's just being defensive. Or maybe the show was indeed profoundly self-divided, both phony and non-phony, an exploration, partly by accident, of the difference, and thus a reflection of the contradictions of pop at the time.

Despite all the dismissals of the Monkees, and the self-denigrating statements by Nesmith and other band members, the producers and the band clearly wanted to be part of what was happening, on TV, in music, and in film. And Rafelson and Schneider seemed to think of themselves as in touch with the underground or avant-garde. And, as you are aware if you've read this book up until now, the Monkees emerged in the same year that Andy Warhol, whose pop art always played at the border of the crassly commercial and the avant-garde, sponsored a band with "Underground" in their name and made them the musical component in his elaborate multimedia mixed-media art project—and, incidentally, thereby ended up collaborating with Tom Wilson for the musical side of the project. The Monkees were no Velvet Underground (to say the least). But the distance between the two acts shouldn't blind us to the fact they were happening at the same time and were closer in some of their (mixed) artistic aims and (conflicted) desires than we might expect.

In 1967, the Monkees began a live concert tour. Then-emergent artist Jimi Hendrix was signed as their opening act. The absurdity of the combination was obvious even at the time, and it's no surprise that Hendrix eventually "gave the finger to everybody in the Monkees' audience at Forest Hills Stadium in New York and walked offstage" before leaving the tour.[21] But the generational, racial, and (sub-)cultural divisions between the Monkees and their audience on the one hand, and the formidable Hendrix on the other hand, have often been exaggerated. Hendrix, expressing his frustration at the audience response to the booking, joked, "I think they're replacing me with Micky Mouse!" The

Daughters of the American Revolution were blamed, in a publicity story made up by Hendrix's manager, Chas Chandler (formerly of the Animals), as the source of an angry morals complaint against the Black psychedelic-rock guitarist.[22] But the musicians themselves got along fine during the tour. Hendrix remained friendly with the Monkees and later showed up to support Nesmith at a difficult press conference.[23] Tork met Hendrix in L.A. and invited him to his house in Laurel Canyon. There is a photo showing the Monkees and Hendrix sitting together in a hotel room with girls and others gathered around. Hendrix is playing Nesmith's white and green Gretsch guitar (upside down/left-handed) as Nesmith listens, sitting beside him on the bed. Tork looks on. Stranger than fiction, maybe. But just the fact of the camaraderie and its casual nature, like the friendships between the Monkees and the Beatles and the admiration expressed by Zappa, reminds us of the porous boundaries at the time between pop and rock, commercial and underground, popular and hip. What happened on the (partial) tour took place along a seam between musical worlds, but it was really no big deal. The double-voicing was there, out in the open. It just overreached in that case, as the dominant audience for the Monkees shouted down any slightly hipper listeners who might have heard what Hendrix was playing.

COMING TO (A) *HEAD*

Raybert Productions—Rafelson and Schneider—along with actor and writer Jack Nicholson, in cooperation with Peter Fonda, went on from *The Monkees* to make *Easy Rider* (1969), *Five Easy Pieces* (1970), and other films in the gray area between popular and hip. If we get beyond the assumption that anything on TV is inevitably trivial, whereas "film" as a form is always serious, we can trace the continuity between *The Monkees* and these Raybert films that followed. The link (not missing, but underappreciated) is the Monkees' movie *Head*.[24] It's often described as the willful obliteration of the Monkees—a collective career suicide. But it was also a declaration of intent on the part of the producers, a kind of dissolution of assets on the way to reconstituting their projects on hipper terms.

Head premiered November 6, 1968. It opened in theaters December 4. Dolenz said later that he associated the premiere of the film with a strange gallery event, at a "psychedelic party" in New York, where the film was running in separate reels on individual Moviola machines. "Each reel was just playing endlessly over and over again, and that's how they kinda screened it for the first big screening in New York City. That was for the hip-oisie, I call 'em, in

New York."[25] The scene recalls Warhol's early showings of his films on a similar gallery setup. The intended audiences were probably not that dissimilar in terms of their being art-conscious and in-the-know. You can hear it in the tone of Dolenz's memory of the event: at that moment in 1968, the Monkees were not in Kansas anymore, which is to say they were no longer trapped on network television.

Dolenz's fuzzy memory of all those Moviola viewing machines is a fit analogy to the way that *Head*, the movie, is constructed. It's a series of loosely connected stitched-together scenes, surreal, hallucinatory, tonally jarring, all looping in the end back to the beginning, in which first Micky and then all four Monkees run onto and jump off a bridge. Like the multiple Moviolas, the early "Ditty Diego" sequence takes place on rapidly multiplying embedded TV screens for the multiplying voices, reinforcing a sense of McLuhanesque fragmentation. The film also splinters into multiple parodies of various Hollywood genres and clichés. One Western scene—with cowboys and Indians and cacti—featured Terri Garr in her debut film role. Snakebit, she suggestively says, "quick, suck it before it reaches my heart!" The scene ends with the Monkees tearing through the painted paper backdrop, Dolenz disgustedly objecting to the "fake arrows! and fake trees!" etc. In another scene, Nicholson and Rafelson, who cowrote the script, "sometimes under the influence of Timothy Leary's little pills,"[26] play themselves walking into the shot and commenting meta-theatrically on the making of the movie. Tork objects to the script that has him punching a waitress in a diner ("it's a movie for kids, they're not gonna dig it, man! . . . me hitting a girl. Especially the way I feel about violence and all that stuff, ya' know?"). Then he walks out off the set onto a soundstage, fake snow begins to fall, and he's transported to a real exterior snowy-mountain setting. After a musical number with the bandmembers singing from different remote locations, billboards appear, harshing the mellow. Shortly thereafter the four find themselves in white jumpsuits, apparently making a shampoo commercial. They only learn mid-action via an unseen director's voice that they are supposed to romp around a giant hairy head—that they're to "be dandruff." They obediently do the bit.

The Monkees had already appeared in real TV commercials that were not much less absurd than this scene. They were featured in commercials for Kellog's Rice Krispies, Black Label aftershave, and Kool-Aid. Many of the spots were written to fit the show's Dada aesthetic. One Kool-Aid commercial (from a later season) prefigures the dandruff scene in *Head*. In a water park, the Monkees first pop up inside the giant head of a clown, peering out from inside its toothy mouth. (Dolenz: "Hey Davy, what's the matter? You look kind of down in the mouth.") Then they stir up a batch of the "new, sugar-sweetened Kool-Aid" to attract a crowd of kids ("make friends with Kool-Aid!"), and everyone slides into the pool as the camera pulls back.

One scene in *Head* features Jones in one of his song-and-dance numbers. He tap-dances with hat and cane yet again, singing a dark Harry Nilsson tune, "Daddy's Song." The melody and lyrics, along with the dim empty set, completely undermine the carefree attitude Jones's hoofing would seem to represent, a kind of visual sarcasm. (Nilsson's "Cuddly Toy," which appeared on *Pisces, Aquarius, Capricorn & Jones Ltd.* [1967], is built on similar ambiguities of tone.) At a press conference, Jones cited Nilsson's music as an example of the genre he called "Broadway Rock" and (wrongly) predicted would be "the next thing," in part, he says, tellingly, because it was a genre that would be accepted by adults, by "mom and dad," without offending them.[27] "Daddy's Song" is the scene Zappa shows up after. He tells Jones he should concentrate less on his dancing and more on his music.

Which brings us to the music on the album, *Head.* It was something more than just the soundtrack for the film. With a shiny metallic cover like one of Warhol's mylar balloons, it reflected the head of anyone who picked it up to take a look. It had lettering running around the border, repeating the word "MONKEES" and, just once, "HEAD." It was produced by the Monkees themselves with Goffin, but was arranged, as it were—you might say edited—by Nicholson. He spliced together bits of dialogue from the already random-sounding script to create found-audio tracks. One example: Nicholson followed Zappa's remark about Jones's song being "pretty white," with Nesmith's declaration: "And the same goes for Christmas!" The album had no songs by Boyce and Hart, but it had a slow psychedelic track by King and Goffin, "Porpoise Song." And it included two psychedelic-rock songs by Tork, both with titles in the form of questions: "Can You Dig It?" and "Long Title: Do I Have to Do This All Over Again?" Another track, "Circle Sky," written by Nesmith, was recorded live in a concert staged for the purpose. Footage of that performance, showing the Monkees playing their instruments and singing, shows up in the film, intercut with shocking photos of atrocities from the war in Vietnam. A new mix of the audio recording of the performance, with an overdubbed vocal, became track 4 on the album.

STILL SPINNING: *33⅓ REVOLUTIONS PER MONKEE*

The Monkees TV show ended in 1968, but there were already plans for one-off TV specials. One was titled after the speed of LP records: *33⅓ Revolutions per Monkee*. It aired April 14, 1969. Nesmith later called it "the television version of *Head* in a way."[28] It continued the movie's act of myth deconstruction. And it continued the use of contradictory tones and genres as a tool toward that end. The Monkees are not technically the stars of the special—those roles are played by British musicians Brian Auger and Julie Driscoll, with their band, the Trinity, in an absurd sci-fi mind-control plot.[29] Just as *Head* had done, the TV special hammers on the problem of authenticity in pop music—which is odd if *Head* was supposed to have already laid the Monkees to rest.

One scene in the special has Nesmith sitting with an acoustic guitar in front of an Old West–style sign: "WANTED FOR FRAUD." He's dressed in a white country-and-western cowboy suit with stars on it. Through the magic of television, another Nesmith moves into the shot, in a business suit, with sunglasses on the top of his head (no green stocking cap), playing an electric guitar. It's a split-screen image of two Nesmiths: one pop-rock, one country. They sing a weird, doubled song ("Naked Persimmon") and angrily debate one another in a kind of proto rap-battle skit. The genre opposition of rock and country frames their debate about the evils of television and fraud. Nesmith later said, "One of the things that I really felt was honest was country-rock. I wanted to move the Monkees more into that because I felt like, gee, you know, if we get closer to country music, we'll get closer to blues, and country blues, and so forth."[30] Even at that late date, for him the blues still represented a route to authentic musical expression, one that might offset the corruption of commercial pop. The "Naked Persimmon" skit is in fact a naked display of Nesmith's own inner contradictions. In religious language ("the devil incarnate runnin' music supervision" obviously refers to Kirshner), makes for painfully earnest self-satire. But it also reveals just how seriously Nesmith took the questions involved, "what was true and what was lies," and how he saw the music and television businesses as exploiting and distorting artistic expression for profit. At the end of the scene, a cowboy figure in silhouette rises up in the foreground, as if from among us in the viewing audience, and shoots both Nesmiths.

33⅓ Revolutions per Monkee also features actual 1950s rock 'n' roll stars, Jerry Lee Lewis, Fats Domino, and Little Richard, performing a medley starting with

"At the Hop," with backup vocals by the Clara Ward Singers. It ends with the rockers playing baby grand pianos stacked on top of one another, presumably making a point about musical lineage and the shoulders of giants, etc. The Monkees themselves sing and dance in silly-looking 1950s garb, by implication either claiming their place in rock 'n' roll history or, more likely, spoofing the possibility of such a thing.

By contrast with all of this, the closing musical number comes across as intensely heartfelt. The genre shifts to contemporary rock—the Monkees' own. It opens quietly, with Tork playing Bach on an electric harpsichord (see? a real musician). Then the other Monkees walk on in silence, tune up, and play their own instruments on a rendition of the Nesmith-penned "Listen to the Band." Jones, as always, dances and sings and plays the tambourine. The band is arranged in front of an old-fashioned jukebox, the kind stocked with vinyl records. The song builds until, as if it were a missing number from *Hair*, hippie-costumed dancers stroll on set and start dancing. The guest performers, along with the Buddy Miles Express, join in a giant jam session. The crowd of dancers—some placed high up on some scaffolding—make the set look like a nightclub or go-go party, reminiscent of the "birthday party" sequence in the movie *Head*, with a psychedelic light show and then-advanced video-editing effects.[31] The song repeats and builds. There's a horn section and gospel singers. Someone holds up a sign behind Nesmith that reads "HE'S REALLY PLAYING THIS." There's an extended percussion break leading to a big noisy climax. It's more like a freak-out than the Beatles, but it's the kind of multi-voiced cacophonous ending viewers would have associated with "A Day in the Life" from *Sgt. Pepper's*.[32]

As Hugh Barker and Yuval Taylor have said, "the really interesting question is why it was so important to the Monkees to prove that they could be a real band."[33] Why *was* it so important to them, but also to the wider culture at the time? What was at stake? It seems like a symptom of something bigger than just the identity crisis of a single TV band. Coming at the end of 1966, it was as if the Monkees franchise as a whole had to be invented to embody the central conflict of pop in that historical moment—the doomed search for authenticity in a music world where genres were multiplying and the very grounds of authenticity were being undermined. By the end of the 1960s, the rebellious Monkees monster had supposedly been killed by its creators, but it showed up again, one more time on the medium that gave it birth, television.[34] (And Nesmith would return to TV of a sort in the 1970s and 1980s, when he helped to develop the music video as a form and contributed to the rise of MTV.) The conflicts the Monkees represented in 1966 have continued to reverberate.

EPILOGUE, CA. 1969

Around the same time the Monkees TV special aired in 1969, Verve Forecast released a *Best of the Blues Project* album. That same year, 1969, Sun Ra and his Astro-Infinity Arkestra released an album titled *Atlantis*, much of it recorded as early as 1967. On the album, Sun Ra played electric Hohner Clavinet, and one whole side is taken up with the title song about the lost city.

In March 1969, the Velvet Underground (with Doug Yule in place of John Cale) released an oddly belated self-titled album, *The Velvet Underground*, that included what became classic tracks, "Candy Says" and "Pale Blue Eyes." Also in March, the Mothers of Invention released a best-of compilation, *Mothermania* (they just couldn't let the Beatles jokes go) produced by Zappa, but also released *Uncle Meat*, an experimental double album and the soundtrack to an underground film in progress. The entire fourth side of *Uncle Meat* is taken up with multiple variations on the song "King Kong" (for example, "King Kong: As Played by 3 Deranged Good Humor Trucks").

Maybe it was the summative end-of-the-decade impulse, but in 1969 Hugh Masekela also released a self-titled album, *Masekela*, including Wayne Henderson on trombone, as well as a *Best of Masekela* album, produced by his business partner, Stewart Levine. The compilation opens with the global pop hit, "Grazing in the Grass," and closes with the traditional "Bajabula Bonke (The Healing Song)."

Contrary to Quentin Tarantino's fantasy timeline, *Batman* had been off the air for a full year by 1969. But the TV show and the craze it inspired were already preserved in the fast-setting amber of pop culture, to be revived (and reviled) decades later as a whole imaginary universe: Batman '66. The darker film franchises remained for the decades that followed.

As for *Batman* fan Tom Wilson, about six months after the show actually did go off the air and a month before the Monkees' *Head* premiered, a *New York Times Magazine* story featured the influential record producer (September 29, 1968).[35] Wilson had that year resigned from MGM and started his own independent talent agency and production company, the Tom Wilson Organization. The magazine story depicts him as a hip executive, a Black producer building a music empire, making about $100,000 a year (in 1968 dollars), with nine bands then in production, ready to launch new albums and careers, new contracts rolling in, dedicated warehouse office space in Brooklyn, and plenty of rented studio time over in Manhattan. It was the end of a year in which, we're told, he had placed eight albums in the top 100—five of them occupying the list at the same time.[36] Photos for the piece show Wilson in the studio, listening to playback, sitting behind the mixing board, discussing an album cover with a staffer, and talking to musicians: "Wilson is now doing two albums a month in an assembly-line style, with singles between," the reporter notes. He's running a music factory, but by design it's as much a Warhol Factory of creativity as a traditional record company.

We're told about his physical appearance and stylish wardrobe, and about the trendy decor of his apartment. As an index of both his income and his coolness, we learn that he drives a blue 1960 Aston Martin DB4. Readers would know that this is pretty close to being a James Bond car (who in the 1960s films drove a DB5). Though the *Times Magazine* doesn't get into his politics, Wilson was in fact a party-of-Lincoln, anti-Dixiecrat Republican from Waco, Texas, and he always chafed at stereotypical expectations of "authentic" Blackness.[37] In the era of the civil rights movement and the Voting Rights Act, he repeatedly spoke out (often mockingly) against examples of racism and discrimination. The story ends with a strange anecdote: the elegant Wilson, driving his blue Aston Martin, chases down a cab on Manhattan's 6th Avenue that he had just seen ignore and pass up a Black man who was trying to hail it. The imposing 6'4" producer cuts off the cab, gets out of his car, steps over and dresses down the driver for his appalling display of prejudice when Black men like the one he had passed up "are fighting and dying in Vietnam." In the end, he "cuffs" the cabbie (though only "lightly," we're told). It's worth remembering, among all the talk of Wilson's affability, that he could be an intimidating presence. And that he had no tolerance for racism.[38]

As for his work as a producer: "He has the knack of building up whatever talent a group or an artist has, by sitting back and letting things happen, guiding them offhandedly." This sounds like putting a positive spin on the common complaint that he was often *too* hands off in the studio, on the phone with a young woman on his lap. Those nine new bands he's producing are mostly rock bands, some leaning toward what would soon be called progressive rock, some playing hybrid jazz-rock or classical rock. The article reports that Wilson, who had started with the Harvard Jazz Society and Transition Records, now says that jazz is dead, that it's rock music that "absorbs musical influences the way jazz did." Absorbing musical influences (plural) from multiple genres and styles, he means. The sign of a vital musical form: everything is everything.

One other detail in the article stands out. Totally unremarkable in 1968, in retrospect it's full of meaning: "Wilson is only interested in self-contained groups, like the Bagatelle, who can write their own material, the ones who have 'woodshedded'—played together for a period to develop some style and maturity—but only one out of every 20 he hears have any talent, he says." Now, think of that ("self-contained groups") in contrast with the 1965 sessions with Bob Dylan, for example, Al Kooper sitting in with the session musicians. Or with most of those same session musicians being hired to electrify "The Sound of Silence." Or with the strange studio pop-music project, *Eric Is Here*. Or, in 1968, with *Head* set to premiere in just a few weeks, think of it in the context of everything the Monkees stood for and worked through in 1966, aiming to remain ironically aware and therefore—it was hoped—meta-authentic, even as they fulfilled their roles and played their parts. It was in the end an impossible goal, an oppositional reaction to the plastic, commercialized environment that gave them birth. But for a couple of years, on TV, in film, in the press, on that first risky tour, and on their highly successful singles and albums, they embodied the conflict, both that elusive ideology and its contradictions. To be authentic but also artfully constructed, hip yet popular, meant everything in 1966.

NOTES

Introduction

1. Amir "Questlove" Thompson, with Ben Greenman, *Music Is History* (New York: Abrams Image, 2021), 118. As he also observes, "The devil may be in the details, but history is in the formats" (71).

2. An FCC (Federal Communications Commission) Nonduplication Rule for the content of AM and FM radio stations was put in place in 1964 and was implemented in full by January 1967. Explicitly meant to encourage competition, this had the effect of encouraging "freeform" and even "underground" FM radio programming in the late 1960s and early 1970s. See https://www.fcc.gov/document/fcc-reinstates-radio-non-duplication-rule-commercial-fm-stations.

3. See Kelefa Sanneh, *Major Labels: A History of Popular Music in Seven Genres* (New York: Penguin, 2021), 141–42, on genre and oppositional definition.

4. On the emergence in the 1960s of a "rock ideology" set in opposition to pop music, see Peter Wilton, "Rock," in *The Oxford Companion to Music*, ed. Alison Latham (London: Oxford University Press, 2011), https://doi.org/10.1093/acref/9780199579037.001.0001.

5. Kembrew McLeod says that "[u]nderground culture and popular culture have traditionally been viewed as diametrically opposed to each other, but the boundaries dividing the two are often blurry. Rather than living in different universes, they developed a mutually constitutive relationship that was transformative." (*The Downtown Pop Underground: New York City and the Literary Punks, Renegade Artists, DIY Filmmakers, Mad Playwrights, and Rock 'n' Roll Glitter Queens Who Revolutionized Culture* [New York:

Abrams Press, 2018], 10). McLeod explores several topics relevant to my book, including, for example, "experimentation, hybridity, and border-crossing" (11), and the "eclectic cross-pollination of people and scenes" (14).

6. Karl Hagstrom Miller, *Segregating Sound: Inventing Folk and Pop Music in the Age of Jim Crow* (Durham, NC: Duke University Press, 2010). Miller builds on the meta-disciplinary work by Regina Bendix, *In Search of Authenticity: The Formation of Folklore Studies* (Madison: University of Wisconsin Press, 1997).

7. Miller, *Segregating Sound*, 3, 187–214.

8. Miller, 5.

9. Miller, 5.

10. Miller, 1–2.

11. Michael Serazio, *The Authenticity Industries: Keeping It "Real" in Media, Culture, and Politics* (Stanford, CA: Stanford University Press, 2023), 82. Chapter 3 is dedicated to pop music.

12. Serazio, *Authenticity Industries*, 1–2.

13. As Serazio puts it, "the more that commerce and capital encroaches, the more necessary these declarations [of authenticity] become" (84).

14. Jon Savage, *1966: The Year the Decade Exploded* (London: Faber & Faber, 2015).

15. Savage, *1966*, ix, 41.

16. Barry Miles, *Zappa: A Biography* (New York: Grove Press, 2004), 151. The Beatles experienced pushback from EMI lawyers to the *Sgt. Pepper's* cover over possible liability for using celebrity images. See Philip Norman, *Paul McCartney: The Life* (New York: Little, Brown, 2016), 265.

17. Norman, *Paul McCartney*, 261.

18. In the parody image, Wilson stands in the position occupied in the *Sgt. Pepper's* collage by a wax figure of the boxer Sonny Liston, perhaps a comment on the producer's "heavyweight" status.

19. Irwin Chusid, ed., *Tom Wilson, Record Producer*: https://producertomwilson.com. This website debuted in 2013 and is still the most reliable single source on Wilson, including the photographs of him described throughout this book, found at https://www.producertomwilson.com/photos/. All quotations from the radio show are from my own transcriptions of audio files at https://www.producertomwilson.com/the-music-factory/.

20. Travis Scott, host, *Invisible Icon: The Tom Wilson Story*, podcast (11 episodes, 2020–2021), Rogue Media Network, https://roguemedianetwork.com/podcast/invisible-icon-the-tom-wilson-story/.

21. Anaïs Ngbanzo, ed., *Everybody's Head Is Open to Sound: Writings on Tom Wilson* (Paris: Éditions 1989, 2025).

22. One blog calling Wilson a "Zelig-like figure" is Johnny Pierre, "Faces in the Crowd: Tom Wilson (Producer)," *Mind Smoke Records*, n.d., https://msmokemusic.com/blogs/mind-smoke-blog/posts/6846982/faces-in-the-crowd-tom-wilson-producer.

23. This catholicity carried over to Wilson's Transition label, which the producer first "envisioned . . . as spanning multiple genres, using catalog codes: J (Jazz), F (Folk),

M (Mood), C (Classical)" (Wolfram Knauer, "Tom Wilson and Jazz, Part I: Transition Records," in Ngbanzo, *Everybody's Head*, 26).

24. Ngbanzo, "Introduction," 11.

25. The 2024 film directed by James Mangold, *A Complete Unknown*, based on Elijah Wald's book, *Dylan Goes Electric! Dylan, Seeger, Newport, and the Night That Split the Sixties* (New York: HarperCollins, 2015), includes a brief fictionalized scene with Wilson (played by Eric Berryman) in the recording booth, though it makes him seem more like a passive sound engineer than the producer in charge.

26. Michael Watts, "The Man Who Put Electricity into Dylan," *Melody Maker*, January 31, 1976, https://www.producertomwilson.com/melody_maker_1976/.

27. Jann S. Wenner, "Bob Dylan Talks: A Raw and Extensive First *Rolling Stone* Interview," *Rolling Stone*, November 29, 1969, https://www.rollingstone.com/music/music-news/bob-dylan-talks-a-raw-and-extensive-first-rolling-stone-interview-90618/.

28. Greil Marcus, *Like a Rolling Stone: Bob Dylan at the Crossroads* (New York: Public Affairs, 2005).

29. Marcus, *Like a Rolling Stone*, 142.

30. Marcus, 142.

31. Marcus, 116.

32. Al Kooper, *Backstage Passes & Backstabbing Bastards: Memoirs of a Rock 'n' Roll Survivor* (London: Backbeat UK, 2008), 36.

33. Kooper, *Backstage Passes*, 33–34.

34. "Intro to Flute Thing (2nd version)," track 18, *The Blues Project 1966, The Matrix, SF* (KSAN FM), https://archive.org/details/the-blues-project-1966-matrix-sf-wor-fm.

35. The Blues Project, *The Sound* (New York: McGraw Hill, 1968), 145.

36. Al Gorgoni cited in Richie Unterberger, "The Columbia Years," in Ngbanzo, 111.

37. *In Restless Dreams: The Music of Paul Simon*, directed by Alex Gibney (MGM+, 2023).

38. Unterberger, "Columbia Years," 111.

39. Tom Wilson, interviewed by John Gilliland, *Pop Chronicles*, KRLA radio, Los Angeles, November 8, 1967, University of North Texas Digital Library, https://digital.library.unt.edu/ark:/67531/metadc1692082/.

40. The *Billboard* notice is quoted by Jon Savage in a discussion of the Velvet Underground (192).

41. Savage, 201.

42. Irving Howe, "The Culture of Modernism," *Commentary*, November 1, 1967, 48–59 (52).

43. Irwin Chusid, headnote to *The Music Factory* radio show, https://www.producertomwilson.com/the-music-factory/.

44. Tom Wilson, *The Music Factory*, program 13, https://www.producertomwilson.com/the-music-factory/.

Chapter 1

1. Roland Barthes, *Mythologies* (New York: Noonday Press, 1957, 1972).

2. See, for example, José Esteban Muñoz, "Ephemera as Evidence: Introductory Notes to Queer Acts," *Women & Performance* 8, no. 2 (1996): 5–16.

3. On the recording and production of the album (the little that's known), see the historical note by Irwin Chusid (2019), https://sunramusic.bandcamp.com/album/batman-and-robin. And see Robert L. Campbell and Christopher Trent, *The Earthly Recordings of Sun Ra*, 2nd ed. (Redwood, NY: Cadence Jazz Books, 2000), 124–25.

4. I've found no external documentation to confirm the date of this non-union session, but my copy of the vinyl disc shows a scratched "runout" number between the playable grooves and the paper label, including "1–66." This may be a "cut date" listing the month and year of the album's pressing (January 1966).

5. Kooper probably did not play on the record. He has sometimes said that he didn't. Sun Ra certainly did, and it seems unlikely the job would have required two organists.

6. Wolfram Knauer, "Tom Wilson and Jazz, Part I," in *Everybody's Head Is Open to Sound: Writings on Tom Wilson*, ed. Anaïs Ngbanzo (Paris: Éditions 1989, 2025), 16.

7. On the classical sources for the tunes on the various tracks, see Campbell and Trent, *Earthly Recordings*, 125.

8. Paul Youngquist, *A Pure Solar World: Sun Ra and the Birth of Afrofuturism* (Austin: University of Texas Press, 2016), notes that Sun Ra "had a soft spot for novelty tunes" (232). Wilson also had a soft spot for novelty, or novelty-adjacent, records. He produced experimental audio demonstration albums, a compilation album of TV commercials, and a number of records that might qualify as exotica or lounge music.

9. Johnny Green, "The Only Man 'Raunchy' Enough to Play Music for the Joker," *Billings Gazette*, October 26, 2013, https://www.youtube.com/watch?v=FGu1Nm4l5jo. Green suggests that "raunchy" meant something like "funky" in musical terms.

10. John F. Szwed, *Space Is the Place: The Lives and Times of Sun Ra* (New York: Da Capo Press, 1998), 144. Interestingly, Williams Sites, in *Sun Ra's Chicago: Afrofuturism and the City* (Chicago: University of Chicago Press, 2020), says that Sun Ra's playing in the strip clubs of Calumet City actually required him to play "Tin Pan Alley standards and even light classical tunes" that the dancers wanted as accompaniment (88–89). His facility with jamming on "light classical tunes"—in juxtaposition with bump and grind—may have contributed to the use of classical melodies on the *Batman and Robin* album.

11. Telephone interview with Jimmy Owens, November 2018.

12. Szwed, *Space Is the Place*, 214.

13. Wilson produced albums of gospel music in 1963, from music performed at the Sweet Chariot nightclub in New York (cf. note 36, chapter 2 below). There's a chance some singers from those records may have been recruited to sing on *Batman and Robin.*

14. Elijah Wald, *Dylan Goes Electric! Dylan, Seeger, Newport, and the Night That Split the Sixties* (New York: HarperCollins, 2015), 209.

15. Val Adams, "Discotheque Frug Pay Heralds Batman's Film and TV Premiere," *New York Times*, January 13, 1966, 79.

16. Susan Sontag, "Notes on 'Camp,'" in *Against Interpretation and Other Essays* (New York: Noonday Press, 1966), 275–92.

17. Sontag, "Notes on 'Camp,'" 292.

18. Jon Savage, *1966: The Year the Decade Exploded* (London: Faber & Faber, 2015), 223.

19. Savage, *1966*, 190. In 1966, a club in Sunnyvale, California called Wayne Manor featured go-go girls in Catwoman and Robin costumes, dancing in front of a giant Bat signal. Susana Guerrero, "One of the Hottest Bay Area Nightclubs in the 1960s Was Batman-Themed," *SF Gate*, December 19, 2021, https://www.sfgate.com/sf-culture/article/Hottest-1960s-Sunnyvale-Batman-bar-16671050.php.

20. "Pop Goes the Joker" and "Flop Goes the Joker," *Batman*, season 2, episodes 57 and 58, March 22 and 23, 1967.

21. The comic-book series, *Batman '66*, first appeared in 2013.

22. Robert Sherman, "Batman to the Rescue in Shea Caper," *New York Times*, June 26, 1966, 72.

23. Gérard Genette, *Paratexts: Thresholds of Interpretation*, trans. Jane E. Lewis (Cambridge: Cambridge University Press, 1997).

24. See M. Consalvo, "When Paratexts Become Texts: De-centering the Game as Text," *Critical Studies in Media Communication* 34, no. 2 (2017): 177–83, for paratext in videogames.

25. As I'm told by Marshall Crenshaw, who has it from a recording sound engineer who worked with Wilson at TTG Studios in L.A., Angel Balestier.

Chapter 2

1. Joel and Ethan Coen, interviewed by Terry Gross, "The Coen Bros. on Writing, 'Lebowski' and Literally Herding Cats," *Fresh Air*, NPR, December 17, 2013, https://www.npr.org/2013/12/17/251638952/the-coen-bros-on-writing-lebowski-and-literally-herding-cats.

2. Dave Van Ronk and Elijah Wald, *The Mayor of MacDougal Street: A Memoir* (New York: Da Capo Press, 2013), 30.

3. Van Ronk and Wald, *Mayor of MacDougal Street*, 30.

4. Hugh Barker and Yuval Taylor, *Faking It: The Quest for Authenticity in Popular Music* (New York: Norton, 2017), 82. As Karl Hagstrum Miller argues, in *Segregating Sound: Inventing Folk and Pop Music in the Age of Jim Crow* (Durham, NC: Duke University Press, 2010), white (and sometimes Black) performers in the minstrel tradition had made early blues records before record companies decided to try to capture the Black consumer market in the mid-1920s (224–27).

5. Steve Katz, *Blood, Sweat, and My Rock 'n' Roll Years: Is Steve Katz a Rock Star?* (Essex, CT: Lyons Press, 2015), 28.

6. Katz, *Blood, Sweat*, 25.

7. In England, the Yardbirds "had struggled with the same problems of authenticity as the Stones: whether to stick with the ever-diminishing repertoire of purist R&B or to go pop" (Jon Savage, *1966: The Year the Decade Exploded* [London: Faber & Faber, 2015], 58).

8. Blues Project, *The Sound* (New York: McGraw Hill, 1968), 58.

9. Frank Mastropolo, "50 Years Ago: The Blues Project Release Their Tour De Force, 'Projections:' Exclusive Interviews," *Ultimate Classic Rock*, November 2, 2016, https://ultimateclassicrock.com/blues-project-projections/?utm_source=tsmclip&utm_medium=referral.

10. Simon Frith, "'The Magic That Can Set You Free': The Ideology of Folk and the Myth of the Rock Community," *Popular Music*, January 1981, 161. Frith says, "the American folk revival was based on a contradiction" (161).

11. Kooper, *Backstage Passes & Backstabbing Bastards: Memoirs of a Rock 'n' Roll Survivor* (London: Backbeat UK, 2008), 55.

12. Kooper, *Backstage Passes*, 53.

13. Kooper, 56.

14. Blues Project, *Sound*, 33; 58.

15. Kooper, 88.

16. Beyonce's sometimes heavily resisted forays into country music are another recent example of the persistence of such divisions.

17. Ulrich Adelt, *Blues Music in the Sixties, A Story in Black and White* (New Brunswick, NJ: Rutgers University Press, 2010), 40.

18. Tom Wilson, interviewed by John Gilliland, *Pop Chronicles*, KRLA radio, Los Angeles, November 8, 1967, University of North Texas Digital Library, https://digital.library.unt.edu/ark:/67531/metadc1692082/m1/#track/5.

19. Katz, 42.

20. Kooper, 60.

21. Robert Shelton, "Folk and Blues Echo over Holiday," *New York Times*, November 29, 1965, 45.

22. Ken Emerson, "Specials: The Blues Project's Mid-Sixties Connection," *Creem*, August 1, 1973, 72, rightly notes the "ostentatious eclecticism" of *Projections*, and also observes that the Project was part of the "the bifurcation of American rock into an above-ground AM audience and an FM underground generally comprised of older listeners who dismissed their junior as teeny-boppers" (72).

23. Blues Project, *Sound*, 80.

24. Murray Kaufman, *Murray the K Tells It Like It Is, Baby* (New York: Holt, Rinehart and Winston, 1966), 36.

25. Blues Project, *Sound*, 80.

26. Emerson, "Specials," 72.

27. Emerson, 72.

28. Emerson, 72.

29. E. P. Thompson, *The Making of the English Working Class* (New York: Vintage Books, 1966), 12.

30. Blues Project, *Sound*, 155.

31. Mastropolo, *Ultimate Classic Rock*, https://ultimateclassicrock.com/blues-project-projections/?utm_source=tsmclip&utm_medium=referral.

32. Mastropolo, *Ultimate Classic Rock*.

33. Kooper, 77.

34. Mastropolo.

35. "Gospel Singers: Pop Up, Sweet Chariot," *Time*, May 24, 1963, https://time.com/archive/6626617/gospel-singers-pop-up-sweet-chariot/.

36. The three gospel albums Wilson produced in 1963 were *Introducing the Sweet Chariot (The Sensational New Pop Gospel Club with "Soul")*, *Shoutin', Wailin', Hard Drivin' Pop Gospel (Recorded Live at the Sweet Chariot)* with tracks by various artists, and *The Herman Stevens Singers, Everybody's Shoutin' Gospel (Recorded Live at the Sweet Chariot)*. Wilson was brought up in the New Hope Baptist church of Waco, Texas, where he likely heard gospel, as well as other genres of traditional and modern sacred music.

37. Katz, 20.

38. *Steve Paul's The Scene*, TV show, September 1967, posted July 20, 2018, by Nick Dauphinais, YouTube, https://www.youtube.com/watch?v=XfvkbYnoGXQ.

39. See Emily Lordi, "The Radical Experimentation of Black Psychedelia," *New York Times, T Magazine*, February 10, 2022, 116, on the differences between Black and white psychedelias: "These innovations, as deployed by Black artists, did not announce a narcissistic break with the status quo (to 'turn on, tune in, drop out,' as Leary said of his LSD-inspired life philosophy) but a thrust toward the utopian." This highlights what we see in most psychedelic music by white artists (and some Black artists) at the time: an internalization of the quest for authenticity.

40. Ryan H. Walsh, *Astral Weeks: A Secret History of 1968* (New York: Penguin, 2018), observes that "the changing lineups" at one cafe in Boston in 1967 "traced the path from Dylan's rebellious act at Newport to the spring of 1967: collegiate folk giving way to garage rock, then morphing into something harder to define" (77). That "something" was very often psychedelic music. Walsh's reading of Van Morrison's *Astral Weeks* incidentally suggests another way to understand the Blues Project's album title, *Projections*, as referring to the out-of-body experience of astral projections.

41. Kooper, 77.

42. Blues Project, "Flute Thing," performed June 18, 1967, as seen in *Monterey Pop*, directed by D. A. Pennebaker (Janus Films, 1968), posted January 18, 2012, by SnookyFlowers1, YouTube, https://www.youtube.com/watch?v=10IE95R09Ms.

43. Larry Fallon, with whom Wilson would collaborate in the 1970s on a planned R&B opera, was the arranger for the strings and flute on *Chelsea Girl*. See Ignacio Juliá, "On Signing the Velvet Underground and Nico," in *Everybody's Head Is Open to Sound: Writings on Tom Wilson*, ed. Anaïs Ngbanzo (Paris: Éditions 1989, 2025), 172.

44. Mastropolo.

45. Jim DeRogatis, *Turn On Your Mind: Four Decades of Great Psychedelic Rock* (New York: Hal Leonard, 2003), 9.

46. DeRogatis, *Turn On Your Mind*, 10.

47. DeRogatis, 11.

48. DeRogatis, 12.

49. DeRogatis, 13.

50. *Aspen* magazine, December, 1966.

51. Katz, 51.

52. Katz, 46.

53. Photo accessed online at Steve Katz's website, https://stevekatzmusic.wordpress.com/more/.

54. One of the photos from San Francisco State appears to show Gail Sloatman (the future Gail Zappa) standing behind Kooper's keyboard while Emmaretta performs with the band. Charles Deering McCormick Library of Special Collections (Digital Collections), Northwestern University Libraries, "Blues Project, San Francisco State Folk Festival," Berkeley Folk Music Festival, https://dc.library.northwestern.edu/items/e9608777-de3f-46a6-8c4a-795604d27218.

55. Chamberlain, in *Aspen* magazine, December, 1966.

Chapter 3

1. John F. Szwed, *Space Is the Place: The Lives and Times of Sun Ra* (New York: Da Capo Press, 1998), 218–19. And see James Gavin, "Inside Slugs' Saloon, Jazz's Most Notorious Nightclub," *Jazz Times*, September 18, 2024, https://jazztimes.com/features/profiles/inside-slugs-saloon-jazzs-most-notorious-nightclub/.

2. Paul D. Zimmerman and Ruth Ross, "The New Jazz," *Newsweek*, December 12, 1966, 106.

3. Zimmerman and Ross, "New Jazz," 106.

4. Paul Youngquist, *A Pure Solar World: Sun Ra and the Birth of Afrofuturism* (Austin: University of Texas Press, 2016), 246–50.

5. Leroi Jones (Amiri Baraka), *Black Music* (Akashic Books, 2010; first publ. 1967), 198–99.

6. Youngquist, *Pure Solar World*, 179; Szwed, *Space Is the Place*, 187–94.

7. Jones (Amiri Baraka), *Black Music*, 199.

8. Mark Dery, "Black to the Future, Interviews with Samuel R. Delaney, Greg Tate, and Tricia Rose," in *Flame Wars: The Discourse of Cyberculture*, ed. Mark Dery (Durham, NC: Duke University Press, 1994), 179–222.

9. Marshall Crenshaw's forthcoming documentary on Wilson includes plans for a recreation of the opera.

10. Michael Watts, "The Man Who Put Electricity into Dylan," *Melody Maker*, January 31, 1976, https://www.producertomwilson.com/melody_maker_1976/.

11. Smithsonian National Museum of African American History and Cuture, *Afrofut-*

rusim: A History of Black Futures, March 24, 2023–August 18, 2024, https://www.si.edu/exhibitions/afrofuturism-history-black-futures%3Aevent-exhib-6648.

12. Youngquist, 249.

13. James E. Smethurst, "'Pat Your Foot and Turn the Corner': Amiri Baraka, the Black Arts Movement, and the Poetics of a Popular Avant-Garde," *African American Review* 60 (2003): 261–70 (261–62).

14. Szwed, 238.

15. William Sites, *Sun Ra's Chicago: Afrofuturism and the City* (Chicago: University of Chicago Press, 2020), pt. 2. Quoting pianist Andrew Hill, Sites characterizes Sun Ra's musical experiences in Chicago in the 1950s as "a time 'before the music got separated' . . . prior to the sorting of music into discrete genres marketed to distinct categories of consumers" (81).

16. Sites, *Sun Ra's Chicago*, 202.

17. Szwed, 231.

18. Val Wilmer, "Like a Cosmic Newspaper: Val Wilmer on Sun Ra," *Quietus*, March 4, 2018, https://thequietus.com/articles/24147-sun-ra-val-wilmer-as-serious-as-your-life-book-extract.

19. Szwed, 203.

20. Marion Brown, review of Sun Ra, *Secrets of the Sun*, *Change*, Fall–Winter 1965, 49; Alton Abraham, Collection of Sun Ra, box 132: scrapbook 1962–67, Hanna Holborn Gray Special Collections Research Center, University of Chicago Library.

21. James Semark, "A Review of Two Sun Ra Recordings," *Change*, Fall-Winter 1965, 53; Alton Abraham, Collection of Sun Ra, box 132: scrapbook 1962–67, Hanna Holborn Gray Special Collections Research Center, University of Chicago Library.

22. On the underground theater and one of the earliest examples of Happenings, Allan Kaprow's *18 Happenings in 6 Parts*, see J. Hoberman, *Everything Is Now: The 1960s New York Avant-Garde—Primal Happenings, Underground Movies, Radical Pop* (London: Verso, 2025), 17–19.

23. Szwed notes that in the 1960s free jazz evolved in parallel with experimental twentieth-century classical music (231).

24. Szwed, 74.

25. Szwed, 275.

26. In 2022, a sixtieth-anniversary reissue of the album was released on vinyl through Craft Recordings. It includes the original cover art, labels, liner notes, etc., with a historical note by Irwin Chusid, who produced the album.

27. Sun Ra, in Alton Abraham, Collection of Sun Ra, box 132: scrapbook 1962–67, Hanna Holborn Gray Special Collections Research Center, University of Chicago Library.

28. Youngquist, 161–68.

29. Youngquist, 163.

30. Youngquist, 165.

31. Youngquist, 171.

32. Sites, 88–89.

33. Irwin Chusid, liner note, *The Magic City* (reissue, 2017), https://sunramusic.bandcamp.com/album/the-magic-city-cd-lp-digital.

34. Szwed, 233–34.

35. Szwed, 212.

36. Robert L. Campbell, quoted in Chusid, liner note.

37. Youngquist, 182.

38. Details can be found in Irwin Chusid's notes to the 2014 reissue, https://sunramusic.bandcamp.com/album/strange-strings.

39. Szwed, 238.

40. Szwed, 112.

41. David Byrne, Playing the Building, Manhattan, 2008, Creative Time, https://creativetime.org/projects/playing-the-building/.

42. Brian Eno's coinage, "scenius," has been widely cited and repeated, including by Eno himself. See, for example, "Brian Eno on Scenius," posted September 28, 2021, by Peter MacDonald, YouTube, https://www.youtube.com/watch?v=77mbz2HbY5Y. The idea that artistic creativity is collective rather than individual was expressed well before; by Max Ernst, for example, as quoted in Hoberman, *Everything Is Now*, which goes on to say that collective creativity was exemplified in New York in the 1960s, where "[b]oundaries were transgressed, new forms created" (1).

Chapter 4

1. *The Velvet Underground*, written and directed by Todd Haynes (Apple, 2021).

2. Haynes, *Velvet Underground.*

3. Victor Bockris and Gerard Malanga, *Up-Tight: The Velvet Underground Story* (New York: Cooper Square Press, 2003), 74.

4. Frank Zappa, interviewed by Frank Kofsky, "The Mothers of Invention: Part II," *Jazz & Pop*, October 1967, 32.

5. Kristine McKenna, "Lots of Aura, No Air Play," *Los Angeles Times*, May 23, 1982, L6.

6. Warhol repeated Cher's remark and said, "we picked it up for our ads" (Bockris and Malanga, *Up-Tight*, 42).

7. Dylan Jones, *Loaded: The Life (and Afterlife) of the Velvet Underground* (New York: Hachette, 2023), 110.

8. Jones, *Loaded*, 110.

9. John Cale quoted in Clinton Heylin, *All Yesterdays' Parties: The Velvet Underground in Print, 1966–1971* (Boston: Da Capo Press, 2006), xii–xiii.

10. Lou Reed letter to Delmore Schwartz, ca. 1964, reproduced as part of *Lou Reed Words & Music Deluxe Edition* (Lou Reed Archive, 2022).

11. Joe Harvard in *Velvet Underground: Under Review*, directed by Tom Barbor-Might (2006).

12. Quoted in Jones, 61.

13. See Regina Bendix, *In Search of Authenticity: The Formation of Folklore Studies* (Madison: University of Wisconsin Press, 1997), on the link between "the quest for authenticity" and the rise of (primarily academic) folklore studies.

14. Tom Wilson, interviewed by John Gilliland, *Pop Chronicles*, KRLA radio, Los Angeles, November 8, 1967, University of North Texas Digital Library, https://digital.library.unt.edu/ark:/67531/metadc1692082/m1/#track/2; https://digital.library.unt.edu/ark:/67531/metadc1692082/m1/#track/5.

15. Wilson interview.

16. Sheila Klein, "John Cale on Ludlow Street," *Velvet Forum*, December 5, 2019, https://velvetforum.com/viewtopic.php?t=145799.

17. Joe Harvard, *The Velvet Underground & Nico*, 33⅓ series (New York: Bloomsbury, 2004): "there was an almost totally successful effort to avoid overtly incorporating the dominant influences of the time—a refreshing absence of hoary 'blooz' riffs prevails" (64).

18. Harvard, *Velvet Underground & Nico*, 134.

19. Harvard, 134–35.

20. Harvard, 135.

21. Tom Wilson, *The Music Factory*, program 3, https://www.producertomwilson.com/the-music-factory/.

22. Interestingly, Wolfram Knauer characterizes Wilson's Triple Play Stereo records as experiments in "mixing genres": "Tom Wilson and Jazz: Part II: After Transition," in *Everybody's Head Is Open to Sound: Writings on Tom Wilson*, ed. Anaïs Ngbanzo (Paris: Éditions 1989, 2025), 64–65.

23. *Music Factory*, program 3.

24. Jones, 121.

25. Bockris and Malanga, 26. Reed's declaration may have something to do with resisting the pop art attitude of the Factory. Warhol and Nico, as Jon Savage points out, liked to tweak people by embracing the label of "phony" (*1966: The Year the Decade Exploded* [London: Faber & Faber, 2015], 190).

26. Jones, 57.

27. Bockris and Malanga, 53.

28. Andy Warhol, interviewed by WNET TV, New York City, 1966, posted March 3, 2019, by Public Delivery, YouTube, https://www.youtube.com/watch?v=p7nw9Up54pg.

29. Bockris and Malanga, 35.

30. The dispute over who invented the light show was another manifestation of the East Coast versus West Coast beef. See Bockris and Malanga, 47.

31. Richard Witts, *The Velvet Underground* (London: Equinox, 2006), 123.

32. Jones, 90.

33. Richard Witts, *Nico: The Life and Lies of an Icon* (London: Ebury, 2017), Kindle ed., loc. 2902.

34. In Todd Haynes's documentary, *The Velvet Underground*, Jackson Browne recalls

that Andy Warhol had at one point wanted Nico to perform inside a plexiglass box, a rather on-the-nose metaphor for the confining sexism she faced.

35. On the date of the encounter between Nico and Emmaretta, Richard Witts says it was in 1970 (*Nico*, loc. 4787–4808). Jennifer Otter Bickerdike, *You Are Beautiful and You Are Alone: The Biography of Nico* (New York: Da Capo Press, 2021), 228–29, says it was 1971. Nico was in Egypt in early 1970 (Bickerdike, 204), recorded *Desertshore* in a few days in 1970 in New York while staying at the Chelsea (Bickerdike, 215), and was back in New York for the album's release later that year. The timeline suggests that the fight probably took place in 1970.

36. Simon Reynolds, "From the Velvets to the Void," *Guardian*, March 16, 2007, https://www.theguardian.com/music/2007/mar/16/popandrock3.

37. In a 1975 interview, Nico referred to Emmaretta as "a young girl, a Black Panther," and said that "the police were looking for me, and the Black Panthers, so I couldn't go back" (quoted in Bickerdike, 228–29).

38. Witts, *Nico*, loc. 5168–5171.

39. Bockris and Malanga, 44.

40. Albums and singles by the Supremes topped the charts in 1966. Like the concept of a "girl singer," the idea of a "girl group" was beginning to seem dated, on the cusp of the rise of women rock stars like Grace Slick and Janis Joplin.

41. Steve Katz, *Blood, Sweat, and My Rock 'n' Roll Years: Is Steve Katz a Rock Star?* (Essex, CT: Lyons Press, 2015), 89.

Chapter 5

1. Pauline Butcher, *Freak Out! My Life with Frank Zappa* (London: Plexus, 2011), Kindle ed., 11.

2. Butcher, *Freak Out!*, 12.

3. Butcher, 36.

4. Butcher, 36.

5. Frank Zappa, "Edgard Varèse, the Idol of my Youth," *Stereo Review*, June 1971, 63, https://www.afka.net/Articles/1971-06_Stereo_Review.htm.

6. Gillian Moore, "Edgard Varèse: In Wait for the Future," *Guardian*, April 8, 2010, https://www.theguardian.com/music/2010/apr/08/edgard-varese-national-youth-orchestra.

7. Frank Zappa, interviewed by Jim Dalahant, "My Favorite Records," *Hit Parader*, August 1967, https://wiki.killuglyradio.com/wiki/My_Favorite_Records.

8. Kurt Loder, "Frank Zappa (1988)," in *Bat Chain Puller: Rock & Roll in the Age of Celebrity* (New York: Cooper Square Press, 2002), 113.

9. Frank Zappa, with Peter Occhiogrosso, *The Real Frank Zappa Book* (New York: Simon & Schuster, 1989), 78.

10. Zappa, *Real Frank Zappa Book*, 78.

11. Frank Zappa (1967), "Psychedelic Music," disc 4, track 7, "The MOFO Project/Object," *Translated Zappa*, https://www.translatedzappa.com/EN/EN/aa077.html.

12. Frank Zappa, interviewed by Matty Biberfeld, WRVR radio, New York City, Summer 1967. Audio excerpt ("Poop Rock") found at "The MOFO Project/Object," *Translated Zappa*, https://www.translatedzappa.com/EN/EN/aa077.html#s59.

13. Zappa, *Real Frank Zappa Book*, 56–58.

14. Dan Sullivan, "Mothers of Invention at the Garrick," *New York Times*, May 25, 1967, 58.

15. Zappa, 97.

16. Zappa, 97.

17. Zappa's music always drew on the conventions of surf music, as well as doo-wop. As evidence, see the 2004 multi-artist Zappa tribute album, *Lemme Take You to the Beach*, which found plenty of surf-ready tunes in his repertoire, including "Memories of El Monte" and "I Ain't Got No Heart."

18. Patrick and Barbara Salvo, "Mother in Lore," *Melody Maker*, January 5, 1974, 23.

19. Zappa, 30.

20. Zappa, 98.

21. Zappa, 99.

22. Joseph Fernbacher, "Concert Review: Mothers of Invention," *Spectrum*, May 7, 1969, https://afka.net/Mags/Spectrum.htm#1969May07.

23. Zappa, 99.

24. He mentions it, for example, with little context, in Zappa, 163.

Chapter 6

1. Hugh Masekela and D. Michael Cheers, *Still Grazing: The Musical Journey of Hugh Masekela* (New York: Crown, 2004), Kindle ed., loc. 3331.

2. Masekela, *Still Grazing*, loc. 3162.

3. Hugh Masekela, *Welcome to South Africa* (BBC 4, February 9, 2018), posted February 17, 2018, by Kosmonooit, YouTube, https://www.youtube.com/watch?v=T8VTGOk3woo.

4. *Monterey Pop*, directed by D. A. Pennebaker (Janus Films, 1968).

5. Masekela, loc. 1948.

6. Masekela, loc. 214.

7. Masekela, loc. 547.

8. Two live albums were recorded in late 1965, *The Americanization of Ooga Booga* (1966) and *The Lasting Impression of Hugh Masekela* (1968). Thirty years later, they were recombined and released on CD as *The Lasting Impressions of Ooga Booga* (Verve/Chronicles, 1996).

9. Masekela, loc. 3444.

10. Masekela, loc. 2455.

11. Dan Epstein has speculated about Arthur Lee's connection to Herb Alpert (Substack Newsletter, *Jagged Time Lapse*, "Love Jumped Through My Window" [July 16, 2024], https://danepstein.substack.com/p/love-jumped-through-my-window). Many of the same session musicians played on different records in different, sometimes dispa-

rate genres. For example, trumpeter Roy Caton appears on Nancy Sinatra's hit single "These Boots Were Made for Walkin'" and on Love's album *Forever Changes*.

12. This experimentation with funk and fusion led to the *On The Corner* album in 1972, and many such forays as the 1970s continued.

13. *Young Man with a Horn*, directed by Michael Curtiz (Warner Bros., 1950).

14. Masekela, loc. 1562.

15. Masekela, loc. 422.

16. For three years starting in 1961, Masekela worked for Harry Belafonte's publishing office, transcribing music on field tapes for copyrighting (Masekela, *Still Grazing*, loc. 2812).

17. Masekela, loc. 3012.

18. Masekela, loc. 3014.

19. Masekela, loc. 2664.

20. Masekela, loc. 2678.

21. Masekela, loc. 408.

22. Hugh Masekela, "Alf Kumalo: A Tribute," https://hughmasekela.co.za/news/alf-kumalo/.

23. Masekela, loc. 3341.

24. Masekela, loc. 3152.

25. Kathleen Boyle's liner notes for *The Lasting Impression of Hugh Masekela* observe that "it is interesting to note in his voice the echoes of his horn phrasing." I would add that this goes both ways: the horn phrasings were likely derived in part from township-music vocal stylings. I spoke with jazz trumpeter and Professor James Suggs about Masekela's style. He said he always tells his students that one strength of the trumpet is that it can so readily mimic the human voice. Wilson himself played trombone and said that "it's the instrument that most nearly resembles the human voice" (Ann Geracimos, "A Record Producer Is a Psychoanalyst with Rhythm," *New York Times Magazine*, September 29, 1968, 68).

26. Masekela, loc. 3160.

27. On the title's Radium typeface and its connotations, see Florian Hardwig, "Hugh Masekela—Hugh Masekela's Next Album Album Art," *Fonts in Use*, August 15, 2021, https://fontsinuse.com/uses/30238/hugh-masekela-hugh-masekelas-next-album-album#:~:text=.

28. Masekela, loc. 3000.

29. Masekela, loc. 3623.

30. Masekela, loc. 3571.

31. Masekela, loc. 3637.

32. Masekela, loc. 3638.

33. Note to "Younger Than Yesterday," *ByrdWatcher: A Field Guide to the Byrds of Los Angeles*, https://web.archive.org/web/20101028072320/http://ebni.com/byrds/lpyty.html.

Chapter 7

1. John Corcoran, "The Animals," Rock 'n' Roll Hall of Fame essay, https://rockhall.com/wp-content/uploads/2024/03/The_Animals_1994.pdf.

2. Eric Burdon, with J. Marshall Craig, *Don't Let Me Be Misunderstood* (New York: Thunder's Mouth Press, 2001), 55.

3. Burdon, *Don't Let Me Be Misunderstood*, 14.

4. Burdon, 55.

5. Tom Wilson, interviewed by John Gilliland, *Pop Chronicles*, KRLA radio, Los Angeles, November 8, 1967, University of North Texas Digital Library, https://digital.library.unt.edu/ark:/67531/metadc1692082/.

6. Burdon, 20.

7. In the 2025 film about Bob Dylan, *A Complete Unknown*, we first see the young Joan Baez in Gerde's Folk City in Greenwich Village, singing a traditional version of "House of the Rising Sun." In fact, Baez recorded the song for her first album in 1960.

8. Brian Ward, "That White Man, Burdon: The Animals, Race, and the American South in the British Blues Boom," in *Transatlantic Roots Music: Folk, Blues, and National Identities*, ed. Jill Terry and Neil A. Wynn (July 2, 2012; online March 20, 2014), 157, https://doi.org/10.14325/mississippi/9781617032882.001.0001.

9. Ward, "That White Man," 156–57.

10. Ward, 157.

11. Ward, 158.

12. Wilson himself said that the Animals' "House of the Rising Sun" was "the original folk-rock record." He added that he considered Dylan's "Subterranean Homesick Blues," which he had produced, to be "the second—the first American-made one" (Richie Unterberger, "The Columbia Years," in *Everybody's Head Is Open to Sound: Writings on Tom Wilson*, ed. Anaïs Ngbanzo [Éditions 1989, 2025], 94).

13. Drummer John Steel insisted that Dylan told the Animals that the song "gave him the connection" and showed "how he *could* go electric" (Sean Egan, *Animal Tracks: The Story of the Animals: Newcastle's Rising Sons*, rev. ed. [London: Askill, 2012], 69). Steel told Richie Unterberger that Dylan had told the Animals their version had "'planted the idea of going electric'" (Unterberger, "Columbia Years," 89).

14. Clinton Heylin, *Bob Dylan: The Recording Sessions, 1960–1994* (New York: St. Martin's Press, 1997), 34.

15. Wilson's overdubbed version of "House of the Rising Sun" was finally released as part of the *Highway 61 Revisited* Interactive CD-ROM in 1995.

16. Dylan and a drunken Price have an uncomfortable set of encounters in the film *Dont Look Back*, including an infamous scene over someone having thrown a glass from a hotel window. The falling out between Price and the Animals seems to have begun when his name was the only one signed on the paperwork as "arranged by" for "House of the Rising Sun."

17. Egan, *Animal Tracks*, 112–13.

18. Egan, 126.

19. Egan, 130.

20. Egan, 130.

21. The song was not included on the U.S. version of the album.

22. Egan, 130.

23. Burdon, 70.

24. Burdon, 71.

25. Frank Zappa, "The Boss Mother Meets the Animals," *Hit Parader*, July 1967, 40.

26. "Frank Kofsky Interviews FZ [1969]," *Zappa Wiki Jawaka*, https://wiki.killugly radio.com/wiki/Frank_Kofsky_interviews_FZ. The reprinted interview on the Zappa-related website is substantially longer than the version printed in *The Age of Rock: Sounds of the American Cultural Revolution*, ed. Jonathan Eisen (New York: Vintage, 1969), 254–68, which does not include the segment about Eric Burdon. I have cited the longer online reprint here and below.

27. Egan, 191.

28. Egan, 191.

29. Bob Dawbarn, "The Ultimate Burdon," *Melody Maker*, October 7, 1967, 5.

30. Burdon, 70.

31. For the history of LSD as the context for psychedelic music, see Jim DeRogatis's *Turn On Your Mind: Four Decades of Great Psychedelic Rock* (New York: Hal Leonard, 2003). Burdon was invited to Dr. Hofmann's 100th birthday party in 2006 but was working and couldn't attend (Alan Clayson, "War Hero," Interview with Eric Burdon, *Record Collector Magazine* [July 24, 2008], https://recordcollectormag.com/articles/war-hero).

32. Egan, 115.

33. The B side to the single version of "San Franciscan Nights" in the United States was "Good Times." In the United Kingdom, it was "Gratefully Dead," a grinding psychedelic blues song with a poetic spoken-word counterpoint to the sung verses.

34. Dawbarn, "Ultimate Burdon," 5.

35. Dawbarn, 5.

36. Clayson, "War Hero," 166.

37. Besides Burdon, the other white member of War was a Danish harmonica player, Lee Oskar.

38. Burdon, 105.

39. Burdon, 107

40. "Kofsky Interviews FZ."

41. "Kofsky Interviews FZ."

Chapter 8

1. The title of Paul Revere & the Raiders' 1965 album, *Here They Come*, a play on the midnight cry at the original British Invasion, may have helped to inspire the song by Boyce and Hart. The Raiders were certainly a model for the Monkees in other ways.

"Catch Us If You Can," by the Dave Clark Five, may also have been an inspiration for the theme (*A History of Rock in 500 Songs*, podcast, episode 144 [February 15, 2022], https://500songs.com/podcast/episode-144-last-train-to-clarksville-by-the-monkees/).

2. Tom Wilson speech, transcribed from typewritten draft by Bronwyn Bishop, https://www.producertomwilson.com/wilson-speech/.

3. See Marshall McLuhan and Quentin Fiore, with J. Agel, *The Medium Is the Massage: An Inventory of Effects* (New York: Random House, 1967).

4. Martin Porter and David Goggin, *Buzz Me In: Inside the Record Plant Studios* (London: Thames & Hudson, 2025), 27. As the authors note, the Music Factory/Record Plant name was likely a "nod" to Warhol's Factory.

5. Hugh Barker and Yuval Taylor, *Faking It: The Quest for Authenticity in Popular Music* (New York: Norton, 2017), 163.

6. Barker and Taylor, *Faking It*, 161.

7. Andrew Sandoval, *The Monkees: The Day-by-Day Story of the '60s TV Pop Sensation* (San Diego: Thunder Bay Press, 2005), 41.

8. "Star Collector" begins as a simple rock song sung by Jones but ends with a then-rare Moog synthesizer solo played by session musician Paul Beaver, who in early 1967 had also played the Moog on a psychedelic-exotica record *The Zodiac: Cosmic Sounds.* "Star Collector" dissolves into atonal electronic noise near the end, followed by Dolenz's chanting "bye-bye."

9. Sandoval, *The Monkees*, 101.

10. Nesmith said he specifically asked for James Burton, and also for another TV-star musician, Ricky Nelson (*Infinite Tuesday: An Autobiographical Riff* [New York: Crown Archetype, 2017], Kindle ed., 85).

11. Nesmith, *Infinite Tuesday*, 79.

12. John Willett, ed. and trans., "Alienation Effects in Chinese Theatre," in *Brecht on Theatre: The Development of an Aesthetic* (New York: Hill and Wang, 1964), 91–99.

13. Philip Norman, *Paul McCartney: The Life* (New York: Little, Brown, 2016), 255.

14. Sandoval, 66–67.

15. Sandoval, 80, 95.

16. Micky Dolenz, interviewed by Bob Girouard, *Modern Drummer*, December 15, 2011, https://www.moderndrummer.com/2011/12/micky-dolenz/#.TupQMWMr2dC.

17. Sandoval, 25.

18. Elijah Wald, *Dylan Goes Electric! Dylan, Seeger, Newport, and the Night That Split the Sixties* (New York: HarperCollins, 2015), 206.

19. "Geegee's Gossip!," *16 Magazine*, April 16, 1967, 50, reprinted at *Sunshine Factory*, https://monkees.coolcherrycream.com/articles/1967/04/16/geegees-gossip.

20. Sandoval, 72.

21. Nesmith, 34.

22. Eric Burdon, with J. Marshall Craig, *Don't Let Me Be Misunderstood* (New York: Thunder's Mouth Press, 2001), 37; Sandoval, 217.

23. Nesmith, 35.

24. Micky Dolenz, interviewed by Billy Corgan, "How the Monkees' Movie 'Head' Bankrolled 'Easy Rider,'" posted July 12, 2025, by The Magnificent Others, YouTube, https://www.youtube.com/watch?v=u_ISUIB4mso&t=152s. Wilson produced a track used for the *Easy Rider* soundtrack: "Don't Bogart Me," by Fraternity of Man (1968).

25. "*Head* (Davy, Micky, Mike, Peter Commentary) Script," reprinted on *Sunshine Factory*, https://monkees.coolcherrycream.com/scripts/head-davy-micky-mike-peter-commentary.

26. Dave Swanson, "Timeline: 1968—'Head'—Career Suicide by Way of Abstract Pop Art Cinema—We Look Back On the Monkees Film, 55 Years On," *Summit FM*, November 30, 2023, https://thesummit.fm/2023/11/30/timeline-1968-monkees/.

27. Sandoval, 205.

28. Sandoval, 218.

29. Brian Auger would later collaborate with Eric Burdon. Before joining the Animals, guitarist Vic Briggs had played with Auger and the Trinity.

30. Sandoval, 118.

31. At the end of 1966, Tork and others from *The Monkees* TV show staff took a field trip to San Francisco to visit clubs and dancehalls and get ideas about light shows they might use on the Monkees' tour (Sandoval, 71).

32. The script/outline for the TV show referred to the conclusion in Zappaesque terms, as "the wild 'Freak-Out' finale" (Sandoval, 218).

33. Barker and Taylor, 167.

34. Nesmith, among others, characterized *Head* as intended by Rafelson and Schneider "to kill the monster they thought they had created" (*Infinite Tuesday*, 103).

35. Ann Geracimos, "A Record Producer Is a Psychoanalyst with Rhythm," *New York Times Magazine*, September 29, 1968, 32–69.

36. Geracimos, "Record Producer," 33.

37. Interviewed for the podcast, *Invisible Icon: The Tom Wilson Story* (1963–1968), episode 5, https://roguemedianetwork.com/podcast/invisible-icon-the-tom-wilson-story/, Tom Wilson III (the record producer's son) clarifies his father's voter registration as a Republican, saying that Wilson's favorite president was the Democrat Lyndon Johnson (primarily because of his support for civil rights legislation) and that he was never a "Nixon-type Republican."

38. The article includes another telling detail when it comes to understanding Wilson's situation during the exchange on 6th Avenue. A police car shows up at the scene and the officers watch through the squad car windows. Wilson remarks (joking), "If you smash my car, I'll kill you" (Geracimos, 33).

INDEX

The letter *n* following a page number denotes an endnote.